WHAT YOUR COLLEAGUE

This is a book for educators by educators. I wish I had had this book during my early years as a science teacher. It provides a wealth of information about the current state of climate education as well as practical advice and resources for educators.

—Blake Touchet
Science Education Specialist, National Center for Science Education
Abbeville, LA

What Teachers Want to Know About Teaching Climate Change delivers *on the promise of its title. Bertha Vazquez, Kimi Waite, and Lauren Madden offer research-based and classroom-tested guidance to equip K–12 educators to teach climate change not only accurately but also effectively. A tremendous contribution!*

—Glenn Branch
Deputy Director, National Center for Science Education
Oakland, CA

The authors deftly explore the facts, feelings, and future needed by every educator to teach climate change accurately and equitably. The book is structured for ease of access where each chapter includes Q-and-A format reinforcement, teaching tips, success stories from schools around the country, reflection questions, and resources. I have already begun to apply things I've learned from this book!

—Anne Farley Schoeffler
President, National Middle Level Science Teachers Association
Cleveland, OH

This critically important book helps teachers consider how climate change relates to the topics they are already teaching today so that students can consider how they can lead the way to a better tomorrow.

—Stephen Hupp
Editor of *Skeptical Inquirer: The Magazine for Science and Reason*
Edwardsville, IL

This book is a powerful resource for STEM educators to implement intentional lessons in climate education for students of any age. It narrates the tools, tips, and how-to in a myriad of contexts so that there's something for everyone.

—Sephali Thakkar
K–12 Education Ambassador, T-Mobile for Education
Allen, TX

A "get ready, get set, go" guide for teaching climate change in your classroom. Thoughtful information on climate change, science literacy, and supporting hope regarding this complex topic.

—Alison Betz Seymour
Biology Teacher, Winchester College
2022–2023 President, National Middle Level
Science Teachers Association
Scottsdale, AZ

Grades K–12

What Teachers Want
to Know About
TEACHING
CLIMATE CHANGE

*To every student who ever walked
through our classroom doors.*

Grades K–12

What Teachers Want
to Know About

TEACHING
CLIMATE CHANGE

An Educator's Guide to
Nurturing Hope and Resilience

**Bertha
VAZQUEZ** **Kimi
WAITE** **Lauren
MADDEN**

CORWIN
A Sage Company

FOR INFORMATION

Corwin

A SAGE Company

2455 Teller Road

Thousand Oaks, California 91320

(800) 233-9936

www.corwin.com

SAGE Publications Ltd.

1 Oliver's Yard

55 City Road

London EC1Y 1SP

United Kingdom

SAGE Publications India Pvt. Ltd.

Unit No 323-333, Third Floor, F-Block

International Trade Tower Nehru Place

New Delhi 110 019

India

SAGE Publications Asia-Pacific Pte. Ltd.

18 Cross Street #10-10/11/12

China Square Central

Singapore 048423

Vice President and
  Editorial Director: Monica Eckman

Senior Acquisitions Editor,
  STEM: Debbie Hardin

Senior Editorial Assistant: Nyle De Leon

Project Editor: Amy Schroller

Copy Editor: Diana Breti

Typesetter: C&M Digitals (P) Ltd.

Indexer: Sheila Hill

Cover Designer: Scott Van Atta

Marketing Manager: Margaret O'Connor

Printed in the United States of America

ISBN 9781071948286

This book is printed on acid-free paper.

25 26 27 28 29 10 9 8 7 6 5 4 3 2 1

CONTENTS

PART I

WHAT DO I NEED TO KNOW TO GET STARTED TEACHING CLIMATE CHANGE?

PART II

HOW DO I OVERCOME THE BIGGEST OBSTACLES TO TEACHING CLIMATE CHANGE?

Chapter 3: The Importance of Data Literacy in Climate Change Education   73

PART III

HOW DO I AVOID ANXIETY AND ENCOURAGE HEALTHY ENGAGEMENT IN MY STUDENTS?

For downloadable resources related to
What Teachers Want to Know About Teaching Climate Change,
please visit the companion website.
companion.corwin.com/courses/TeachingClimateChange

EDITOR'S NOTE

The summer of 2024 was the hottest on record. We saw extreme storms, flooding, fires around the world, and damage into the tens of billions of dollars, much of which was attributed to human-induced climate change. Climate change is one of the greatest threats humanity has collectively faced. Time is running out on our ability to attenuate its threats to human life on this planet. We believe understanding climate science and its potential solutions is essential learning for our students. But when researching the state of climate change education, we were puzzled by recent research that indicated a disconnect between teacher beliefs in the need to teach climate change and their classroom behavior.

A recent report by the North American Association for Environmental Education Research indicates that 74% of U.S. teachers and 80% of administrators agree that climate change will have an overwhelming impact on students' futures.[1] In addition, the survey found that more than half of middle school and high school teachers reported that their students have expressed a deepening anxiety over the climate crisis, including worrying about the future and how climate change will affect their lives. Almost half of the elementary teachers surveyed say students raise the issue in class. Likewise, parents overwhelmingly agree that students should be taught climate change in school: More than 80% of parents in the United States support the teaching of climate change—and that support crosses political divides for the majority of people, according to the results of an NPR/Ipsos poll: Whether they have children or not, 66% of Republicans and 90% Democrats agreed in this survey that the subject needs to be taught in school.[2]

However, the same NPR poll indicates that most teachers aren't actually teaching climate change in their classrooms. According to the survey of more than 1,000 teachers, only 42% of teachers say they even mention climate change in the classroom.

To get a better understanding of what's happening in the classroom and to find ways to support teachers in their efforts to teach climate change, we at Corwin did our own market survey to find out what teachers really want

---

[1]Braus, J., & Morales Garcia, M. (2023). *Students have climate anxiety. Here's what educators need to be able to help them.* EducationWeek. https://www.edweek.org/teaching-learning/opinion-students-have-climate-anxiety-heres-what-educators-need-to-be-able-to-help-them/2023/04

[2]Kamenetz, A. (2019). *Most teachers don't teach climate change; 4 in 5 parents wish they did.* NPR. https://www.npr.org/2019/04/22/714262267/most-teachers-dont-teach-climate-change-4-in-5-parents-wish-they-did

to know about teaching climate change and to try to understand how we can best help teachers approach this difficult topic. We sent a survey questionnaire to more than 135,000 teachers and school leaders and received responses from around the country and Canada outlining the issues classroom teachers face. The three concerns most consistently expressed by the respondents were as follows:

- 65% of respondents said the content was "not related" to the subject they teach. (Another way this was expressed was that teachers felt climate change would be an additional topic that they didn't have time for in their already busy school day.)

- 20% of respondents said children were too young/too vulnerable to be exposed to such an upsetting topic. Teachers reported being anxious about managing the students' social and emotional well-being during such lessons.

- 17% expressed a lack of confidence in their own understanding of the science behind climate change.[3]

We decided to build this book around these concerns, as well as others expressed in our survey. To give teachers the tools and the confidence they need to teach climate change, our book addresses these issues in turn, demonstrating how climate change can be taught across disciplines and how it can be aligned to the existing standards across the curriculum, so that it is not an additional course on top of an already extended course load.

To ensure we truly captured what teachers want to know about teaching climate change, we also asked our survey respondents

1. Do you have any tips for reducing our collective carbon footprint?

2. Can you share any success stories you've had with your students around teaching climate change?

We present these tips and success stories as a source of inspiration, so that you can learn from what other classroom teachers have found most useful.

* * *

We hope this truly addresses the questions teachers have about teaching climate change, and we invite you to learn more by checking out additional resources listed in the appendix and online at https://companion.corwin.com/courses/TeachingClimateChange.

---

[3]Ibid.

PREFACE

. . . .

Why Students Need You to Teach
Climate Change Now More Than Ever

Climate change is a complex, rapidly evolving field, and many educators today find themselves stepping into the classroom to teach a subject they never formally learned in school.

If you're passionate about preparing your students for the future but feel anxious about navigating the ever-growing mountain of data and the emotional complexities of the issue, this book is here to help.

Climate change is not just a scientific concept; it's a reality that touches every aspect of our lives, from extreme weather events to food security and social justice to the emotional well-being of our students. Our students, the generation that will inherit the consequences of our actions, deserve to be informed, engaged, and empowered to take action. As educators, we have a responsibility to equip them with the knowledge and skills to understand and address this global challenge.

ABOUT THE BOOK

We wrote this book as a team, with each coming to the party with our own expertise, unique viewpoints, cultural history, and regional allegiances. Bertha, who taught middle school science in Miami-Dade County for 34 years, wrote Parts I and II and curated the appendix and online content. Bertha is the education director at The Center for Inquiry, an international nonprofit organization that promotes reason and science. Her multifaceted approach to teaching climate science has been featured in the *New York Times*, NPR, *Earth* magazine, and in a book and film series by Lynne Cherry titled *Empowering Young Voices for the Planet*. Her efforts led to her being awarded the 2008 National Environmental Education Charles C. Bartlett Award, among other awards. Kimi wrote Part III. She is an assistant professor of child and family studies at California State University, Los Angeles. A former elementary teacher in South Los Angeles and a K–12 STEM curriculum specialist in Compton, her approach to climate change focuses on interdisciplinary climate/environmental justice. An Asian American educator-activist-scholar, she was named a North American Association for

Environmental Education EE 30 Under 30 in 2019 and the 2021 California Council for the Social Studies Outstanding Elementary Social Studies Teacher of the Year. Lauren, who wrote Part IV, is a former middle school science teacher who has worked in New Jersey for the past 13 years as a professor of elementary science education. In recent years, her teaching and research has centered on New Jersey's adoption of comprehensive climate change standards across subject areas and grade levels K–12, and she was the lead author on the New Jersey School Board Association & Sustainable Jersey for Schools *Report on K–12 Climate Change Education Needs in New Jersey*. She was voted the Association for Science Teacher Education (ASTE) Science Teacher Educator of the Year in 2021 and the Alliance for New Jersey Environmental Education Outstanding Environmental Educator in Higher Education in 2023.

How to Use the Book

In Part I we set the foundation for what teachers need to know before they start teaching climate change. Chapter 1 dives deep into the history of climate science. The chapter explores the connection between climate change and economic health and sets up the theme of hope that will carry through all chapters. The chapter also initiates a discussion of equity that threads throughout the rest of the book. Chapter 2 addresses the most common misconceptions surrounding the science of climate change and looks at how teachers can help their students overcome any misunderstandings they bring to the topic. It is our hope that this chapter also provides confidence to teachers who will be teaching the science of climate change.

In Part II we discuss ways to overcome obstacles to teaching climate change. Chapter 3 explores the need for data literacy when teaching climate change and provides examples of different types of graphs and infographics that can be used to teach data literacy in the classroom. Each example is followed by sample questions and possible answers, uncovering a pathway to add data literacy to the curriculum. (You will find the graphs, tables, and infographics along with the accompanying questions reproduced on our companion website, for easy reproduction. The answers to all accompanying questions, including the extension questions, can be found in Chapter 3.) Chapter 4 delves into the politics of climate change, offering advice on talking with students, parents, and administrators who are uneasy about the topic. We introduce the idea of how our own biases and preconceptions influence how we present and process information in our daily classroom instruction. Strategies for fostering open, productive discussions in the classroom are laid out, with humility at the center of all debate.

In Part III we discuss how to foster hope in students and how to acknowledge climate anxiety and channel this into activism and meaningful action that provide hope and an outlet for students. In Chapter 5 we explicitly discuss the reality of climate change impacting some populations more than others, focusing especially on the disproportionate impacts on women and girls around the world. At the same time, we offer examples of women who have taken back the narrative and written themselves into myriad climate change solutions. Chapter 6 further explores student activism as a way to combat climate anxiety.

In Part IV we focus on the practicalities of fitting climate change into existing educational frameworks, such as the Next Generation Science Standards and the Common Core State Standards, and we look at ways you can advocate for climate change in your schools and districts. Chapter 7 discusses integrating climate change across the curriculum and focuses on interdisciplinary instruction. Chapter 8 offers a roadmap for advocacy in climate change by looking first at New Jersey's climate standards. Recognizing the urgency of this issue, New Jersey emerged as the first state in the United States to integrate climate change education across all K–12 content areas. We also look at work done in California, Maine, New York, and city-specific measures.

Each chapter features Success Stories submitted by educators from around the United States and Canada, from which you'll learn about inspiring climate change lessons and school-based activism on topics ranging from planting a pizza garden on campus to attract birds and other pollinators, to one girl's effort to replace the fleet of gas-guzzling buses in her district with electric vehicles, to a long-term ecological study on plant and animal interaction in a local forest. We also provide a vignette feature called Learning From Our Colleagues at the end of every chapter, which walks through how a climate change lesson might play out. The vignettes are set in a variety of classes, from kindergarten through middle and high school, and tackle lessons such as how electricity is provided for a city, using persuasive writing to teach climate change, and activism for the very youngest students around inequity in the proximity to greenspace.

Throughout the book there are questions from educators like you who asked us tough questions about teaching climate change—and we answered them—and along the way provided all the additional resources you should need to help you work through any challenges you face in teaching this important content. We also scatter throughout the pages Tips to Make a Difference, offering tons of suggestions for reducing our carbon footprint, reducing waste, and preventing the release of additional greenhouse gases into the atmosphere. Most of these tips were provided by educators, too. We really couldn't have written this book without *you*!

The book ends with a wealth of classroom resources in the appendix, with links to the free curriculum mentioned in each chapter. We also provide content on our companion website at https://companion.corwin.com/courses/TeachingClimateChange.

About the Language Used in This Book

Jamila Lyiscott asks in her TEDx talk *Why English Class Is Silencing Students of Color*, "What if I told you that the way you use language every day had the power to either uphold or disrupt social injustice? What if I told you that because language is saturated with history and culture and memory, the way that it is policed within our classrooms and our communities is deeply connected to racism and colonialism?"

As lifelong students of anti-racism, central to our writing and collaborative process was ensuring we respect how groups of people and individuals want to be identified. To make language decisions explicit, we outline our language choices and reasoning below, which were created with the consultation of the APA Style and Grammar Guideline for Bias-Free Language:

1. Black, Indigenous, and People of Color (BIPOC) people: A term referring to "Black and/or Indigenous People of Color." BIPOC explicitly leads with Black and Indigenous identities, which helps to counter anti-Black racism and the erasure of Indigenous communities. (Racial Equity Tools Glossary: https://www.racialequitytools.org/glossary)

2. Historically and contemporarily marginalized people: The presence of structural racialization and racism in the present day and also throughout history is evidenced in differences in lifespan, family wealth, educational attainment, etc. In our writing we emphasize the historical and contemporary injustices that exist.

3. Black, White: We are following the APA Style Guide's principles of writing about race and ethnicity, which stipulates that racial and ethnic groups are designated by proper nouns and are capitalized. For example, "Black," and "White" instead of "black" and "white."

4. Community science: Until recently, *citizen science* referred to projects where the general public participates in scientific research. It's a way for people to contribute to scientific discovery and data collection

alongside professional researchers. However, there is debate about the term *citizen science*, and "citizen and community science" or "community science" is now commonly used. (https://www .calacademy.org/community-science)

5. Latin and Hispanic: The cultures of Latin and Hispanic people are extremely diverse, and there is no singular Latin or Hispanic experience. Although imperfect, this term will be used to refer to people whose origins are from Mexico, Central and/or South America, and the Spanish-speaking countries of the Caribbean (Lopez et al., 2023).

* * *

In so many ways, the future is uncertain, but one thing is clear: Our students need climate change education, and they need it now. This book is your roadmap to becoming a confident, informed climate change educator, empowering the next generation to build a more sustainable, hope-filled future. The urgency of this issue cannot be overstated, and your role in addressing it is vital. Let's embark on this journey together.

—Bertha, Kimi, and Lauren

ACKNOWLEDGMENTS

Bertha: My deepest gratitude goes to my colleagues at the Center for Inquiry and to Melanie Trecek-King, who, like beacons in the dark, champion science and reason. In the science classroom, my lifelong partnership with Ana Driggs, Mary Martinez, and Elia Valdes helped me navigate climate education in a state lacking climate science standards. We supported each other and instilled this knowledge in our students. It's a joy to witness so many of them now actively shaping a better world, including my own son, Brendan. At Corwin Press, my thanks go to senior acquisitions editor Debbie Hardin, one of the most competent professionals with whom I've ever had the pleasure of working, and to senior editorial assistant Nyle De Leon, whose patience helped bring this project to life. I'm grateful to Kimi Waite and Lauren Madden, my co-authors, and to the teachers who contributed valuable content to my chapters. It was a pleasure to work with you. Finally, to my friends Kelly Dawson and Michelle Drucker, tireless climate activists, moms, and engaged citizens—their work inspires not only me but countless children they encounter. They are true role models.

Kimi: Thank you to my grandfather, who taught me how to be an environmentalist and that my history and culture as a Japanese American are part of environmental history. I would also like to thank my former kindergarten students in South Los Angeles, who inspired my research and practice in environmental justice. I thank my mentors, who have encouraged my leadership in sustainability education throughout my professional career. From the California Global Education Project: Emily Schell, Barbara Doten, Lisa McAllister, and Tom Herman. From Prescott College: Emily Affolter, Kimberley Greeson, Scott Ramsey, Dianna Gielstra, and Calvin Centáe Richards. I would also like to acknowledge all of my fellow teachers who were frontline workers during the COVID-19 pandemic and teachers around the country who dare to teach the truth, whether about systemic racism or climate change. I'm honored to collaborate with two amazing co-authors, Bertha Vazquez and Lauren Madden, and the teachers who contributed to our book. Thank you to the Corwin Team: Debbie Hardin, for her amazing support and encouragement, and Nyle De Leon.

Lauren: I appreciate the guidance and partnership of Sarah Sterling-Laldee at the New Jersey Department of Education and vision and inspiration from New Jersey's First Lady, Tammy Snyder Murphy. Your leadership has shifted conversations and made climate change education a viable and fruitful solution to this tremendous issue. My heartfelt gratitude goes to the current and future teachers of New Jersey who have allowed me to learn alongside them. Your work on the front lines lets us tell the story of what widespread climate change education is. It has been an honor and a joy to work alongside Bertha Vazquez and Kimi Waite in creating this book. To the Corwin Team: Debbie Hardin and Nyle De Leon for bringing this story to life. I am forever grateful to my family, especially my sons Connor and Luke Madden. Your creativity is unmatched. I'll fight forever to make the world a better place for you.

PUBLISHER ACKNOWLEDGMENTS

Thank you to Rebecca Burton, professor emerita of biology and environmental science, Alverno College, for fact-checking the science throughout. We appreciate your meticulous eye and insightful suggestions.

Thank you to the many educators and school leaders who took the time to respond to our survey about teaching climate change; we thank you for your thoughtful questions, helpful tips, and inspiring stories of success. We especially thank the following individuals, who allowed us to reproduce their questions, tips, and success stories in this book: Janett Akerman, Angela Anthony, Shirley Anthony, Jamie Ashburn, Bradley Barton, Todd Bloch, Debbie Bond, Jamie Bothwell, Kate Breitschwerdt, Georgia Brewer, Christine Briske, Shanna Burcham, Lynn Connor, Brittany Crawley, Kylie Currie, Kim Decker, Kim Demarest, Luke Douglass, Shanna Dowd, Elizabeth Duff-Russo, James Earley, Naomi Elliott, Andrea Finley, Megan Fullerton, Joan Gillman, Jacki Grady, Jennifer Grolemund, Renae Henry, Allyson Israel, Natalye James, Ebony Jamison, Veranda Johnson, Kristina Klammer, Katherine Korn, Lanette Lanchester, Teresa Madewell, Tracy Majors, Graeme Marcoux, Morgan Massey, Andrew McCullough, Cindy Moore, Karen Nichols, Harvey Norris, Katie O'Connor, Helena Paisley, Renee Pascale-Reynolds, Mario Patino, Amber Pitts, Liam Plybon, Terry Neal Purvis, Preston Reeder, Shannon Rine, Mrs. Rogers, Loretta Rowland-Kitley, Jennifer Skrobisz, Aaron D. Sloboda Kathleen Small, Katie Smith, Andrea Strouse, Benjamin Taylor, Eric Tharp, Anthony Tournis, Robert E. Tufts, Janet Villas, Wendy L. Welshans, Georgina Whalen, Joel Wickert, Ellen Wilder, John Winkler, Michael Winship, Debra Yliniemi, Seth Yosef, Marianne Zupanc.

We also thank our reviewers:

Glenn Branch
Deputy Director
National Center for Science Education
Oakland, CA

Amanda Clapp
Teacher
The Catamount School
Sylva, NC

Alison Betz Seymour
2022–2023 President of the National Middle Level Science Teachers
Association
Biology Teacher
Winchester College
Scottsdale, AZ

Sephali Thakkar
K–12 Education Ambassador
T-Mobile for Education
Allen, TX

Blake Touchet
Science Education Specialist
National Center for Science Education
Abbeville, LA

ABOUT THE AUTHORS

Bertha Vazquez is a retired science teacher who taught middle school for 34 years in Miami-Dade County Public Schools. She is the education director at The Center for Inquiry, an international nonprofit organization that promotes reason and science. She runs a teacher-led network of more than 100 teachers who have presented more than 400 professional development sessions for their fellow teachers in all 50 U.S. states. Her multifaceted approach to teaching climate science has been featured in the *New York Times*, NPR, *Earth* magazine, and in a book and film series by Lynne Cherry titled *Empowering Young Voices for the Planet*. Her efforts awarded her the 2008 National Environmental Education Richard C. Bartlett Award, among others. She is the editor and contributing author of the book *On Teaching Evolution*, published in 2021. She has also worked on several translation projects, including the translation of Maria Jinich's book into English, *A Brief History of Four Billion Years of Evolution: Understanding Darwin*. She is a regular speaker at skeptical and humanist conferences and is a Fellow of the Committee for Skeptical Inquiry.

Kimi Waite is an assistant professor of child and family studies at California State University, Los Angeles. A former elementary school teacher in South Los Angeles and a STEM curriculum specialist in Compton, she has received both national and state recognition for her leadership in environmental education, social studies, and climate change education. She is an early career fellow with the UCLA Center for Diverse Leadership in Science; the 2021 California Council for the Social Studies Outstanding Elementary Social

Studies Teacher of the Year; a 2021 Public Voices Fellow on the Climate Crisis with the OpEd Project and the Yale Program on Climate Change Communication; and the recipient of a 2019 Environmental Education 30 Under 30, awarded by the North American Association for Environmental Education. Since 2019, she has been a steering committee member for California's statewide climate change initiative, the Environmental and Climate Change Literacy Projects (ECCLPS). Her work has been published by outlets such as PBS, the *Boston Globe, Grist, Ms. Magazine,* the *Progressive Magazine,* the *Journal of Curriculum & Pedagogy,* and more.

Lauren Madden is a professor of elementary science education at The College of New Jersey. She holds a BA in Earth Sciences-Oceanography, MS in Marine Science and PhD in Science Education. In recent years, her work has focused directly on K–5 climate change education, and she was the lead author on the New Jersey School Boards Association & Sustainable Jersey for Schools *Report on K–12 Climate Change Education Needs in New Jersey.* Her work advocates for scientific literacy and the health of our planet through teaching and learning. Her research has been supported by grants from the New Jersey SeaGrant Consortium, National Science Foundation, and the U.S. Environmental Protection Agency. She has written a textbook on elementary science teaching methods along with more than 50 peer-reviewed journal articles and book chapters. Her expertise has been cited widely in media venues including the *New York Times, Washington Post,* and PBS *Weekend News Hour.* She was named the 2021 Outstanding Science Teacher Educator of the Year by the Association for Science Teacher Education and received the inaugural I CAN STEM Role Model Award by the New Jersey STEM Pathways Network.

PART I

WHAT DO I NEED TO KNOW TO GET STARTED TEACHING CLIMATE CHANGE?

Source: istock.com/Don Mennig

CHAPTER ONE

THE FOUNDATIONS OF TEACHING CLIMATE CHANGE

The best time to plant a tree was 30 years ago, and the second best time to plant a tree is now.

—*Anonymous*

THIS CHAPTER WILL DISCUSS

- The history and evidence that scientists have long cited to sound the alarm about climate change
- The importance of incorporating green technology into the 21st-century economy
- Why some teachers are reluctant to teach climate change
- How to teach climate change without causing anxiety in students; and
- Where to find excellent classroom resources for empowering students

The best time for humanity to have made a serious course correction and addressed the dangers of climate change was 30 years ago—probably earlier. There's no question that the second-best time to commit to corrective action is now.

LOOKING BACK

Many of us well-versed in the science of climate change play a morbid thought experiment when the reality of today's climate crisis keeps us up at night. We wonder how different the world would be today if policymakers worldwide had heeded the warnings of scientists from generations ago. The world we envision in our midnight musings is not economically depressed or worse off because humanity chose environmental preservation over the economic growth of specific sectors, such as fossil fuel companies. On the contrary, this imagined world that altered its course to clean energy decades ago is filled with astounding energy innovations and thriving global industries. The atmosphere is not polluted and the constant news of climate disasters does not appear on our media screens.

Interestingly, the history of climate science begins in the 19th century. Eunice Newton Foote, born in 1819, was an American scientist, inventor, and a vocal advocate for women's rights. She became the first person to demonstrate that certain gases trap heat from sunlight, potentially causing the atmosphere to warm. This phenomenon, now known as the greenhouse effect, is a key principle in understanding climate change. Despite the significance of her work, Foote's contributions were largely overlooked for many years. However, her research is now recognized as a vital stepping stone in our understanding of climate science.

Fast forward to 1957 and Roger Revelle, one of the pioneering scientists to research human-caused global warming. Unfortunately, his warnings 70 years ago went largely unheeded. He played a significant role in establishing the International Geophysical Year (IGY) and founding the first Committee on Climate Change and the Ocean (CCCO). Along with Hans Suess, he authored a study and subsequent article in 1957 that was the first to suggest that gas emissions as a result of human activity could potentially alter the balance of the planet, leading to what they called a "large-scale geophysical experiment" (Revelle & Suess, 1957). At the time, Revelle also warned the U.S. Congress about the dangers of rising seas and desertification. His research was the first to use the phrase "global warming" to describe the potential consequences of a large-scale warming trend.

Revelle's testimony went mostly unheeded.

. . . .

Q&A   **Q:** How far back do we have actual scientific data?

Shanna Burcham, Health Academy High School, Chesapeake, OH

A: The oldest continuous temperature record is the Central England Temperature Data Series, which began in 1659. The Hadley Centre has some measurements beginning in 1850, but there is too little data before 1880 for scientists to estimate average temperatures for the entire planet.

The greenhouse effect was first theorized in the early 1800s by Foote and other scientists like Joseph Fourier and John Tyndall. In the late 19th century, Svante Arrhenius provided quantitative calculations demonstrating that increased carbon dioxide could lead to global warming (NASA, 2024).

. . . .

Twenty years later in 1979, under the leadership of President Jimmy Carter, a panel of climate scientists warned that greenhouse gas emissions could cause changes in climate (Alter, 2020). Carter himself was the first global leader to recognize climate change—and during his administration, there were fourteen environmental statutes passed, including the first funding for research into alternative fuels, the first fuel economy standards, and the first federal toxic waste cleanup (known as Super Fund). However, subsequent administrations failed to act, even taking backward steps. Carter's successor, President Ronald Reagan, metaphorically and literally took the solar panels off the roof of the White House, and Carter's energy initiatives, such as tax credits and research funds around alternative energy, were eliminated from the budget (Wihbey, 2023).

In a letter to the editors of *Scientific American* in 1982, Revelle stated that there was still considerable uncertainty about the extent of the impact of increased atmospheric CO_2 on climate change. He concluded, "If the modelers are correct, such a signal should be detectable within the next 10 or 15 years" (Revelle, 1982).

As hypothesized, 10 years later, during a U.S. Senate Committee hearing on June 23, 1988, another respected scientist, James Hansen (1988), who worked for NASA, declared that the record temperatures that year were most likely not due to natural causes and reported his findings with a 99% confidence level. This was the first instance when a prominent scientist had enough data available to correlate human activities, pollutants in the atmosphere, and global warming.

"It's time to stop waffling so much and say that the evidence is pretty strong that the greenhouse effect is here," Hansen said. He cited the Villach Conference (held in Austria in 1985), which concluded that an increase in global mean temperature greater than any in history could occur in the first half of the 21st century due to increasing greenhouse gases (World Meteorological Organization, 1986). The hearings received a lot of media attention, with the *Washington Post* featuring them on their front page. And yet again, little action was taken.

Teachers, the Zinn Education Project has created an interactive timeline of how we arrived at this inflection point in the history of climate action. The timeline encourages teachers and students to explore the decisions and implications that drive the climate crisis and collaborate on effective resolutions. qrs.ly/c5g36sv!

Although climate scientists are frustrated that their warnings have been ignored for decades, they are not surprised by the current situation. And for the first time ever, a Gallup survey conducted before the heat wave of 2023 showed that a majority of Americans prioritize protecting the environment (52%), even if it negatively impacts the economy (Gallup, 2023).

WE HAVE REACHED THE TIPPING POINT

TIPS TO MAKE A DIFFERENCE: Ditch the Plastic!

Christine Briske, Ronan High School, Ronan, MT

1. Stop selling plastic water bottles at school.

The Importance of Teaching Climate Change

Here we are, nearly 70 years after Revelle sounded the first warning. His hypotheses and the hypotheses of others have been validated, and the impact of a warming planet has been evident since the late 20th century. This evidence and conclusion are supported by an *overwhelming majority* of actively publishing scientists. Ninety-seven percent of active scientists agree that human activity is causing global warming and climate change (Cook et al., 2016). Likewise, the vast majority of leading science organizations around the world agree, including international and U.S. science academies and the UN Intergovernmental Panel on Climate Change (IPCC). Many believe we've already reached the tipping point. In November 2023, James Hansen published a new study predicting that the average increase in global temperature can pass 2°C in as little as 6 years unless we take action to reduce the energy imbalance (Hansen et al., 2023). A survey of 380 climate scientists revealed that 77% of these experts expect a 2.5°C increase between now and 2100 (Carrington, 2024b).

The term *tipping point* refers to the point when minor alterations become significant enough to trigger a more substantial and critical change that can have abrupt, irreversible consequences, leading to a cascade of effects. Initially, the IPCC believed that tipping points would only occur if global warming reached 5°C, but recent assessments have suggested that such points could be reached at much lower levels of warming, between 1°C and 2°C. Scientists look at several tipping points, including the effects of the deforestation of the Amazon rainforest (see Figure 1.1), the melting of Antarctic ice shelves, and changes in ocean currents (IPCC, 2021).

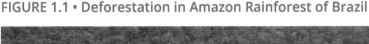

FIGURE 1.1 • Deforestation in Amazon Rainforest of Brazil

Source: istock.com/luoman

Despite agreement on the cause and effects of climate change, we are still not going far enough to take the actions required to reverse warming trends. Since 1970, global surface temperatures have risen faster than in any other 50-year period over the past 2,000 years (IPCC, 2021).

The report released by the IPCC in March 2023 revealed that the Earth's climate is undergoing unprecedented changes due to human-induced global warming, which has caused a rise of 1.1°C since 1900. The report states that the impact of climate change on ecosystems and people is more severe and widespread than anticipated, and the risk will increase with every fraction of a degree of warming.

The IPCC (2023) report concluded that it is now imperative that we implement comprehensive changes to achieve a net-zero, climate-resistant future. (Net zero means the amount of carbon emitted into the atmosphere is equal to the amount of carbon removed from it.) Reducing carbon emissions is no longer enough to limit global temperature increase; carbon removal from the atmosphere is now a necessity. It may seem like a small number, but a 1.5°C increase in global temperature would significantly impact our planet. We can expect harsher weather, rising seas, stressed ecosystems, water scarcity, food insecurity, and health problems (IPCC, 2023).

According to the IPCC (2023) report, nations worldwide need to increase their financial commitment to combatting climate change if humanity is to effectively address both mitigation and adaptation. The somber report addressed how climate change will affect some countries and communities more than others, and some populations within communities will suffer more. Inequality will only worsen as we strive to deal with the effects of climate change.

A survey completed by the *Guardian* newspaper reveals the despair felt by many of the world's leading climate scientists. They've witnessed the increasing frequency and intensity of extreme weather events, rising global temperatures, and melting glaciers. For example, data show that warmer ocean temperatures fuel stronger tropical cyclones. On September 23, 2024, Hurricane Helene encountered sea surface temperatures in the Gulf of Mexico that were about 1.26°C (2.3°F) warmer than the 20th-century average. According to Climate Central's Climate Shift Index, those temperatures are 300 times more likely due to climate change (Climate Central, 2024). Hurricane Helene demonstrated that even places we consider climate havens, like Asheville, NC, are not safe from climate change. And just two weeks later on October 7, 2024, Hurricane Milton explosively intensified from a Category 1 to a catastrophic Category 5 storm near the Yucatan Peninsula in less than 24 hours, with sustained winds of 290 kilometers per hour (180 miles per hour; Gramling, 2024).

Despite their research and warnings, many say they feel the world's response to climate change has been inadequate. They see the devastating effects on ecosystems, communities, and economies, yet they feel the world isn't taking the necessary actions to mitigate the crisis (Carrington, 2024a).

If we continue on the current path, those still living—including many of our students of today—will feel the full effects of climate change and will undoubtedly question why we allowed this to happen.

 Q: How do we teach the history of what has and has not happened over the past 100 years so students can make claims, collect evidence, and then come to a conclusion?

Debra Yliniemi, Little Falls High School, Little Falls, MN

A: Teaching the history of climate change can help students enhance their critical thinking and empower them to actively participate in ongoing conversations about climate change.

1. **Start with historical awareness.** Using primary sources, introduce students to historical data like weather records, scientific papers, photos, and oral histories. Analyze these sources to see how understanding of climate change has evolved.
2. **Focus on evidence collection and data analysis.** Use interactive tools to show how climate has changed. Let students identify trends and patterns in different data sets.
3. **Focus on local stories.** Connect climate change history to your local area, making it more relatable for students.
4. **Explore diverse perspectives.** Include voices from various communities and cultures. Consider the social, economic, and political factors shaping societies' understanding of climate change.
5. **Promote critical thinking.** Encourage students to question assumptions, analyze bias, and consider limitations in different sources of evidence.

The Financial Costs of Climate Change

Climate change is expensive.

Between 2019 and 2023, the United States averaged 20 climate disasters per year for a total cost of more than $600 billion. These disasters included severe storms, catastrophic fires, and record flooding (see Figure 1.2), and it's clear from the statistics that such "once in a lifetime events" are happening more frequently and with greater intensity. Contrast this to an average of 3.3

Have any of the effects of climate change affected your community?

climate disasters per year in the United States from 1980 to 1989, which caused $21.9 billion per year in damage, adjusted for today's economy (NOAA, 2023).

FIGURE 1.2 • A new weather phenomenon, known as a Bomb Cyclone, touched down in 2023 in Pacifica, California, just south of San Francisco.

Source: istock.com/JasonDoiy

 Q: How does climate change affect the economy of an area?

Georgina Whalen, DuVal High School, Lanham, MD

A: It depends on where you live. Stronger storms, floods, and fires can damage roads, homes, and the overall infrastructure of a location. Rising sea levels and warming waters will negatively affect beaches and docks in coastal areas, impacting tourism and local fisheries. Heat waves, air pollution, and waterborne diseases will increase healthcare costs and decrease worker productivity across the country. And as we will see throughout this book, climate change disproportionately affects people with the lowest incomes. But there is hope: Policymakers can improve an area's economic future by investing in green tech and infrastructure upgrades.

Because the costs of climate change are enormous, investment in alternative energy sources could be the key to a thriving 21st-century U.S. economy. The United States is experiencing a surge in clean energy development, leading to increased investment and job opportunities nationwide. The 2023 U.S. Energy and Employment Report from the Department of Energy reveals that almost 300,000 new energy jobs were created in 2022, with 114,000 in clean energy technologies such as renewables and zero-emission vehicles.

Clean energy jobs grew 3.9% in 2022 compared to the previous year, surpassing the 3.1% growth rate for jobs nationwide. The solar energy sector is a significant contributor to this growth, employing 263,883 workers in all 50 states, the District of Columbia, and Puerto Rico in 2022, with a 3.5% increase in jobs since 2021 (IREC, 2023).

The majority of people who will be working in the climate sector by 2030 have not yet started their careers, creating a demand for a diverse range of professionals, including engineers and technicians. This represents an enormous opportunity for our students.

> What skills should you teach your students when preparing them for exciting careers that don't even exist yet?

Q&A

Q: Why do the seasons seem to be pushed back? For example, it used to snow here in October, and now it doesn't start until December; April used to have rain showers, and now those are in June.

Andrea Finley, Endeavor Academy, Centennial, CO

A: Climate change is the primary driver behind the shifting seasons we're experiencing. As the Earth's average temperature rises due to the increasing concentration of greenhouse gases, we see a domino effect on weather patterns. Winters are becoming warmer, leading to later first snowfalls and shorter overall winter durations. This warmth also delays the onset of spring rains, pushing them closer to summer months. Additionally, summer heat lingers longer, extending the season and further compressing the window for spring and fall. These changes are likely to become even more pronounced in the years to come (USDA, 2024).

Success Story: Green Champions Club

Helena Paisley, MAST Academy, Key Biscayne, FL

In 2017, a group of students, parents, and teachers formed the Green Champions Club at the Maritime and Science Technology (MAST) Academy, a middle and high school in Key Biscayne, Florida.

"A big part of MAST's original mission was to teach our kids to be responsible stewards of the environment," says Helena Paisley, a 32-year veteran teacher at MAST and one of the club's founders. "The Green Champions really brought that aspect of our philosophy into the limelight again."

FIGURE 1.3 • Photograph of one of the solar panels installed at MAST Academy with grant money.

The Green Champions goal is to work toward making MAST the first zero energy and zero waste school in Florida. The club secured a $40,000 grant for a 26-kilowatt solar array to power the school's athletic field (see Figure 1.3)—and the club's impact hasn't stopped at the gates of MAST Academy. Parent Michele Drucker, environmental chair of the Miami-Dade County Council's Parent Teacher Association, and the students introduced a resolution that called on their district to commit to 100% clean energy by 2030. The resolution was presented to the School Board of Miami-Dade County and passed unanimously.

Source: Michelle Drucker

In August 2023, the Green Champions racked up another success when Miami-Dade Public Schools received 20 electric school buses, the first of 125 electric buses they'll have on the road by 2026. The funding came through a $8.8 million Clean School Bus grant from the Environmental Protection Agency (MDCPS 2024).

Holly Thorpe, a Green Champion team member, was a seventh grader when she began studying the health hazards diesel fuel fumes posed for the students and bus drivers exposed to them daily. She measured the excessive levels of CO_2 inside the buses and in MAST's bus loading zone in a science fair project and began attending school board meetings, lobbying Miami Dade County Public Schools to purchase electric buses.

"This experience has helped me feel more confident as a person and better as a person that I helped to do something like this for the environment and for the people of Miami," says Holly.

Holly counts her determination and her membership in Green Champions as critical to her success:

"I think that finding a good group that supports you is really important. And then also just being determined and not giving up. I understand that problems are solved with solutions and not by complaining. I understand that we have to fight for a livable future. People are going to try and push you away, but you just have to keep trying and speaking on what you stand for, and eventually, you can make a change."

NOW WHAT? HOW THIS BOOK CAN HELP

The purpose of this book is climate science education, not climate policy and solutions. Therefore, the question is not, "Now what?" but rather, "Now what, teachers?"

The answer to this question is now is the time to prepare our young people for a future of consistently more extreme weather events and more general changes in climate, such as permanent changes in precipitation levels and air temperatures, as well as to prepare them for the future economy. These are complex issues, making climate education very challenging (see Figure 1.4).

MAST Academy's successes have been featured by many news media outlets. Check out the following article to learn more about the electric buses that the students lobbied for:

- Montoya, P. (2021, February 3). Yellow and green: MAST students bring electric buses to Miami. *The Beacon*. qrs.ly/z3g36vm

FIGURE 1.4 • Images of Climate Change in 2023 From Around the World

a. Flooding in Australia

Source: istock.com/Beyondimages

b. Dead Coral Reef in Thailand

Source: istock.com/Johan Holmdahl

c. Air Pollution in New York City from Fires in Canada in 2023

Source: istock.com/James Andrews

d. Extreme Drought in Turkey

Source: istock.com/Selçuk KARABIYIK

Nevertheless, parents and students want climate change to be taught in schools. More than 80% of parents in the United States say they want their children to learn about climate change in school—and 79% of kids report that they want to learn this content (Will & Prothero, 2022). Whether they have children or not, 90% of Democrats and 66% of Republicans agree that climate change should be taught in school (Kamenetz, 2019), and 86% of teachers agree. So why are some of us reluctant to teach climate change?

You'll see from Figure 1.5 that according to a widescale poll, the biggest issue preventing teachers from tackling the subject is that they see it as distinct from the subjects they teach. The next biggest concern teachers express is that students are too young to understand the content and they are likely to be overwhelmed with a feeling of hopelessness. The last two concerns reported by more than a small fraction of responding teachers are that teachers feel like they don't understand the science behind climate change well enough and that they don't have the materials needed to teach the subject. (This is why we wrote this book! We will be addressing each of these issues in turn throughout the book.)

FIGURE 1.5 • Reasons Teachers Say They Don't Teach Climate Change

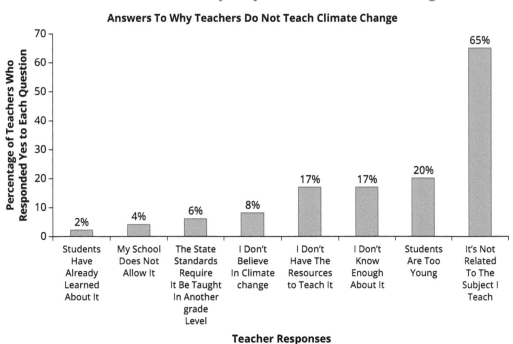

Note: NPR conducted a poll in March 2019 asking teachers whether they teach about climate change. The answers in the figure refer to the 55% of teachers who responded that they did not teach climate change in their classrooms.

TIPS TO MAKE A DIFFERENCE:
Actions Speak Louder Than Words!

1. You don't have to start from scratch: There are plenty of worthy organizations who can help you get started on your school's climate journey.

   - The Climate Initiative (https://www.theclimateinitiative.org/)

   - Organization180 (https://generation180.org/)

   - Kids Fight Climate Change (https://www.kidsfightclimatechange. org/)

2. Your students may ask you what they can do right now; the United Nations offers these nine things you can do right now.

   - Join the United Nations' #ActNow campaign for climate action and sustainability (qrs.ly/jeg3gk1).

   - Calculate your carbon footprint (qrs.ly/bbg3gk4).

   - Learn from your peers on the Reach Not Preach platform (qrs.ly/ n1g3gk7).

   - Educate yourself on the impact of climate change through an online course offered by UNICEF (qrs.ly/vkg36w0).

   - Be a Climate Superhero! (qrs.ly/m3g3gka)

   - Read the Global Youth Statement on Climate Change and COP26 Outcomes (qrs.ly/n6gd299).

   - Join YOUNGO, a global network of children, youth activists, and youth NGOs on climate change (qrs.ly/2fg3gkg).

   - Speak up! Share this information through social media.

We teachers today face many obstacles, including crowded classrooms, student behavioral problems, constant state assessments, and teaching multiple courses. Frankly, we have more than enough on our plates as it is. But let's reflect on an aphorism commonly used by people trying to make an environmental difference in their communities: "Don't let the perfect be the enemy of the good."

This book aims to meet you where you are and help you build your skills around teaching climate change. We will address the three most-cited concerns: finding time to teach a new curriculum (spoiler alert: you don't have to!), addressing the social and emotional needs of students learning about climate change, and providing the science background needed to teach the content. Our companion website (https://companion.corwin.com/courses/TeachingClimateChange) will address the fourth concern, lack of resources, by offering an extensive index of free lesson plans and other resources on climate change. These resources can also be found in the appendix at the end of this book.

Other chapters in this book will address how to identify reliable scientific content; how to navigate political and community pressure; how to tie climate change to existing national standards; and how one state (New Jersey) has created standards and a curriculum around climate change (and what other states have done subsequently). We'll also look at climate justice—acknowledging areas and groups of people most vulnerable to the effects of climate change, especially women and girls.

The Need to Invite Communities Most Affected by Climate Change to Participate in the Solutions

BIPOC communities in the northern hemisphere are more likely to suffer from the effects of climate change due to their proximity to pollution sources and contaminated water (Patnaik et al., 2020). Despite their high level of concern about climate change, these communities are often absent from climate conversations. Moreover, research and articles contributing to climate policy and action predominantly focus on the northern hemisphere despite the southern hemisphere experiencing more immediate and severe environmental impacts. Diverse perspectives and inclusive approaches in climate science are crucial for comprehending intricate climate challenges and engaging policymakers and the public effectively (Ballew et al., 2021).

What Are Teachers Teaching Today?

The first step in understanding what information and training teachers need is to gauge the state of climate education in the United States today. In March 2016, the National Center for Science Education (NCSE) published a report called "Mixed Messages: How Climate Change Is Taught in America's Public Schools." The NCSE is a nonprofit organization in the United States that defends the teaching of evolution and climate change in public schools. This report investigated the accuracy, comprehensiveness, and balance of the materials, textbooks, and curricula used in teaching students about climate change in U.S. public schools. The report aimed to determine whether there are inconsistencies, gaps, or biases in how this critical topic is taught across different schools or regions in the United States.

The study showed that approximately 75% of public-school science teachers cover climate change, with students receiving education about recent global warming. Teachers who dedicate at least one class hour to the topic cover important aspects such as the greenhouse effect, carbon cycle, and consequences of climate change. Positive steps to alleviate recent global warming are also discussed by many educators. However, up to 30% of teachers who teach about climate change believe that there are different perspectives regarding the primary causes of global warming (see Figure 1.6).

FIGURE 1.6 • Polled Teachers' Personal Acceptance of the Existence and Causes of Global Warming

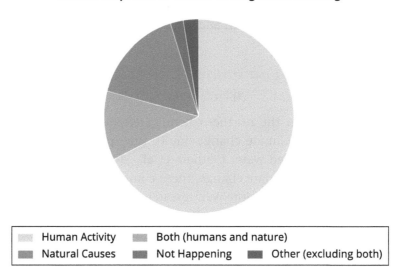

Teacher Responses to What is Causing Global Warming

| Human Activity | Both (humans and nature) |
| Natural Causes | Not Happening | Other (excluding both) |

Source: Data from Plutzer and Hannah (2016).

The research also reinforces the idea that many teachers are not confidant about the adequacy of their understanding of the science behind climate change. Many teachers rate their expertise in climate models as lower than their peers and relatively less than their knowledge of other science topics. This is not surprising because less than half of all teachers polled had any formal coursework on climate change, and less than half are aware that more than 97% of practicing scientists believe that global warming is primarily caused by human activities.

The conclusion of NCSE's report was that the complex nature of climate change education calls for a coordinated and cumulative approach:

• Current teachers require assistance to stay updated with the latest scientific knowledge through effective teaching materials and professional development opportunities.

- Authors of teaching resources should not assume that educators using their materials have completely grasped the underlying science.

- Teacher education programs must also prepare future teachers to handle the politicization of science in general, and educators, administrators, and community members must remain watchful for attempts to introduce denial into the classroom.

Any publisher or organization that aims to help educators present climate science accurately and engagingly must recognize the ideological diversity of educators and tailor climate change education to be inclusive at all levels of instruction. According to the survey, no single policy or program can fundamentally change how climate change is taught in U.S. schools. However, the survey results can guide those who aim to provide today's students and future generations with the scientific knowledge required to tackle the challenges of climate change (Plutzer & Hannah, 2016).

REASONS FOR HOPE

. . . .

Q&A   Q: How do we communicate the severity of the climate change situation without making it too scary?

Kylie Currie, Classical Preparatory Academy, Springhill, FL

A: This may be one of the most important questions answered in this book. It is not an easy task. In this section, some of the strategies that teachers can implement are addressed. We also delve deeper into climate anxiety in Chapter 6. The short answer is to provide students with agency and to remind them that scientists and innovators are working on solutions. Our fellow humans who engage in scientific inquiry are capable of great achievements; they are responsible for rocket ships, computers, and hospitals. Our species has the potential to solve the climate crisis, and young people are part of the equation.

. . . .

Before any discussion about climate change education can take place, we must address how to proceed with the mental health of our students in mind. The Centers for Disease Control (2023) reported that even before the COVID-19 pandemic, there was a mental health crisis among students for well over a decade: Young people have experienced a 40% increase in feelings of sadness, hopelessness, and suicidal thoughts and behaviors since 2010.

This crisis was amplified by the pandemic, which resulted in additional social isolation, academic disruption, loss of parents and other caregivers, and abuse at home. In addition, concerns about wars, mass violence, racial injustice,

Those of us living today often take for granted advancements like lifesaving breakthroughs in antibiotics, vaccines, water filtration, and medical procedures. Other breakthroughs have made our lives easier, like electricity and automobiles. Your students can use the lesson *Science Saves Lives* at https://qrs.ly/7ng36wk to come up with creative solutions for specific climate problems, like pollution, ocean acidification, and glacial melting (Vazquez, 2021).

natural disasters, political polarization, depersonalization through social media, and climate change have added to the already difficult challenges that children and teenagers face.

These factors can be overwhelming for those of us who work with children daily in the classroom. How do we cover this important concept without making the situation worse? One way is to present climate solutions along with the facts. Helping students find their agency is a proven strategy (Stevenson & Peterson, 2015). In each chapter of this book, you will find success stories that exemplify how teachers around the country have promoted student agency around the topic of climate change. Share these with your students and look for similar success stories in your local news.

Another way to present the reality of today's climate crisis in a way that fosters hope is to discuss how quickly technology is changing. An excellent exercise is to invite retired volunteers to speak with students. Children's eyes grow wide when they hear about people who lived to see the first smart phones, computers, and astronauts. If we were to transport a person living in 1950 to today, they would not recognize the world. Technology advances at an astonishing rate (see Figures 1.7 and 1.8, which demonstrate innovative approaches to alternative energy based on the unique locales in which they are based). Even a time traveler from 1990, a seemingly recent year, would be shocked when presented with the latest AI technology.

FIGURE 1.7 • Geothermal Pipes at the Krafla Power Station in Iceland

Source: istock.com/Travel_Motion

Note: Reminding students that scientists and engineers are working on the climate crisis and that the decades ahead hold innovations we cannot even begin to imagine might ease their climate anxiety. Indeed, those of us alive today would likely be astonished if we time-traveled to encounter the world of 2050.

FIGURE 1.8 • A Field of Wind Turbines in Palm Springs, California

Source: istock.com/Ginton

TIPS TO MAKE A DIFFERENCE: Pack It In, Pack It Out
Angela Anthony, Oklahoma Union High School, South Coffeyville, OK

1. When possible, reuse or recycle food packaging (deli cups, plastic cutlery, etc.).

2. Support environmentally friendly companies.

3. Find ways to talk about conservation and environmentally friendly practices with students, regardless of the subject that you teach.

4. Become involved in research and/or citizen and community science projects that aim to educate, conserve, and restore.

WHAT SHOULD STUDENTS KNOW?

Today, climate action across North America is real. Local municipalities, states, and the federal government are showing that the transition to a carbon-free future is possible. For example, the government leaders of Miami, Florida, came to a unanimous decision in April 2021 to aim for a net-zero reduction in greenhouse gases by 2050, with a 60% reduction target by 2035 (City of Miami, 2021). The Austin Climate Equity Plan was adopted by the City Council of Austin, Texas, in September 2021. The plan's objective is to achieve net-zero communitywide greenhouse gas emissions by 2040 (City of Austin, 2021).

Many states are also taking action. In January 2023, the Minnesota House of Representatives passed a significant bill mandating that the state's electric utilities obtain all their electricity from carbon-free sources by 2040 (Marohn, 2023). From December 2022 to May 2023, California Climate Investments invested almost $511 million in 7,326 projects, which are expected to reduce greenhouse gas emissions by 3.3 million metric tons. More than 84% of the implemented funds are being utilized for the benefit of priority populations, including low-income communities and households (CCI, 2024).

 Q: Are there any easy-to-access and up-to-date simulations that will help teaching climate change?

Tracy Majors, Wyoming High School, Wyoming, OH

A: Yes! Climate science is very complex, but thankfully, numerous interactive tools are accessible online that help students link different concepts, visualize abstract ideas, and anticipate the future.

The Climate Reality Project reviews six of these excellent simulations on their website.

- Our favorite: En-ROADS is a climate simulator that operates worldwide and enables individuals to investigate the effects of numerous policies, such as carbon pricing, electrification of transportation, and advancements in agricultural practices, on numerous factors, including energy costs, temperature, air quality, and sea level rise (https://qrs.ly/k1g378q).

- *The Guardian's* Fossil Fuel Interactive shows how much coal, oil, and gas the world extracts every day (https://qrs.ly/i8g379q).

- The Climate Time Machine tool by NASA offers a visual representation of the link between our emissions and the subsequent increase in temperatures. It also shows some of the possible effects of global warming (qrs.ly/hqg3gno).

- The Yale Climate Opinion Maps illustrate the diversity of Americans' views on climate change (https://qrs.ly/exg378v).

- Discover how climate change is affecting your country with the *New York Times'* Climate Risk by Country (https://qrs.ly/2sg3791).

- The Earth Overshoot Day Calculator helps individuals understand their own impact on the environment by calculating how many Earths would be needed if everyone lived the same lifestyle as you (qrs.ly/ghg3gki). (The Climate Reality Project, 2021)

All in all, more than 600 local governments in the United States have developed climate action plans (Markolf et al., 2022). As of the end of 2023, a minimum of 147 bills have been presented in 24 states with the aim of lowering emissions and enhancing energy efficiency in buildings (National Caucus of Environmental Legislators, 2023).

At the level of the U.S. federal government, the current most significant legislation touching on climate change in U.S. history (Environmental Protection Agency, 2023), The Inflation Reduction Act (IRA), was signed into law by President Joe Biden on August 16, 2022 (see Figure 1.9). The IRA provides funding, programs, and incentives to facilitate the transition to a clean energy economy. It is expected to drive the deployment of new clean electricity resources and reduce renewable energy costs for various organizations, including Green Power Partners. Utilizing the incentives offered by the IRA, such as tax credits, will be crucial in accelerating the clean energy transition and lowering greenhouse gas emissions. In 2023, the U.S. Department of the Treasury reported that IRA investments are taking off in "Energy Communities"—areas with a history of fossil fuel production. Clean investments have increasingly been directed toward economically disadvantaged counties, with more than 80% of such investments allocated to counties with below-average wages and more than 85% to counties with below-average college graduation rates (U.S. Department of the Treasury, 2024; see Figure 1.10).

FIGURE 1.9 • Growth in Clean Investments After the IRA Passed (U.S. Department of the Treasury, 2024)

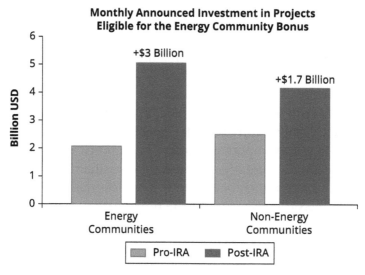

Source: U.S. Department of the Treasury (2024).

FIGURE 1.10 • Where Clean Investment Dollars Are Flowing (U.S. Department of the Treasury, 2024)

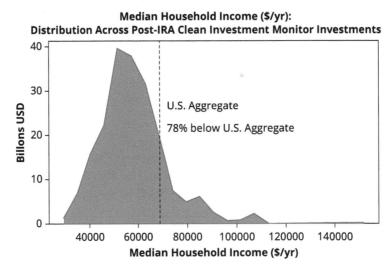

Source: U.S. Department of the Treasury (2024).

Carbon capture technology is one exciting part of the climate solution that is receiving a lot of attention recently. Under President Biden, the U.S. government is investing billions of dollars in demo projects, research, and tax breaks to incentivize carbon capture. Private companies, including venture capitalist firms and energy giants, are also making large investments. There have been some big wins in this space, with millions of dollars being awarded for capturing CO_2 from power plants and gas wells. In December 2023, the Department of Energy awarded $890 million to support carbon capture projects at natural gas and coal plants. ExxonMobil also announced a $100 million investment in a carbon capture and storage project in Wyoming in October 2023 (U.S. Department of Energy, 2023). Heirloom Carbon Technologies, a U.S. climate champion, launched a direct air capture plant in Tracy, California, in November 2023. This innovation can pull up to 1,000 tons of CO_2 from the air each year and is critical in our fight to keep global warming below 1.5°C (Chase, 2024). Carbon capture technology offers a great opportunity to address climate anxiety in the classroom. Students can research important aspects of carbon capture and explore its different methods, limitations, and future possibilities, which will foster a sense of agency and empower students to learn more about potential solutions. Teachers can also connect the rise of carbon capture technology to potential career paths, discussing the need for scientists, engineers, and policymakers in this growing field.

At the time of publication, another promising development emerged in Europe. Carbon capture technologies gained significant momentum, particularly in countries like Norway and the Netherlands. The European Union has committed to continue substantial funding to scale up carbon capture and storage (CCS) infrastructure, positioning it as a key tool for addressing climate change (Earth.org, 2024).

Young people are leading the charge in many places. In a landmark settlement, Hawaii agreed to decarbonize its transportation system by 2045 after 13 youths sued the state, arguing its policies threatened their future due to climate change (Raymond, 2024). And a lawsuit filed by young Montanans forced the state to consider the climate impact when issuing permits for fossil fuel projects. In BREAKING NEWS: The Montana Supreme Court has just ruled that the young people who sued the state in that climate-change lawsuit have a constitutional right to "a clean and healthful environment."

In Canada, the government has passed a number of economic plans, including The Pan-Canadian Framework on Climate Change and Clean Growth (PCF) in 2016 and 2020's Healthy Environment Healthy Economy plan (HEHE). The country has also seen a steady increase in carbon pricing, which is crucial in tackling climate change, and it has also pledged to phase out coal-fired power entirely by 2030.

Carbon pricing is a system that charges polluters for their greenhouse gas emissions. The goal is to make those who cause pollution pay for the damage it creates, such as extreme weather events and rising sea levels. Putting a price on carbon encourages businesses and individuals to reduce their emissions to save money. For example, the Energy Innovation and Carbon Dividend Act of 2023 would put a fee on carbon pollution from fossil fuel companies and then return 100% of the net fees to households as a dividend. The dividend would be paid directly to eligible individuals, who are defined as residents with a Social Security number or TIN. According to the Citizens' Climate Lobby, about two-thirds of Americans would receive more in dividends than they would pay in higher prices. They also say that the act could inject billions into the economy, protect family budgets, and encourage innovation (Citizens' Climate Lobby, 2024).

Here are some other well-known solutions to climate change that students can explore that can reduce carbon emissions and help the world prevent climate change's worst effects. Think about assigning a writing project to report on any of the following.

1. **Electrifying the Grid** involves shifting energy generation away from fossil fuels to cleaner sources like renewables, reducing carbon emissions as electricity production becomes less reliant on fossil fuels (Union of Concerned Scientists, 2021).

2. **Decarbonizing the Grid** calls for removing or offsetting the carbon emissions associated with electricity generation, using carbon capture technology or implementing reforestation projects that absorb atmospheric carbon dioxide (IEA, 2020).

3. **Agriculture Solutions** involves adopting practices that reduce emissions from farming and livestock operations (World Resources Institute, 2020).

4. **Protecting Nature** refers to preserving and restoring ecosystems like forests, wetlands, and oceans, which act as carbon sinks by absorbing and storing carbon dioxide (United Nations Environment Programme, 2021).

5. **Plastics Cleanup** addresses the issue of plastic waste and its environmental impact (Ocean Cleanup, 2021).

6. **Cement Technology** focuses on reducing the carbon emissions associated with cement production by using alternative materials (Global Cement and Concrete Association, 2020).

7. **Carbon Capture Technology** captures CO_2 emissions from sources like power plants and stores them deep underground in geological formations to prevent them from entering the atmosphere (Carbon Capture and Storage Association, 2021).

If students are provided with hopeful examples like these and are given agency and ways to be a part of the solution, they are more likely to have hope for the future (Stevenson & Peterson, 2015), and we as teachers may be able to present this difficult subject in a way that does not lead to hopelessness.

The key is trying to build a narrative for people which is positive. It's "This is the world we can build. We can address climate change alongside other issues. It's not going to cost you a ton of money. It might save you money. We'll have cleaner air. We'll have more energy security." This is more appealing than "We're all going to die from climate change."

—Hannah Ritchie, PhD, data scientist and science communicator, University of Oxford. Author of *Not the End of the World.*

The year 2024 had many depressing climate milestones, such as being the hottest year since records began in 1940. Global carbon emissions reached 45.8 billion metric tons, a new high. Emissions remain on an upward trajectory globally, emphasizing the need for rapid, global action to achieve a peak and then reduce emissions significantly to meet climate targets. (Friedlingstein et al., 2024).

On a positive note, according to a recent study on global electricity generation, renewable energy is growing quickly and is almost at the pace required to triple capacity by the end of the decade (IEA 2023).

 Q: Where can I find good lesson plans about climate change?

Andrea Strouse, Wes Del High School, Gaston, IN

A: Many trusted organizations offer free ready-to-go lessons on climate change.

- The NASA Climate website (https://climate.nasa.gov/for-educators/) offers lessons and activities designed for students in grades K–12 that are aligned with both Next Generation Science Standards and Common Core Math Standards.

- Teachers can utilize NASA's Climate Kids (https://climatekids.nasa .gov/) as a valuable resource for teaching about global climate change. The Big Questions section can provide essential background information, while games like Offset can make learning about the carbon cycle more engaging. Videos such as "What Is Happening in the Ocean" can spark whole-class discussions, and the Activities page is full of resources and links that teachers may find useful for planning lessons.

- The CCL Climate Classroom curriculum is divided into three modules: Impacts of Climate Change, Climate Solutions, and Taking Action. Students learn about the impacts of climate change around the world and in their own communities, as well as potential solutions and how to take action to address climate change. The program includes activities such as creating climate stories, contacting members of Congress, and lobbying. https://qrs.ly/ygg3798

 TIPS TO MAKE A DIFFERENCE: Keep It Simple
Katherine Korn, Williamsville East High School, East Amherst, NY

1. Don't waste food.
2. Take shorter showers.
3. Don't overconsume goods (you don't need a new phone every year).
4. Reduce, reuse, recycle (in that order).
5. Avoid fast fashion. Buy local.

Success Story: The Power of Collaboration at George Washington Carver Middle School, Miami, Florida

Bertha Vazquez, formerly of George Washington Carver Middle School, Miami, FL

This is my story.

It all started in 2007 when a friend gave me a ticket to see former Vice President Al Gore speak at the University of Miami. He was presenting a screening of *An Inconvenient Truth,* his incredibly influential documentary about climate change (Guggenheim, 2006). It really hit me. I lost sleep.

The school where I taught for 33 years, George Washington Carver Middle School, sits just 8 feet above sea level; several of the surrounding neighborhoods are even lower. Miami is often cited as the city with the most to lose economically because of climate change, not just in the United States, but globally.

In 2007–2008, I asked my colleagues at Carver to join me in a schoolwide effort to show our students that change was possible. The results were astounding. I developed and conducted several initial workshops on energy-saving strategies and environmental curriculum with the principal's permission. The first step was building awareness and encouraging a sense of the school community. I included everyone, creating workshops for my school's faculty, cafeteria employees, custodial staff, students, and parent-teacher association.

Science teachers focused on basic climate science in their classes (e.g., units on energy and energy transfers, ecology, and meteorology). Students in other disciplines participated in engaging lessons, ranging from art installations to writing pen pal letters to children in other countries.

As a result of what the school community learned, we made several efforts to reduce our energy consumption:

- Increased efforts to reduce and recycle. For example, the PTSA and school administration switched to digital communications to save paper.

- Swapped in energy-efficient light bulbs

- Added smart thermostats in the cafeteria and auditorium

- Added weather stripping around doors and windows

- Collaborated with a local business that donated labor and materials to paint a school roof white (which reflects heat and keeps buildings cooler)

Every department at Carver participated in our green efforts. For example, the art students created "trash monsters" out of the litter they found near the school (see Figure 1.11).

As a result of schoolwide initiatives, the school's electric bill decreased by $52,700 from September 2007 to September 2008. Our carbon emissions were reduced by 297,000 lbs., as calculated by Dream in Green (2008). This was an enormous accomplishment, and it was the beginning of continued work by the school community that goes on to this day.

And lest you think this work is thankless: The school community and I received enormous publicity around our achievements (leading to my opportunity to coauthor this book!). George Washington Carver's successes were highlighted in the film series *Young Voices for the Planet,* written and produced by Lynne Cherry (2013).

FIGURE 1.11 • A Trash Monster, Titled "Warming Earth."

Source: Alexandra Garcia

Photo Credit: Janas Byrd

TIPS TO MAKE A DIFFERENCE:
Carpools and Composting

Andrew McCullough, Brunswick High School, Brunswick, ME

1. Create a school carpool for teachers.
2. Unplug appliances over vacations.
3. Start a compost collection in the cafeteria.

LEARNING FROM OUR COLLEAGUES
How Do We Provide Electricity to the World?

After the bell rings, it takes a few minutes for the students to settle down. The usual round of requests for bathroom passes and trips to the Lost and Found ensues before Ms. V starts her class.

"Can somebody tell me what their favorite electronic device is?" The hands shoot up immediately.

"I love my cell phone!" cries Massimo.

"Yeah, but I prefer the computer,' says William, "or my Xbox."

"Wait a second, what about your refrigerator? That's more important, in a way," answers Sophia.

"So are the lights," counters Aiden.

Microwave ovens, heaters, car chargers, hair dryers, the list continues to grow.

"You know, all of these things are important. And let's not forget air conditioning. I don't know if we could live here without it," says Ms. V. The students nod in agreement. "So, it's okay to say electricity is an important part of our lives. I mean, in addition to all the devices you mentioned, think about how important electricity is in a hospital. Now, if it's such a big deal, tell me, how do we generate electricity?"

The teacher smiles as silence ensues. She's done this before. And she knows that not a single seventh grader in her Honors Physical Science class will know the answer. She will lovingly tease her class now. "You mean, you guys all love everything electricity gives you, but you don't know how humans provide electricity for our city? You know all the words to your favorite songs, but you don't know where the electricity in your homes comes from?"

Slowly, the students will begin to work out the answers; they'll guess that their electricity comes from solar or wind energy. "A small percentage may come from those alternative sources, but the majority does not," replies Ms. V.

Ms. V pulls a flashlight out of her desk drawer similar to the one in Figure 1.12. "I can generate electricity right now; this flashlight has no batteries in it." The students are stunned. "I only need two things to generate electricity, sort of. What's in this flashlight?" Ms. V asks probing questions as the flashlight goes around the room and the students discuss the possibilities. Eventually, the answer emerges.

FIGURE 1.12 • A handheld flashlight powered by the mechanical energy of the human hand.

Source: istock.com/Garry518

"You have to turn a magnet around a copper wire or the other way around!" exclaims Josephine.

"Great! We call the copper wire/magnet thingy a generator. Now for the tough part. How do we do that? How do we get it to turn? That requires energy. I know Jose mentioned wind energy earlier. The wind can turn the generator. Solar panels do not use copper wires and magnets to make electricity, we'll learn more about that soon. But most cities turn the generators another way."

Another round of probing questions begins as students are reminded of their unit on energy transfers. It takes 15 minutes before the answer becomes clear. Ms. V asks John to summarize the answer for the others.

"We light fossil fuels on fire or use uranium in a nuclear power plant to create heat. Either way, the heat boils water, which produces steam. The steam is used to turn the generator."

Ms. V has set the foundation for her next lesson. The students will learn how different sources of energy generate electricity. They will compare their costs and benefits. The project will include how the burning of fossil fuels contributes to climate change.

Reflection Questions

1. What's your biggest concern about teaching climate change? Can you see that changing after you read this book?

2. How do you feel when you think about the opportunities lost to correct environmental damage earlier?

3. How would you help your students work through their feelings about climate change? Can you think of actions that can be done at your own school or in the local community to give your students agency?

4. Why do you think it's important to talk about climate change and other societal challenges on a personal level?

5. Have you taken any personal steps to address the climate crisis? If so, what were they and which one was the most challenging for you? What inspired you to make these changes in your life?

6. When it comes to combating climate change, which do you think is more crucial: individual behavior change or broader policy change? Or do we need both to make a significant impact?

7. What is your connection with nature and the climate? What do you think this relationship will look like in the future?

8. Are you concerned about climate change? If yes, what worries you the most? And what measures would you like to see taken to combat it?

9. Have you ever experienced or witnessed the effects of climate change directly?

For Further Reading

FOR TEACHERS

Doerr, J. E. (2021). *Speed & scale: An action plan for solving our climate crisis now*. Portfolio.

Hayhoe, K. (2021). *Saving us: A climate scientist's case for hope and healing in a divided world*. One Signal Publishers/Atria Books.

Figueres, C., & Rivett-Carnac, T. (2020). *The future we choose: Surviving the climate crisis* (1st ed.). Alfred A. Knopf.

Ritchie, H. (2024). *Not the end of the world: How we can be the first generation to build a sustainable planet*. Little Brown Spark.

FOR STUDENTS

Ages 8 and up

Gilles, R. (2021). *Climate change in infographics*. Cherry Lake.

Ages 7–10

Jackson, T., & Kordić, D. (2022). *How do we stop climate change?* Weldon Owen Children's Books.

CHAPTER TWO

DEBUNKING 10 MISCONCEPTIONS ABOUT CLIMATE CHANGE

. . . .

The brain is like a muscle. When it is in use, we feel very good. Understanding is joyous.

—*Carl Sagan*

THIS CHAPTER WILL DISCUSS

- Whether we should introduce students to climate misconceptions
- The most common misconceptions surrounding climate change, and
- How teachers can use this information in a lesson

One of the goals of this book is to help teachers equip their students to untangle common misconceptions about climate change, separating fact from fiction with critical thinking skills. Students can learn to analyze evidence and sources like detectives, distinguishing reliable information from misleading claims. The goal is for students to be able to communicate their understanding effectively and contribute to informed solutions.

SHOULD WE INTRODUCE STUDENTS TO CLIMATE MISCONCEPTIONS?

Yes.

Believing climate misconceptions may confuse students. Helping our students understand why there are misconceptions can help students identify misinformation and therefore enable them to seek out reliable scientific content.

Our students will walk out of our classrooms and be exposed to more information in a single day than our grandparents were in their lifetimes. Not all this information will be credible. And thanks to social media and monetized sources of news, misinformation spreads faster than the truth (Vosoughi et al., 2018).

Approximately 402.74 million terabytes of data are created each day. If we imagine a standard DVD holds 4.7 gigabytes (GB) of data, 402.74 million terabytes would be equivalent to roughly 85,689,148,894 DVDs! That's a stack of DVDs reaching from the Earth to the moon over 280 times! (Duarte, 2024). (Remember DVDs?)

- An average internet user generates about 146.8 gigabytes (GB) of data daily. That's like creating a new high-definition movie every single day! In a household of four, that jumps to more than half a terabyte (TB)— that's enough to store hundreds of thousands of movies!

- Facebook churns out a whopping 4,000 TB daily. X, with its constant stream of tweets (around 500 million daily), generates 560 GB of data. TikTok's daily video content adds another 7.35 TB to the mix.

- YouTube, with its massive library of user-uploaded videos, sees more than 720,000 hours of content added daily! This translates to 4.3 petabytes (PB) of data—that's like storing the entire Library of Congress in digital form, every single day.

- Google, the world's search engine giant, processes 3.5 billion searches daily, contributing 20 PB of data!

(Edge Delta, 2024)

Teachers cannot begin to address individually the amount of misinformation included in those astounding numbers. Our role as educators is to help young people learn to distinguish credible from noncredible claims. And the topic of climate change is particularly rife with noncredible claims.

Let's start with where climate misconceptions come from.

There is no single cause that can be pinpointed for the spread of climate misconceptions. For example, disinformation campaigns are often used by groups with a vested interest in maintaining the status quo. Some fossil fuel companies or political factions might spread false information about climate change to sow doubt and delay action. These campaigns often cherry-pick data and misrepresent scientific findings to further their agenda.

Another factor that contributes to the spread of misinformation is confirmation bias (Trecek-King, 2022; see Figure 2.1). We all tend to seek information that confirms our existing beliefs, and this can lead to selective exposure to climate change information that aligns with our worldview. Social media algorithms are echo chambers that can exacerbate this, creating information silos where misinformation circulates freely. It's very easy for us to see biases in others; it's much harder to turn the lens inward and check our own biases. And we all have biases, which may not be immediately apparent to us. We may hold opinions that are based on our culture, upbringing, or personal experiences. By acknowledging these biases, we can take steps to overcome them (Sylvie, 2021).

FIGURE 2.1 • We Seek Information That Confirms Our Beliefs

Source: istock.com/PeopleImages

A lack of scientific literacy can also contribute to the spread of climate misconceptions. Understanding complex scientific concepts like climate change requires some level of scientific literacy. Not everyone has access to quality science education, and gaps in knowledge can leave people vulnerable to misleading narratives. Misinterpretations of scientific findings can also contribute to the spread of climate misconceptions, even among well-meaning individuals. This is why it's crucial to use reliable sources that present information in a clear and accurate way. This issue will be addressed in depth in Chapter 3.

Can you think of a time when you've found yourself looking for media that confirms one of your biases?

Sensationalized media coverage is another factor that can distort the public's perception of climate change. Media outlets often focus on extreme weather events or dramatic predictions, which can downplay the long-term and complex nature of the issue. This sort of media coverage brings in viewers/listeners/readers, but it can be misleading. (Have you ever watched national coverage of a natural disaster going on in your hometown? That's often a good example of how the media can distort the reality of the situation.)

Emotional responses can also play a role in the spread of climate misconceptions. Fear and anger can cloud our judgment and make us more susceptible to misleading information. Understanding the emotional dimensions of climate change communication is important for crafting clear and truthful messages.

Finally, social and cultural factors can influence how people perceive climate change. For example, cultural values and political ideologies can influence the acceptance of climate change. People in more individualistic cultures might be less receptive to collective action on climate change compared to those in more communal cultures (Xiang et al., 2019).

To effectively address climate misconceptions with our students, we need to take a comprehensive approach that involves promoting scientific literacy, avoiding misinformation, and developing critical thinking skills.

An opening classroom discussion on climate misconceptions might include questions such as the following:

- Why are these misconceptions so common?

- Are they innocent claims?

- Have some of them been promulgated to perpetuate doubt around the threat of climate change?

- How do my feelings about climate change affect my understanding of what is going on?

- How do we learn to honestly assess any new misconceptions that crop up in the future?

 Q: How do scientists know what the climate was like prior to today?

Shanna Burcham, Health Academy High School, Chesapeake, OH

A: Directly measuring the Earth's climate before the advent of thermometers is impossible, but scientists have come up with resourceful ways to reconstruct past climates using proxies—indirect clues found within the Earth's natural records. Here are some examples and how they're used:

- Tree rings: Wider rings on trees indicate favorable growing conditions, usually associated with warmer temperatures.

- Coral reefs: Coral skeletons show growth patterns and isotopic ratios that help track changes in temperature and ocean acidity.

- Ice cores: Ancient ice layers contain air bubbles that reveal past atmospheric composition, providing information on temperature and greenhouse gas levels.

- Ocean sediments: Different types of shells or pollen in layers of ocean sediments indicate past ocean temperatures and vegetation.

- Speleothems (cave formations): Stalactites and stalagmites' layers reflect past rainfall and temperature patterns.

By analyzing these proxies and comparing them across different sources, scientists can piece together a detailed picture of past climates. It's like solving a mystery with multiple clues that offer glimpses into the bigger picture (see Figure 2.2).

FIGURE 2.2 • Scientists use ice core data as if it were an Earth history book, deciphering ancient atmospheres and climates locked in layers of ancient ice.

Source: US Geological Survey

TIPS TO MAKE A DIFFERENCE: Small Changes!

Jennifer Grolemund. The Rumson Country Day School, Rumson, NJ

1. Include water stations at schools to refill reusable bottles.
2. Create a schoolyard habitat on your school grounds.
3. Encourage kids to bring reusable containers for lunch instead of plastic bags.

THE 10 MOST COMMON MISCONCEPTIONS

Misconception 1: The Fluctuations in Temperature Over the Last Hundred Years Can Be Attributed Solely to Natural Cycles

Your students may argue that the climate of the Earth has always changed, so we shouldn't worry about climate change now. Scientists agree that natural phenomena have always contributed to the complex nature of the Earth's climate system. The Earth has undergone a series of ice ages and warming periods over geological time scales. Ice ages, or glacial periods, involve the expansion of ice sheets and glaciers, leading to cooler temperatures and lower sea levels. Interglacial periods follow, characterized by warmer temperatures and the retreat of ice. These cycles are influenced by factors like variations in the Earth's orbit, volcanic eruptions, and ocean currents. Variations in the Earth's orbit can affect the amount of solar radiation received, leading to long-term climate changes. Volcanic eruptions release particles and gases into the atmosphere, impacting sunlight penetration and temperature. And finally, ocean currents play a vital role in redistributing heat around the planet, influencing regional climate patterns.

But while it's true that the climate has changed naturally in the past, we need to understand that the changes happening now are mostly because of human activities like burning fossil fuels and cutting down trees. Think of a boat sailing along a river with a steady current, representing natural climate changes. You make slight adjustments to the sails to stay on course, symbolizing adaptations to past climate shifts. However, if a severe storm were to suddenly push the boat off course, representing anthropogenic (human-caused) climate change, simply acknowledging the current and ignoring the storm wouldn't be enough to get back on track. To stay on course, we must actively address the ongoing and more significant climate changes caused by human actions.

MULTIPLE LINES OF EVIDENCE

To debunk this line of argument and several other misconceptions, we can teach our students the importance of what scientists call "multiple lines of evidence." When making a claim, having multiple, different lines of evidence supports scientific understanding and decision making. Complex issues like climate change require this approach. Relying on a single study, experiment, or observation can be problematic because it may be flawed, biased, or misinterpreted. Gathering evidence from different sources and methods and seeing that all the evidence converges builds confidence in the overall conclusion. It reduces the effects of bias, errors, and limitations of individual sources. It also helps identify any inconsistencies or contradictions in the data. A great way to explain this to our students is to compare it to the work of police detectives and district attorneys trying to solve a crime and prosecute the defendants. They may not be satisfied with just one eyewitness report. They know that the strongest cases have lots of evidence all pointing to the same person: DNA, fingerprints, bank records, video, witnesses, etc.

TIPS TO MAKE A DIFFERENCE: Saving Paper, Saving Fuel

Naomi Elliott, Auburn School District, Auburn, WA

1. Use electronic writing devices to reduce paper waste.
2. Teach keyboarding earlier.
3. Become a "Green School" in cooperation with your local county.
4. Create a garden at school or home.
5. Use timers for lights and other electronic devices.

The multiple lines of evidence converging on the fact that climate change is caused by human activity include the following:

- The increase of greenhouse gas concentrations, the warming of the atmosphere and oceans, and other climate-related impacts all point to human-caused climate change.

- The rate of climate change is much faster now than it has been in the past. The average rate of increase in the combined land and ocean temperature has been 0.14 degrees Fahrenheit (0.08 degrees Celsius) per decade since 1880. Since 1981, the rate of increase has been more than twice as fast, at 0.32°F (0.18°C) per decade (National Centers for Environmental Information, 2022).

- Data from tree rings (Figures 2.3), satellites (Figure 2.4), ice core studies, sediment layers, weather station records, observations of glacier retreat (Figure 2.5), and sea level rise all point to an abnormal temperature increase.

FIGURE 2.3 • Tree rings can be used to estimate the temperature and precipitation over the course of the tree's lifespan.

Source: istock.com/Ja'Crispy

FIGURE 2.4 • Satellite imagery captures the Earth's temperatures, ice coverage, vegetation, and oceans.

Source: istock.com/FrankRamspott

In this image, the MODIS Terra satellite data from NASA reveals anomalies in land surface temperatures in February 2022 relative to the average conditions recorded in the same month between 2001 and 2010 (NASA, 2022).

FIGURE 2.5 • In 2022, Swiss glaciers experienced their most significant melting rate since the start of record-keeping over a century ago, losing 6% of their volume throughout the year (Revill & MacSwan, 2022).

Source: Istock.com/sgoloyunin

Natural cycles do not explain these changes. Scientists emphasize that when this consistency across diverse sources exists, it greatly strengthens the conclusion that recent climate change is primarily driven by human activities.

In addition, even though the Earth's climate has changed before, we need to remember that our modern way of life has developed during a time of otherwise stable climate. The Earth's climate has been relatively stable for the last 10,000 years (Schmidt & Hertzberg, 2011). The climate anomalies we are witnessing are not just random fluctuations but compelling evidence of a changing climate system. The increasing magnitude, frequency, and global consistency of these anomalies, along with their alignment with scientific predictions, strongly suggest that big changes now could cause problems for people and nature.

> **CIRES Education and Outreach has a free online lesson titled "What Was Earth's Temperature Like in the Past?"** Students are taught to explore historical temperature trends and assess whether there have been recent changes in temperatures globally. https://qrs.ly/vjg379u

Q&A   Q: Is the climate really changing or is it cyclical?

Cindy Moore, Elgin High School, Elgin, TX

A: The Earth's climate has undergone changes in cycles throughout history, but there's a crucial difference now. Although natural cycles still play a role, the current rate of climate change is far more rapid, and converging evidence points to the increased change in climate being caused by human activities like burning fossil fuels. Natural factors such as the Earth's orbit, volcanic eruptions, and ocean currents still affect the climate, but they are not enough to explain the current rate of climate change. Evidence from various sources, including temperature records, ice cores, and sea levels, supports the hypothesis that human activity is contributing to current climate change trends. So although some natural fluctuations still exist, it is the rapid increase in greenhouse gas emissions that is the dominant factor driving climate change.

Misconception 2: The Sun Is Solely Responsible for Temperature Fluctuations

Students may have read that the Sun is responsible for temperature fluctuations. It's an easy explanation, and we as humans tend to look for simple yes-or-no answers to problems (Konnikova, 2013). Unfortunately, climate change is very complex, and we need to help students see that blaming the Sun is a gross oversimplification. According to the United Nations' Intergovernmental Panel on Climate Change (IPCC), the current scientific consensus is that long- and short-term variations in solar activity play only a very small role in the Earth's climate. Warming from increased levels of human-produced greenhouse gases is actually many times stronger than any effects due to recent variations in solar activity.

For more than 40 years, satellites have recorded the Sun's energy output, which has gone up or down by less than 0.1% during that period. Since 1750, the warming driven by greenhouse gases coming from humans burning fossil fuels is more than 270 times greater than the slight extra warming coming from the Sun itself over that same time interval. Solar flares and sunspots are also sometimes mentioned when this misconception pops up. Solar flares are brief eruptions of intense energy from the Sun's surface, and sunspots are temporary phenomena indicating areas of magnetic activity. Although they are powerful phenomena on the Sun and can influence space weather and impact satellite communications, they do not play a significant role in causing climate change on Earth (Forster et al., 2021).

> The concept of the "illusion of explanatory depth" refers to the tendency we have to overestimate how much we know about a particular topic. In other words, it is natural for us to think we know more than we do. It's not until we're asked to explain a given topic in detail that we realize how limited our understanding actually is (Fernbach, 2013). The reasons for global temperature variations cannot be accurately explained with simple answers. And unfortunately, simple answers often lead to misconceptions.

 Q&A   **Q:** How does climate affect different regions?

Seth Yosef, Austin Independent School District, Austin TX

A: Different regions are experiencing climate change in a number of ways.

Overall warming:

- The Arctic is warming two to three times faster than the global average, leading to rapid sea ice loss, glacier retreat, and permafrost thaw, disrupting the delicate Arctic ecosystem and impacting polar bear populations and indigenous communities reliant on the sea ice.

- In mountain regions, glaciers are retreating at an alarming rate, altering water availability downstream and impacting hydropower generation. For example, the Himalayas are experiencing rapid glacial melt, impacting water availability for downstream communities in countries like India, Nepal, and Pakistan. Short-term risks of melting glaciers include increased flooding in low-lying areas. In the long term, glacier melt could result in water scarcity. The changes in water flow may also have adverse effects on downstream ecosystems, impacting fisheries and biodiversity.

- Rising temperatures in mountain regions also affect winter sports tourism and increase the risk of avalanches.

Droughts and changes in precipitation patterns:

- Parts of East Africa have faced prolonged droughts in recent years, leading to food insecurity, malnutrition, and displacement of communities.

- The ongoing megadrought in the western United States has caused severe water shortages, agricultural losses, and ecological damage. The Mediterranean region is also experiencing more frequent and severe droughts, impacting agriculture, tourism, and water resources.

- In South Asia, monsoon rains have become more erratic, leading to devastating floods that displace communities, damage infrastructure, and spread waterborne diseases. Southeast Asia is also experiencing increased flooding due to heavier precipitation events, impacting coastal communities and agricultural lands.

Heat waves:

- Urban areas are experiencing more frequent and intense increases in temperature, due to the urban heat island effect.

Sea level rise:

- Low-lying island nations like the Maldives and Kiribati face an existential threat from rising sea levels. This leads to coastal erosion, inundation of land, and displacement of communities.

- Major coastal cities around the world are facing risks from rising sea levels, which threaten infrastructure, coastal communities, and tourism industries.

Aridification:

• Already arid regions like the Sahara Desert are likely to experience further aridification due to climate change, worsening existing challenges of water scarcity and desertification. (Allan et al., 2021)

· ·

Misconception 3: Colder Winters in Some Areas Means That the Earth Isn't Warming

The late senator James Inhofe, a Republican from Oklahoma, brought a snowball to the floor of the U.S. Senate in February 2015 as a symbolic gesture to express skepticism about climate change. Inhofe was a prominent climate change skeptic who often questioned the scientific consensus on anthropogenic global warming. The snowball was meant to imply that because it was cold on that particular day, global warming couldn't be occurring.

Students have probably heard this misconception over and over, and it's an important one to help them understand. The misconception that colder winters in some areas mean that the Earth isn't warming stems from a misunderstanding of the difference between *weather* and *climate*. *Weather* refers to short-term atmospheric conditions, including temperature, precipitation, and wind patterns, that occur over a specific period and in a specific location. On the other hand, *climate* refers to long-term patterns and trends in weather over extended periods (decades to centuries) and across larger geographic scales.

Climate scientists study long-term trends in average global temperatures, not short-term variations in local weather. There will always be temperature fluctuations, with some areas experiencing colder-than-average conditions in a given year. However, these fluctuations do not negate the broader trend of global warming.

> Unfortunately, a recurring theme regarding climate misinformation will be the influence of monied interests. Senator Inhofe, for example, received $395,455 in campaign contributions from oil and gas companies from 2017–2022 (OpenSecrets, 2023).

Many arguments that misrepresent climate change use what are known as *logical fallacies,* patterns of reasoning that contain flaws, either in their logical structure or in their premises (Trecek-King, 2024). *Cherry-picking* is one of the most common logical fallacies; this is when someone focuses only on evidence that supports their stance while ignoring all the evidence that contradicts it. Pointing out that a snowy day in April must mean climate change is not real is a classic example of cherry-picking.

Success Story: Rumson Country Day School

Jennifer Grolemund, The Rumson Country Day School, Rumson, NJ

My science curriculum for second-grade students includes the water cycle, the rock cycle, weather, and other Earth science topics. My students take part in an exciting STEAM project every year in which they use climate change as a springboard to design and build models of elevated homes that can withstand hurricane-force winds and flood waters (Figure 2.6a and b). As climate change continues to alter storms and weather patterns, this type of lesson has real-life implications, especially since my school is so close to the New Jersey shoreline.

FIGURE 2.6a and b • Second graders build and test their hurricane houses.

Photo Credit: Jennifer Grolemund

The lesson includes an exploration of how hurricanes form, how climate change is affecting the intensity of these types of storms, and how this impacts people and the environment. Through the use of maps, the students learn about the movement of hurricanes and study the communities and ecosystems that have been historically most impacted by these storms. They also explore how climate change is contributing to increased storm frequency and intensity across the globe, leading to a critical need for better storm preparedness and storm damage mitigation.

Over several weeks, the class works together to understand the difference between weather and climate; how climate change is impacting people, wildlife, and ecosystems; and which areas are most vulnerable. By focusing on hurricanes specifically, the students gain a deeper understanding of the components that shape climate patterns and drive storm formation. This project provides students with a unique opportunity to learn about climate change and its impact on our world, develop important problem-solving and critical thinking skills, and apply the engineering design process to a meaningful, real-life scenario.

Extensions to the lessons change a little every year as I assess what aspects of the project the current students find most interesting. For example, sometimes the students want to learn more about what humans can do to help mitigate climate change and protect coastal areas, such as engaging in habitat restoration projects and making changes to environmental laws. Other times, they are more curious about researching examples of how engineers improve structures to keep people safe during storms or examining the types of tools scientists use when studying climatology and meteorology. The opportunities for cross-curricular connections include math, social studies, geography, technology, and so much more. When possible, we take a field trip to our local beach for hands-on science activities to complement our studies. Over the years, we've been featured in the local newspaper and in the school newsletter.

TIPS TO MAKE A DIFFERENCE: Seal the Deal
James Earley, Roseburg High School, Roseburg, OR

1. Close your fireplace damper when the fireplace is not in use, to prevent drafts.

2. Apply for government and private subsidies to pay for solar panel installations.

3. When you reroof a house, use lighter colored roofing materials to reflect the heat.

4. Get a free energy audit of your home from your power company to learn additional ways to save.

5. Consider buying American-made products to reduce global transportation emissions.

Misconception 4: A Few Degrees Warmer Won't Make a Big Difference

This misconception assumes that climate change is linear when, in fact, it's nonlinear. What's the difference between a linear and nonlinear relationship? Tell your students to imagine riding a bike on flat ground. If you push the pedals harder (input), you consistently go faster (output). The harder you push, the faster you go in a perfectly straight line on a graph (see Figure 2.7a). The relationship is linear. Now, imagine climbing a hill. Pushing the pedals harder (input) might make you go faster at first, but as the slope gets steeper, the effort you put in won't translate to the same increase in speed (output). Your progress would look like a curved line on a graph, not a straight line (Figure 2.7b). In this case the relationship is nonlinear.

FIGURE 2.7a • Linear Relationship

FIGURE 2.7b • Nonlinear Relationship

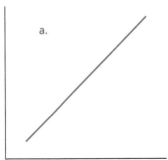

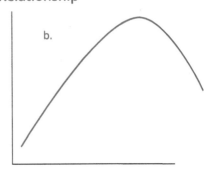

A Linear vs Non-Linear Relationship

Graph a in Figure 2.7 shows how a few degrees can, indeed, make a difference. It depicts a linear relationship. Graph b depicts a nonlinear relationship. Climate is a nonlinear, complex system with many interacting parts. A small temperature rise can disrupt weather patterns, ocean currents, and ecosystems in unpredictable and potentially devastating ways.

The misconception that a few degrees warmer won't make a big difference underestimates the significant and far-reaching impacts of even small increases in global temperatures. Why? Because climate change isn't just about temperatures rising a few degrees uniformly in a linear progression as shown in the graph. Warming, even seemingly small amounts, disrupts complex environmental systems, leading to nonlinear changes.

Share these disruptions with your students to help them understand the misconception.

Disruptions	Examples	More Information
Extreme and unpredictable weather events	Heatwaves, droughts, floods, storms	Unbalanced: How Climate Change Is Shifting Earth's Ecosystems (https://education .nationalgeographic.org/resource/ unbalanced-how-climate-change- shifting-earths-ecosystems/)
Rising Sea Levels	Changes in the strength of ocean currents and wind; redistribution of ocean heat	Climate Change: Global Sea Level | NOAA (https://www.climate.gov/ news-features/understanding- climate/climate-change-global-sea- level)

The nonlinear effects of climate change include the following:

- Climate change disrupts complex environmental systems, leading to extreme and unpredictable weather events: heatwaves, droughts, floods, and storms.

- Rising sea levels threaten coastal communities and ecosystems.

- Ocean acidification harms marine life and disrupts food webs.

- Warmer water temperatures disrupt the delicate balance between corals and their symbiotic algae, leading to coral bleaching and, ultimately, death.

- Loss of biodiversity alters entire ecosystems. For example, keystone species are vital to their ecosystems. They are species that have a disproportionately large effect on their environment relative to their abundance. The polar bear is a prime example. As a top predator, it helps maintain balance in the Arctic. However, climate change is melting sea ice, disrupting the polar bear's habitat and food sources. This decline threatens not only polar bears but the entire Arctic ecosystem of which the polar bear is an integral part.

- Small temperature increases can push the Earth's climate system toward critical thresholds and tipping points, potentially causing abrupt and irreversible changes like melting ice caps.

- Ocean currents are disrupted. For example, as the cold fresh water from melting ice enters the ocean in the North Atlantic, it can affect the Gulf Stream, an important ocean current. If the Gulf Stream slows down, the warm air it carries over Europe will disappear and the temperatures in Europe will drop. The rainfall in South America will decrease, causing a potential disaster for agriculture (Turner, 2023).

- Additional greenhouse gases are released from thawing permafrost, which in turn causes an acceleration of warming.

Your students will have questions about the global impacts of such disruptions, which include the following:

- Food security: Warmer temperatures, altered precipitation patterns, and extreme weather events like droughts and floods threaten global food security by reducing crop yields and challenging agricultural productivity in some regions.

- Health:
  - Higher temperatures can contribute to the spread of diseases—for example, climate change is a significant factor influencing both mosquito migration and malaria transmission. Rising temperatures, altered rainfall patterns, and changes in land use can create more suitable conditions for mosquitoes and increase the risk of malaria outbreaks.
  - Heat and climate change can worsen air and water quality. Rising temperatures intensify air pollution by increasing ground-level ozone and particulate matter from wildfires. Extreme weather events like droughts and floods contaminate water sources with pollutants, harmful algae, and sediment. Additionally, warmer water temperatures promote harmful algal blooms, further degrading water quality. Finally, increases in the frequency of heat-related illnesses like heat stroke can also impact vulnerable populations.

- Socioeconomic consequences: The cumulative effects of warming can have widespread social and economic consequences, including the displacement of populations and increased migration.
  - There will be potential conflicts over resources due to changing environments.
  - There will be challenges to infrastructure and economic stability because of the shifting availability of resources.

Because of these grim predictions, it's important for teachers to mitigate students' reactions to this overwhelming news by creating a safe space for open dialogue and focusing on the actionable steps described.

It's also important for your students to understand that the global impacts of climate change are affected by feedback loops:

- Small temperature increases can trigger feedback loops that amplify warming. For example, melting ice reduces the Earth's reflectivity (albedo), leading to more heat absorption and further warming (which leads to more melting ice).

- As temperatures rise, permafrost melts, exposing organic matter. Microbes break down this matter, releasing methane, a potent greenhouse gas. This methane traps more heat, accelerating warming and thawing more permafrost, releasing even more methane. This cycle amplifies global warming and is a major concern due to the vast amount of methane trapped in permafrost.

Speaking of feedback loops, a twist on misconception #4 involves carbon dioxide levels. Skeptics frequently downplay the role of CO_2 in climate change, often citing its low percentage (0.04%) in the atmosphere. They argue that such a small amount cannot have a significant impact on global temperatures (Cama, 2023). However, scientists emphasize that small changes in atmospheric components can trigger large-scale effects due to complex feedback loops within the climate system. For example, a small increase in global temperature can lead to significant melting of Arctic sea ice. As the ice melts, darker ocean water is exposed, which absorbs more sunlight, leading to further warming. This creates a positive feedback loop, amplifying the initial warming and causing even more ice melt.

> **What climate changes have you experienced or heard about in the news? How have your local average temperatures changed over the past 100 years?**

Q&A **Q:** We keep hearing about global warming, yet the weather seems to be even more wet and cold. Why?

Kate Breitschwerdt, St. Mel Catholic School, Fair Oaks, CA

A: You're right, experiencing cold and wet weather can feel contradictory to global warming. But the Earth's temperature is more like a bumpy road than a smooth line. The overall trend is warming, but there are still ups and downs along the way. Here are some things to consider:
- Global warming refers to the average increase in the Earth's temperature over time, but specific regions can experience temporary dips in temperature due to complex atmospheric interactions.
- Climate change disrupts established weather patterns, which can push cold air masses out of the Arctic and southward, causing colder spells in some regions.
- Warmer temperatures lead to increased evaporation, making more moisture available in the atmosphere. This moisture can condense

and fall as rain or snow, potentially contributing to wetter seasons in some areas.

- Weather cycles through periods of warmth and cold, wetness and dryness. Even within a warming trend, occasional cold or wet seasons are normal.

Focusing on long-term trends is crucial when considering climate change. A single cold or wet winter doesn't negate global warming. The consistent rise in average temperatures across the world over decades is evidence that global warming is a reality.

Misconception 5: Many Scientists Disagree on the Cause of Climate Change

The *overwhelming* consensus among climate scientists is that human activities, particularly the release of greenhouse gases, are the primary drivers of recent climate change. Although there may be discussions and ongoing research on specific details of the climate system, the scientific community's core understanding that humans are causing global warming is well-established (IPCC, 2021).

If your students question how we know that climate change has been caused by human activity, help them understand by discussing the following:

- Emphasize again that multiple sources of evidence from climatologists, including temperature records, ice core data, satellite observations, and climate models, support the explanation of climate change as human-induced. So do research contributions from various scientific disciplines, including physics, chemistry, biology, and earth sciences. The consistent agreement on the human influence on climate change across these scientific disciplines underscores the robustness of the scientific understanding.

- Several reputable scientific organizations across the globe, such as the IPCC, NASA, NOAA, and others, agree that human activities are the primary cause of the observed warming since the mid-20th century. In addition, major scientific organizations worldwide, such as the American Association for the Advancement of Science (AAAS), the Royal Society, and the World Meteorological Organization (WMO), have issued statements supporting the understanding that human activities significantly impact the climate.

- The IPCC, a renowned global organization dedicated to evaluating climate science, periodically issues detailed assessment reports that reflect the combined expertise of numerous scientists. These reports consistently link the recent climate changes to human activities, with a strong emphasis on the burning of fossil fuels and deforestation.

- Most climate scientists publish their research in peer-reviewed scientific journals, and studies investigating the causes of climate change continuously affirm that human activities, primarily the emission of greenhouse gases, are the primary causes of recent warming (Cook et al., 2013).

- Attribution studies examine the changes in climate that have been observed and aim to identify the different factors that have contributed to them. These factors can include both natural and human activities. These studies have consistently shown that it is not possible to explain the warming trend observed solely through natural factors and that human activities have clearly had an impact on climate change (Columbia Climate School, 2021).

- More than 99% of climate scientists agree on the human impact on climate change, with only a tiny number of dissenting views that don't reflect the general opinion of the scientific community (Schulte, 2023). These dissenting views are often presented in the media (and those espousing these contradictory views are often employed by businesses and interests that stand to gain if climate change is left to continue unabated).

There is a need for the greenhouse effect to trap the Sun's heat within our atmosphere—this is one of the reasons our planet is hospitable to life as we know it (i.e., dependent on oxygen and water). But human-induced climate change is leading to a runaway greenhouse effect. How do we help students understand this idea? In my class, I begin by drawing a stick figure of one of my students sleeping in their bed, covered by a single, cozy bed sheet. Students think this is hilarious. Adding a stick dog never fails to draw even more laughs. My sleepy stick figure has a smile on their face, and I let the students know the bedsheet keeps them at just the right temperature. I draw piles of blankets under the bed and start bringing them to the surface with arrows and covering the figure. More blankets come up, and then more, until the figure and the dog are completely blotted out. The takeaway: the Earth's natural greenhouse effect is the single bedsheet. Taking fossil fuels from underground and burning them for energy is like adding more and more blankets on top of our friend. It starts getting too hot!

Misconception 6: Chlorofluorocarbons Are Overwhelmingly Responsible for the Greenhouse Effect

If I had a dollar for every time a student told me that the ozone layer and CFCs were important considerations when considering climate change, I'd be a wealthy woman. I can confidently say that the ozone layer was mentioned in every single opening discussion about climate change I ever had with my students.

Say it with me: Chlorofluorocarbons (CFCs) are *not solely* responsible for the greenhouse effect. CFCs are potent greenhouse gases, but they are a minor player in greenhouse warning. Their overall impact on global warming is currently estimated to be around 5–10% compared to carbon dioxide's 60–70%. This is because CFCs were banned under the Montreal Protocol in 1987 due to their ozone-depleting effects, and their atmospheric concentrations have been steadily declining ever since (EPA, 2022).

So although the effects of CFCs are often misunderstood, this is a good place to stop and reflect with students. The Montreal Protocol is an example of how global leaders united in the past to address an international environmental problem. An undisputed success story, the Montreal Protocol led to a 99% reduction in the consumption and production of ozone-depleting substances (ODS), primarily CFCs (United Nations Environment Programme [UNEP], 2023). It resulted in the recovery of the ozone layer and prevented 0.5°C of global warming by 2100 (UNEP, 2023).

With 198 countries as parties, the Montreal Protocol demonstrates the power of international cooperation and scientific evidence in addressing environmental challenges. It provides us with a valuable blueprint for addressing other global environmental issues, not to mention a powerful learning tool to demonstrate what is possible to our own students. It shows that there is hope!

TIPS TO MAKE A DIFFERENCE: Make It Relatable!

Shannon Rine, Tri-County Career Center, Nelsonville, OH

1. When teaching climate change, use examples that students can relate to, such as invasive species they can find in their area or ways that climate change has impacted them personally.

Misconception 7: Carbon Dioxide Can't Be Dangerous Because Plants Require It

The adage "Too much of a good thing can be bad" is appropriate when discussing this misconception with your students. Plants *do* require carbon dioxide for photosynthesis (see Figure 2.8). But excessive amounts of CO_2 can be harmful. When CO_2 concentrations become too high, it can disrupt the internal processes of plants, leading to reduced growth, nutrient deficiencies, and increased susceptibility to pests and diseases.

FIGURE 2.8 • Photosynthesis is the process by which plants capture light energy and convert it into chemical energy stored in sugars, using water and carbon dioxide as raw materials and releasing oxygen as a byproduct.

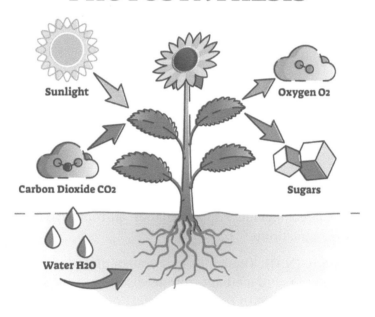

Source: istock.com/VectorMine

The *rate* at which CO_2 is increasing in the atmosphere is also a problem. Plants have evolved to adapt to specific atmospheric CO_2 concentrations. The problem is the rapid rise in CO_2 concentrations that we're currently experiencing due to human activities like burning fossil fuels outpaces the ability of plants to adapt, causing widespread stress and disruptions in ecosystems.

To help our students understand how CO_2 is important for plant growth but can also cause climate change, a couple of points can be discussed in class:

1. Instead of stating that CO_2 can't be dangerous, a more accurate statement would be, "Plants need CO_2, but excessive and rapidly increasing CO_2 concentrations due to human activities pose a threat to both plants and the entire planet."

What other examples of "too much of a good thing" can you come up with?

2. Emphasize the importance of balance and sustainable practices: "Although plants need small amounts of CO_2, we must find ways to reduce atmospheric CO_2 levels to a sustainable level for the well-being of all living things."

3. Water is a good analogy: Remind your students that plants need water to grow, but too much water will kill them.

Misconception 8: Carbon Dioxide Is the Only Greenhouse Gas

Carbon dioxide (CO_2) has become synonymous with the term "greenhouse gas," but it does not stand alone in its influence on the Earth's climate. A diverse collection of gases exerts a warming effect, each with its own unique character and contribution to this complex system (see Figure 2.9).

- **Methane (CH_4):** Possessing a potency 28 times greater than CO_2 over a century, methane plays a significant role in atmospheric heat retention. Its primary sources include natural wetlands, anthropogenic landfills, and livestock agriculture.

- **Nitrous Oxide (N_2O):** Though its atmospheric abundance pales in comparison to CO_2 and methane, nitrous oxide has a warming potential 265 times that of CO_2 over the next century. Fertilizer application and fossil fuel combustion are major contributors to its presence in the atmosphere.

- **Water Vapor (H_2O):** As the levels of carbon dioxide and methane increase, the Earth's temperature increases. That means more evaporation from both water and land areas, which increases the amount of water vapor in the atmosphere. This water vapor absorbs the heat radiated from the Earth, which in turn warms up the atmosphere even more, causing more evaporation and more water vapor to accumulate in the atmosphere. This positive feedback loop more than doubles the warming that would be caused by increased carbon dioxide alone (NASA, 2022). Remember, a positive feedback loop in climate change accelerates warming. Instead of stabilizing the system, it amplifies the initial change.

- **Fluorinated Gases (F-gases):** These synthetic compounds, employed mostly in refrigerants and propellants, have a warming potential thousands of times higher than CO_2. Thankfully, their emissions are increasingly regulated due to their substantial impact on global warming.

What sources are available to help teachers wade through the overwhelming amounts of climate misinformation? Inside Climate News is a Pulitzer Prize-winning nonprofit news organization established in 2007 to provide essential reporting on climate change. They monitor the government, industry, and advocacy groups, holding them accountable for their policies and actions regarding climate change. https://insideclimatenews.org/

Although these gases have varying warming potentials, their actual contributions to climate change depend on their concentrations and lifetimes in the atmosphere. Carbon dioxide, for instance, remains in the atmosphere for centuries, while methane breaks down within a few decades. So, even though methane is more potent per molecule, its overall impact is lower due to its shorter lifespan (EPA, 2020).

FIGURE 2.9 • Common greenhouse gases depicted with plastic ball-and-stick models. Top, left to right: nitrous oxide, ozone, methane. Bottom: pentafluoroethane, carbon dioxide, water.

Source: istock.com/Cristina Moliner

Success Story: Focusing on Heat Waves

Bradley Barton, Maplewood K-8 Co-Op, Edmunds, WA

As a middle school science teacher, I am always looking for ways to connect my students to other concerned members of their community. In 2022, when Jeremy Suzuki, a high school junior (featured in Figure 2.10), reached out to me to share his concern and knowledge about global warming with my students, I jumped at the chance. Jeremy told my class he was looking forward to his summer abroad in Madrid, Spain. He wanted to work on his Spanish and take in the culture of this majestic city. But he was horrified by the deaths caused by the unusually high temperatures that summer.

FIGURE 2.10 • Jeremy Suzuki (at the U.S. Capitol in Washington, D.C.) has made a difference by teaching younger students about climate change and by lobbying the U.S. Congress.

Photo credit: Mark Vossler

In Puget Sound, our hometown of Edmunds, WA, also experienced intense heat waves for the last few summers. Jeremy felt he needed to do something, so he joined the Youth Outreach program of the nonprofit organization Citizen's Climate Lobby (CCL) in September 2022. Thanks to his efforts, he soon became CCL's assistant state director for Washington State. With the help of the Youth Action Team's adult supervisor, Gwen Hanson, Jeremy was able to present to middle school students in his area. He told my class, "I want young people to know they can affect leadership decisions." I find it very meaningful when kids learn about climate change from other kids. My students feel like adults have been dropping the ball on this crucial issue, and it's up to them to do something about it. I tell them to join CCL, join United Student Leaders, or start their own organization and just take action. My students know that *kids aren't just the future; they are the changemakers of today.*

Misconception 9: The Majority of Living Things Will Adapt to All Climate Change

Some plants and animals can adapt to climate change, but it's crucial to dispel the misconception that this means all will adapt successfully or that adaptation alone is enough to solve the problem (Iowa State University, 2019). Explain to your students that the ability of species to adapt to changes in their environment is limited in several ways.

- Evolution takes *a lot of time*, and some populations of organisms simply don't have the necessary genetic variations to adapt quickly enough to survive changing environmental conditions. Mutations in a population do not happen because the species wants or needs them.

- Human activities such as deforestation and urbanization can restrict the movement of many species and limit their ability to find suitable new habitats with better conditions.

- In some cases, after habitat is destroyed there are *no* suitable new habitats.

Species rely on specific interactions with other species to survive, so if some species adapt differently or disappear due to climate change, it can disrupt entire ecosystems, leading to cascading negative effects. For example, the temperature is the primary factor affecting the timing of natural events such as tree leafing and insect emergence, whereas the length of the day triggers bird migration. Climate change results in earlier spring temperatures, but the day length remains constant. As a result, a mismatch may arise because birds may arrive earlier than the optimal food availability, affecting ecosystems where species depend on synchronized timing for survival (Forschungsverbund Berlin, 2019).

The bottom line is that evolution can't run as fast as climate change is galloping. Help your students understand that expecting animals will adapt to climate change is like expecting a marathon runner to keep up with a speeding car. Species evolved over millennia to survive in their environment, but these adaptations may not be sufficient to cope with the rapid pace of human-induced global warming.

Critics who claim that if animals adapted in the past they can adapt today are committing another logical fallacy, the fallacy of false equivalence. Comparing fast, anthropogenic climate change to the gradual, natural climate change of the past is comparing apples to oranges. In addition, let's not forget that 99.9% of species that have ever existed have gone extinct, sometimes as a result of the relatively slower, natural climate changes (Greshko & National Geographic Staff, 2019).

We can help by identifying and protecting areas where species display genetic variation, such as conserving marine and land-based ecosystems in their natural state. This includes intentionally enhancing connectivity between natural habitats and creating pathways for animal migration.

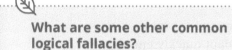

What are some other common logical fallacies?

Try Cranky Uncle with your students. It's a free educational game developed by scientist and cartoonist John Cook to teach people about common misconceptions and denial tactics surrounding climate change.

The Cranky Uncle Teacher's Guide is available at https://qrs.ly/tog379z

These measures would allow species to move to cooler regions, while also promoting the growth of larger, more interconnected populations that can foster genetic diversity. Dan Majka, a cartographer and analyst at the Nature Conservancy, has created a series of maps that illustrate the corridors that mammals, amphibians, and other animals will need to use as they move to new habitats under current models of projected climate change. Majka's interactive map enables both scientists and the general public to visualize the continent-wide impact of climate change on animals and the corridors they will require for movement. qrs.ly/yeg3dh8

Misconception 10: It Will Be Hundreds of Years Before Climate Change Affects Humanity

It's tempting to brush off climate change as a future problem, but unfortunately, the truth is far more urgent.

We're already experiencing the effects of climate change. From intensifying heatwaves and droughts (and resultant fires), to floods, to rising sea levels, and increased intensity in storms, climate change is leaving its mark across the globe. These aren't just distant statistics; these climate change events are disrupting lives, livelihoods, and entire ecosystems right now. In the next 5 to 10 years, we can expect a warmer atmosphere, a warmer and more acidic ocean, higher sea levels, and larger changes in precipitation patterns (World Meteorological Organization, 2024).

Tell your students to think of the proverbial ostrich with its head in the sand. Ignoring the issue won't make it disappear. In fact, delaying action now will only intensify the problem later. The longer we wait, the harder and costlier it becomes to adapt and mitigate the effects. We risk crossing irreversible tipping points and jeopardizing the future for generations to come.

And unfortunately, vulnerability to climate change isn't distributed equally. Low-income communities and countries often lack the resources to cope with these changes, bearing the brunt of the consequences while contributing the least to the problem. It's a matter of social justice as much as environmental responsibility (IPCC, 2022).

HOW CAN I USE THIS INFORMATION IN A LESSON?

Here are some trustworthy resources available to address climate misconceptions in your classroom:

1. **Skeptical Science** is a website that aims to debunk common misconceptions about climate change by providing evidence-based responses. This chapter has only addressed the 10 most common climate misconceptions, Skeptical Science covers more than 200 more. The website also offers a variety of resources, including articles, infographics, and teaching materials suitable for use in classrooms. https://qrs.ly/jlg3gkk

2. **Generation Skeptics** is an education program of The Center for Inquiry. They provide lessons to help students navigate today's media world. Two of their lessons help address climate misconceptions:

   • **How Do You Know if It's a Climate Misconception?** In this lesson, students will identify common misconceptions and learn how to debunk them. You can assign some of these misconceptions to your students. They can work individually or in groups. https://qrs.ly/83g37a2/

   • **Follow the Money Trail.** An important way to spot climate misinformation is to determine whether the source of the information comes from an organization with vested interests in promoting climate change denial. This lesson teaches students to research an organization and determine its money source. https://qrs.ly/ohg37a0

3. **Subject to Climate** is a nonprofit organization dedicated to providing K–12 educators with free, high-quality resources about climate change. Their mission is to make comprehensive climate

education accessible to all students and inspire the next generation to take meaningful climate action. Their lesson, **Fighting Climate Myths**, is a ready-to-use resource for tackling climate misconceptions in your classroom. https://qrs.ly/utg3gkt

4. **A Scientific Guide to the Skeptic's Handbook** is an online resource that you can use to address some of the key questions that skeptics often use to raise doubts about climate change. This guide presents the evidence that humans are causing global warming. https://qrs.ly/t2g37a7

If you prefer to develop your own lesson on misconceptions, here are some things you might want to include:

1. **Pre-evaluation:** Prompt students to share their existing perceptions of climate change before delving into the lesson. This can be achieved through methods such as anonymous surveys, discussions, or concept maps. That way, you'll know where to start when discussing misconceptions.

2. **Dispelling misconceptions:** Actively address prevalent misunderstandings about climate change throughout any lesson. Use clear language, factual evidence, and engaging activities to dismantle inaccurate information.

3. **Exercises in critical thinking:** Pose challenging questions and scenarios that prompt students to critically assess their own beliefs and the information presented. This will be further discussed in Chapter 4, but here are some examples:

   • Who is the source of your climate information? Is it a reputable scientific organization, a news outlet with a known bias, or an individual with no expertise?

   • What is the purpose of this information? Is it designed to inform, persuade, or sell something?

   • What evidence is used to support the claims? Is it based on scientific studies, anecdotal stories, or cherry-picked data?

   • Can you find evidence from other sources that supports or contradicts this information?

   • Where did you learn your initial beliefs about climate change? Were they from family, friends, school, or the media?

   • Are you willing to update your beliefs if presented with new evidence?

   • How can you encourage others to be more informed and engaged in climate action?

4. **Personal relevance:** Help students grasp how climate change affects their lives, communities, and surroundings. Establishing an emotional connection and personalizing the issue makes it more relatable and impactful.

5. **Action-oriented approach:** Move beyond theoretical knowledge to explore solutions and actions individuals and communities can take to address climate change. This empowers students to feel like agents of change. (See Chapters 5 and 6.)

Here are a few ways to continue the journey:

1. **Curated resources:** Supply students with a list of reliable sources such as scientific organizations, documentaries, and climate news outlets to further their learning. You can find more on this in the appendix.

2. **Critical evaluation of information:** Equip students with tools to assess information, identify bias, and verify source credibility before accepting information as factual. (See Chapters 3 and 4 for more on this.)

3. **Lifelong learning:** Motivate students to view the learning process about climate change as continuous, fostering a sense of personal responsibility and ongoing engagement with the issue throughout their lives.

By promoting reflection, dispelling misconceptions, and encouraging sustained learning, we can enable students to become informed and proactive citizens. It's essential to recognize that the primary goal is not only to impart knowledge but also to initiate a critical conversation, foster a deeper understanding of the issue, and empower students who want to take action to do so.

· ·

 Q: Why aren't we teaching that climate change is the clear and present danger that it is?

Anthony Tournis, Mary Gage Peterson Elementary, Chicago, IL

A: To answer this question, I highly recommend one of the books given as an additional resource at the end of this chapter: Katie Worth's *Miseducation.* Worth explores how climate change is currently taught in the United States.

· ·

LEARNING FROM OUR COLLEAGUES
It's Not That Simple!

As the students file into their ninth-grade science class on Monday morning, they are surprised to see images of baseball players on the Smartboard. Some students smile with anticipation as the bell rings; what will Mr. Koogan come up with today? They know the class is supposed to be about energy, and the topic of climate change was introduced last week. What's with the baseball?

The second slide appears on the screen; it's of a young man standing next to their teacher. By the scenery, they appear to be somewhere in Europe.

"OK, class, I'd like you to meet my friend, Stanislas, whom I met on a trip to Slovakia last summer. He is visiting our town and is excited to learn about American culture. I've decided to take him to a baseball game. I'd like to give him a quick primer about the sport, and I need your help. Raise your hand if you can explain baseball to my friend in two or three sentences."

Everyone in the class seems to think this is a very simple task. "Oh! That's easy, Mr. Koogan," replies Peter, the star shortstop on the school team. "You have two teams; one hits the ball with the bat and runs around the bases while the other team tries to stop them."

Mr. Koogan pretends to look perplexed. "What are bases? What's a bat? Does the batting team all hit the ball and run at the same time?"

The students laugh and answer these questions, but Mr. Koogan keeps probing. "How do you stop the batting team?"

Martina answers, "If you catch the ball, you throw it at the player with the baseball glove standing with their foot on first base. If they catch it, the runner is out."

"Not if the runner makes it there before the ball," says Jamar.

"And not if you catch the ball in the air. Then that's it. Then, if any player on the batting team is on a base and runs off their base, they are called out if you throw it to the player on that base," adds Anna.

"Huh?" replies Mr. Koogan. "I don't get it. Can the batter run to another base if the ball is thrown to first base?"

"No, you have to run the bases in order," answers Miranda.

"How many bases are there?" asks Mr. Koogan.

"Three, plus home plate. And you better explain foul balls," adds Brendan.

"And stealing bases," answers Valentina.

"Whoa," says Peter, "This is much more complicated than I thought. I don't think you can explain baseball in two or three sentences, Mr. Koogan."

The class knows their teacher is up to something. They are in the middle of a unit on energy, not baseball. The smile on Mr. Koogan's face lets them know there's a connection somewhere.

"Well, sometimes things seem simple. But when you dig a little deeper, you realize you can't explain them in a few sentences. People try to simplify topics all the time, and that can lead to misunderstandings. Take climate change, for example."

Mr. Koogan lifts the stack of papers on his desk. "Last Friday, at the end of class, I asked you to write down questions about climate change. Here are some of the questions you wrote down."

- *It was freezing last winter; doesn't that mean climate change is not happening?*

- *Carbon dioxide is not dangerous; plants need it. Why are people saying it's dangerous?*

- *I read that the Earth has always gone through temperature cycles. What's the big deal?*

- *Don't some scientists disagree about climate change?*

Mr. Koogan reads several more questions out loud before looking up. "It's natural for people to look for easy answers to questions, but sometimes it takes effort to really understand something. Climate change, like baseball, may seem straightforward, but it's not. We must be willing to take the time to learn about it. That's what scientists do. Be humble. Read. Research. Listen. I can't answer your questions in a couple of sentences. So are you all ready to dig deeper to understand?"

Reflection Questions

1. In what ways can education help tackle and rectify climate change misconceptions?

2. How do climate change misconceptions affect public attitudes toward environmental policies and initiatives?

3. How do scientists come to a consensus on complex issues like climate change?

4. How is climate change already affecting your local community, and what are the potential consequences for future generations?

5. How can we have constructive and respectful conversations with people who might have different views on climate change?

6. How do media and false information contribute to the proliferation of climate change misconceptions?

7. Can personal beliefs and biases influence the way individuals perceive climate change?

8. How can we distinguish between valid skepticism and false information in climate change conversations?

9. What are the economic implications of climate change, and how might misconceptions impact policy decisions?

For Further Reading

FOR TEACHERS

Beach, R., Share, J., & Webb, A. (2017). *Teaching climate change to adolescents: Reading, writing, and making a difference*. Routledge.

Berger, J. J. (2013). *Climate myths: The campaign against climate science*. Northbrae Books.

Berger, J. J., Ehrlich, P. R., & Ehrlich, A. H. (2014). *Climate peril: The intelligent reader's guide to understanding the climate crisis*. Northbrae Books.

Masri, S. (2018). *Beyond debate: Answers to 50 misconceptions on climate change*. Dockside Sailing Press.

Worth, K. (2021). *Miseducation: How climate change is taught in America*. Columbia Global Reports.

FOR STUDENTS

Ages 3–6

Cherry, L. (2020). *The great Kapok tree: A tale of the Amazon rain forest*. Houghton Mifflin Harcourt.

Munsch, R. N., & Martchenko, M. (2020). *The paper bag princess*. Annick Press.

Ages 5–9

Paul, M., & Zunon, E. (2020). *One plastic bag: Isatou Ceesay and the recycling women of the Gambia*. Findaway World, LLC.

Ages 9–12

Part, M. (2019). *The Greta Thunberg story: Being different is a superpower*. Sole Books.

PART II

HOW DO I OVERCOME THE BIGGEST OBSTACLES TO TEACHING CLIMATE CHANGE?

Source: istock.com/johnandersonphoto

CHAPTER THREE

THE IMPORTANCE OF DATA LITERACY IN CLIMATE CHANGE EDUCATION

Start where you are. Use what you have. Do what you can.

—Arthur Ashe

THIS CHAPTER WILL DISCUSS

- Data literacy
- Identifying credible resources; and
- Cutting through the misinformation maze: reliable fact-checking sites

Data literacy is the ability to understand, work with, and convey information through data in a meaningful manner. Our students don't need to be data scientists or computer programmers; they do need to possess the basic skills that enable them to understand how data is presented and analyzed. Data literacy enables students to question the source of data, comprehend its limitations, and avoid misinterpretations. If data were a foreign language, data literacy would be the fundamental vocabulary and grammar needed to comprehend that language, identify patterns, and engage in conversations. These skills will make the science behind climate change accessible, empowering the students to engage with this critical issue (Leve et al., 2023).

TEACHING DATA LITERACY

Data, data everywhere!

The study of climate change relies heavily on accurately interpreting data in the form of tables, graphs, infographics, models, and so on. We have included various examples in this chapter for classroom use. Each example is followed by discussion questions to encourage deeper understanding. You will find the graphs, tables, and infographics along with the accompanying questions reproduced in our companion website, for easy photocopying (https://companion.corwin.com/courses/TeachingClimateChange). The answers to all accompanying questions, including the extension questions, can be found in this chapter. Let's look at some data representations and how they can be used to teach students about climate change (or anything else, really!).

Reading Graphs

Graphs are excellent resources for teaching climate science. Research shows that the brain processes visual information more efficiently and tends to retain it longer than text alone. Graphs can serve as visual anchors for students, helping them remember key concepts and data points related to climate change (Mayer, 2012).

Graphs help students see trends and patterns over time, enabling them to discern the "big picture" and identify cause-and-effect relationships more readily. Students should understand which type of graph is most suitable for different types of data. Let's look at the three main types of graphs and some examples that will encourage discussion in the classroom.

LINE GRAPHS

Line graphs are effective for showing trends or changes over time, like tracking monthly temperature changes. Figure 3.1 illustrates the temperature anomaly trends from the available historical data, showing variations in global temperatures from 1880 to 2010. Line graphs make it easy to identify peaks and valleys visually.

FIGURE 3.1 • Line graphs effectively show change over time (data from NASA, 2024).

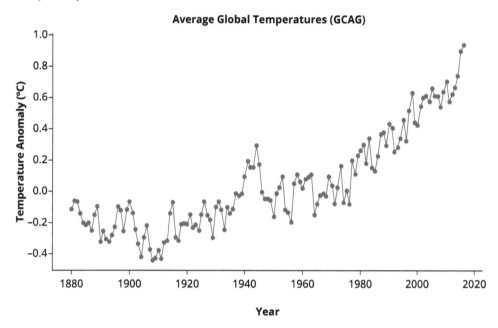

Source: NASA (2024).

The line graph in Figure 3.1 is fairly straightforward. To help build their ability to interpret data, ask students the following questions:

Q: What is shown on the *x*-axis of the graph?

A: Years (1880–2020)

Q: What does each point on the graph represent?

A: A temperature anomaly

Q: What is shown on the *y*-axis of the graph?

A: The *y*-axis displays the annual mean temperature anomaly, or how far off the temperature is from the long-term average. A positive anomaly indicates that the observed temperature was warmer than the reference value, while a negative anomaly indicates that the observed temperature was cooler than the reference value. Students will understand this better with an analogy. Imagine you usually wear a sweater in October because of the average temperature for that month (the reference value). A positive anomaly has you wearing a t-shirt in October; the temperature is warmer than usual (warmer than the reference value). If you still need your sweater in October because it's colder than usual, that's a negative anomaly. The temperature is cooler than the reference value.

Q: What units are used to measure the data on the *x*-axis?

A: Years, with every 20 years marked

Q: What units are used to measure the data on the *y*-axis?

A: degrees Celsius

Q: Can you observe any patterns or trends by looking at the graph?

A: The temperature anomalies go up and down consistently.

Q: What is the *main* trend depicted in the graph?

A: The temperature anomalies show an upward, positive trend. The average global temperatures are getting warmer.

The line graph in Figure 3.2 shows a similar but slightly more complicated line graph.

FIGURE 3.2 • Global Land-Ocean Temperature Index

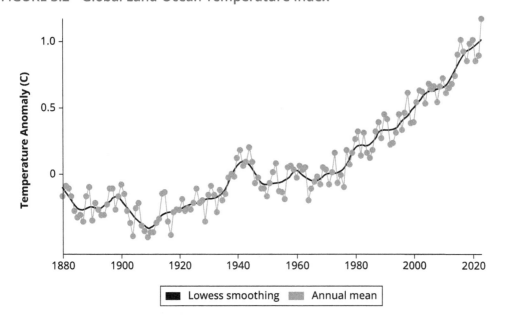

Source: NASA/GISS (2023).

Ask the following questions about the graph in Figure 3.2:

Q: How many lines are on this graph?

A: Two, a light green line and a solid black line

Q: What does the green line represent?

A: The green line is the same annual mean temperature anomaly as in Figure 3.1.

Q: What does the smooth black line represent?

A: The second line, the black line, is a smooth line that depicts the general trend of the temperatures.

Q: What trends can be seen on this graph?

A: This is an excellent graph to address the fact that although the general trend is clear, there are fluctuations from year to year. It also is an opportunity to address the misconception of pointing out a single year or one daily temperature as proof that the Earth's temperatures are not rising. For example, scientists believe the peak in 1940 and the dip that followed until the 1970s was likely caused by variations in the Sun's radiation or by random volcanic eruptions (Niels Bohr Library & Archives, 2023).

The *New York Times* has a weekly feature called "What's going on with this graph?" Teachers can use these graphs to try out some of the suggestions presented in this section. https://qrs.ly/u5g37aa

Another valuable webpage is "Teach About Climate Change With 30 Graphs From the *New York Times*" https://qrs.ly/elg37ab

BAR GRAPHS

Bar graphs are effective for comparing discrete categories and make it easy to visually compare the magnitudes of different categories. They can be used to represent ranked data. Figure 3.3 highlights the significant presence of CO_2 and CH_4 in the atmosphere compared to N_2O and fluorinated gases.

FIGURE 3.3 • Bar graphs are used to compare data (data from Environmental Protection Agency [EPA], 2020).

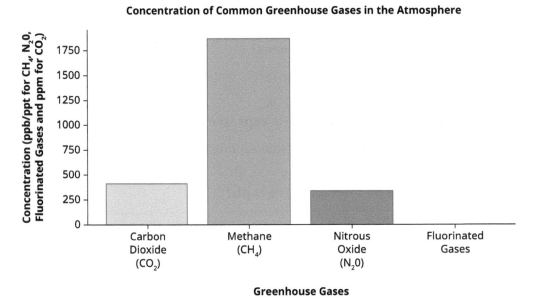

Ask the following questions about the graph in Figure 3.3:

Q: What does the graph show?

A: The x-axis shows the three main greenhouse gases: carbon dioxide (CO_2), methane (CH_4), and nitrous oxide (N_2O). The y-axis shows their concentrations, in parts per million (ppm) for CO_2, and parts per billion (ppb) for CH_4 and N_2O. (Note: While fluorinated gases are less abundant, they have longer atmospheric lifetimes with warming potentials thousands of times higher than CO_2).

Q: What are the main sources of these greenhouse gases?

A: Carbon dioxide (CO_2) is primarily emitted from human activities such as burning fossil fuels (coal, oil, natural gas) for energy production, transportation, and industrial processes. Land use changes like deforestation also contribute to CO_2 emissions.

Methane (CH_4) is emitted from agriculture (rice cultivation, livestock), waste decomposition in landfills, and the fossil fuel industry.

Nitrous oxide (N_2O) comes from agricultural practices using fertilizers, industrial processes, and the burning of fossil fuels.

More questions, though not directly linked to the information on this graph, can be used to prompt student understanding:

Q: Let's do some research on the trend in these greenhouse gas concentrations over time.

A: Carbon dioxide concentration has risen from around 280 ppm in 1750 to over 420 ppm in 2024. (CO2.Earth 2024) Similarly, methane and nitrous oxide concentrations have also increased significantly.

Q: Why is the increase in greenhouse gases a concern?

A: Greenhouse gases trap heat in the atmosphere, causing a gradual warming of the planet. This phenomenon is known as the greenhouse effect. Scientists believe the significant rise in greenhouse gas concentrations is the primary driver of global warming observed over the past century.

Q: What are the potential consequences of global warming?

A: The continued rise in global temperatures can have several negative consequences:

- More extreme weather events like heatwaves, droughts, floods, and storms
- Rising sea levels that threaten coastal communities and ecosystems
- Changes in precipitation patterns leading to water scarcity in some regions
- Ocean acidification harming marine life
- Loss of biodiversity due to habitat changes

Q: What can be done to address climate change?

A: There are several approaches to address climate change, including

- Mitigation: Reducing greenhouse gas emissions by transitioning to renewable energy sources, improving energy efficiency, and adopting sustainable practices in agriculture and industry.

- Adaptation: Implementing strategies to prepare for the inevitable impacts of climate change, such as building seawalls to protect coastal areas or developing drought-resistant crops.

References for this bar graph and discussion:

- National Aeronautics and Space Administration (NASA): https://climate.nasa.gov/

- Environmental Protection Agency (EPA): https://qrs.ly/n3g37b7

- Intergovernmental Panel on Climate Change (IPCC): https://www.ipcc.ch/

PIE CHARTS

Pie charts offer a visually appealing and easy to understand way to introduce students to climate science concepts. For example, Figure 3.4 can be introduced in a classroom discussion to explore renewable energy.

FIGURE 3.4 • The Global Renewable Energy Mix: Pie charts display parts of a whole (data from IEA, 2024).

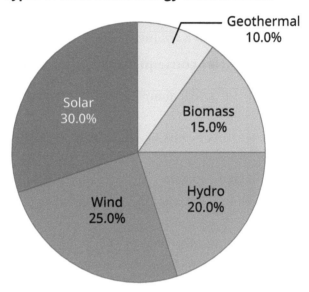

Types of Renewable Energy Contributions

Source: "Renewable - Energy System" at IEA, www. Iea.org, CC BY 4.0. https://creativecommons.org/licenses/by/4.0/

Ask the following questions about the graph in Figure 3.4:

Q: What are the different renewable energy sources represented in the pie chart?

A: Prompt students to identify the percentage of each slice and its corresponding energy source, solar, wind, hydropower, biomass, and geothermal.

Q: What is the largest source of renewable energy contribution, according to the pie chart?

A: Solar energy.

Q: Why do you think solar energy makes up a larger portion of the renewable energy mix compared to geothermal or wind energy?

A: Discuss affordability and a wider geographical suitability of solar energy. Solar energy has become a more prominent player in the renewable energy mix compared to geothermal and wind energy for a couple of key reasons: (1) Affordability—The cost of solar panels and installation has decreased significantly in recent years. This makes solar a more attractive option for homeowners, businesses, and utilities. (2) Geographical suitability—Solar panels can be installed in most locations that receive sunlight, making it a widely accessible renewable energy source. In contrast, wind energy is dependent on location, needing consistent wind speeds to be efficient.

Q: What are some of the challenges of using geothermal energy as a source of renewable energy?

A: Geothermal energy has higher upfront costs. It also requires specific geological conditions like underground hot springs or volcanic activity.

Envisioning the Future Energy Landscape:

Q: How do you think the global energy mix might change in the future? What factors might influence this change?

A: Technological advancements, government policies promoting renewables, public concern about climate change, and economic considerations like storage solutions

Q: Imagine you are an engineer designing a new power plant for a community. What factors would you consider when choosing a renewable energy source?

A: Students should consider available local resources, land constraints, cost-effectiveness, community needs, and environmental impact.

Q: Why do you think it's important to diversify the sources of renewable energy used to generate electricity?

A: Diversification reduces dependence on any single source and its vulnerabilities, allows for leveraging different resources in different locations, and can provide more consistent energy generation.

Q: Choose a kind of renewable energy depicted in the pie chart that you would like to research further.

A: Encourage research and discussion of current events.

Like bar graphs, pie charts can be used to compare and contrast data. Figure 3.5 shows two pie charts depicting the change in the energy mix (fossil fuels vs. renewables) over the last 25 years. A discussion involving these two charts can encourage students to engage in critical thinking.

FIGURE 3.5 • Pie Charts of the Global Energy Mix, Years 2000 and 2024

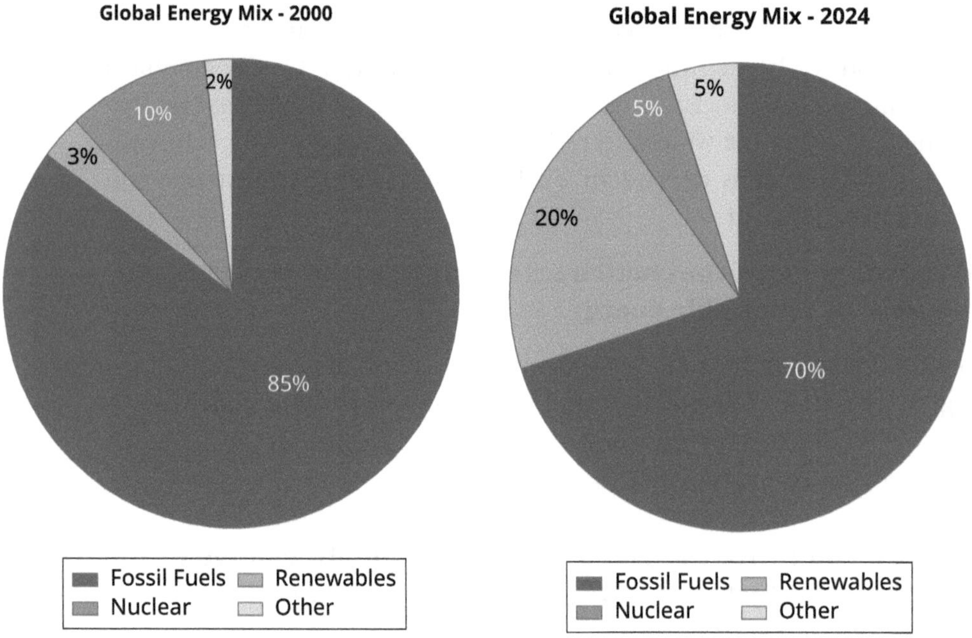

Global Energy Mix - 2000

Global Energy Mix - 2024

| Fossil Fuels | Renewables |
| Nuclear | Other |

| Fossil Fuels | Renewables |
| Nuclear | Other |

Data Source: Ritchie et al. (2024).

Ask the following questions about the graphs in Figure 3.5:

Q: What is the largest section of each pie chart?

A: Fossil fuels represent the largest section of each pie chart—85% and 70%, respectively.

Q: How does the 2024 pie chart compare to the 2000 pie chart?

A: Fossil fuels represent 15% less of the 2024 pie chart, while the use of renewable energy sources have increased.

Q: What is the trend you observe in the use of renewable energy sources?

A: There is an increase in renewables from 2000 to 2024.

Q: What factors might have contributed to the growth of renewable energy?

A: Technological advancements, environmental concerns, and government policies

Q: Imagine we have a pie chart for 2050. How do you think it might differ from these two? Why?

A: Encourage students to predict a continued rise in renewables and a decline in fossil fuels due to advancements and climate concerns.

Q: **What can we do as individuals or communities to promote a shift toward renewable energy sources?**

A: We can promote energy-saving appliances and cars. Buildings can become more energy efficient with simple measures such as adding window stripping and smart thermostats. We can support renewable energy initiatives and advocate for climate action.

Beyond the pie charts:

- Use these discussions as springboards for exploring other climate science topics like the impact of greenhouse gases and the consequences of climate change.

- Encourage students to research specific renewable energy sources and their potential.

 Q: Is there an easy way to teach the Milankovitch cycles?

Eric Tharp, Henry County High School, Carrollton, KY

A: The Vostok Core & Milankovitch Cycles Climate Applet includes a simulation about Milankovitch Cycles, which explain how changes in the Earth's orbit affect global temperature. The three main orbital parameters that affect temperature are eccentricity, precession, and tilt. Each parameter can be explored individually or in combination. Students can compare the orbital parameters to the Earth's past temperature and consider what the future holds. qrs.ly/y9g3gkw

Reading Tables

Climate science involves a vast amount of data on temperatures, precipitation patterns, greenhouse gas emissions, and other factors. Data tables present this information in clear and organized ways, which makes it easier for students to grasp the key concepts. Data tables connect climate science to real-world situations. Students can see how climate data is used by scientists and policymakers to understand and address the challenges of climate change.

Analyzing data tables will teach students to

- Read and interpret the information presented in rows and columns,

- Compare and contrast data points across different categories or time periods,

- Calculate basic statistics (e.g., averages, ranges) if the data table includes numerical values, and

- Identify patterns and trends within the data.

Data Tables 3.1a and 3.1b show the average global sea level rise in millimeters and the impacts of sea level rise. Note that the sources are cited, highlighting the importance of credible sources.

TABLE 3.1a • Global Sea Level Rise (mm)

Year	Sea Level Rise in mm (compared to 1900)	Source
1990	2.2	National Oceanic and Atmospheric Administration (NOAA) Tides & Currents: https://qrs.ly/qtg37an
2000	5.6	National Oceanic and Atmospheric Administration (NOAA) Tides & Currents: https://qrs.ly/qtg37an
2010	7.6	National Oceanic and Atmospheric Administration (NOAA) Tides & Currents: https://qrs.ly/qtg37an
2020	8.4	National Oceanic and Atmospheric Administration (NOAA) Tides & Currents: https://qrs.ly/qtg37an
2023	8.8	National Oceanic and Atmospheric Administration (NOAA) Tides & Currents: https://qrs.ly/qtg37an

TABLE 3.1b • The Causes and Impacts of Global Sea Level Rise

Factor	Impact on Coastal Communities	Impact on Ecosystems and Human Communities
Rising Sea Level	Increased flooding, erosion, inundation	Loss of habitats, saltwater intrusion, ecosystem disruption Island nations with limited land area are at high risk of inundation and displacement due to rising seas. They may face threats to their economies, infrastructure, and food security. Examples include Maldives, Tuvalu, and Kiribati. Coastal regions with high population densities face significant challenges from flooding, erosion, and infrastructure damage. Examples include Jakarta, Indonesia; Miami, Florida, USA; and Tokyo, Japan.
Thermal Expansion	Rising sea levels	Changes in ocean temperature, affecting marine life
Melting Glaciers and Ice Sheets	Rising sea levels	Changes in ocean salinity, impacting marine ecosystems

Ask the following question about Table 3.1a:

Q: Based on the data, describe the trend in global sea level rise over the past few decades.

A: The data shows a clear upward trend in global sea level rise since 1990. In 2023, the sea level had risen by an estimated 8.8 millimeters compared to 1900. This indicates an accelerating rate of sea level rise in recent years.

Data Table 3.1b can prompt further study and classroom discussion about the effects of climate change on coastal communities and other low-lying areas. Some prompts and questions to encourage further discussion are as follows:

Q: Let's learn about how rising sea levels might impact coastal communities and ecosystems

A: Rising sea levels can have several negative consequences for coastal communities and ecosystems:

- Inundation: Low-lying coastal areas, islands, and beaches are at risk of being submerged by rising waters.
- Increased flooding: Storm surges and high tides can cause more frequent and severe flooding in coastal zones.
- Saltwater intrusion: Rising seas can push saltwater farther inland, contaminating freshwater sources and harming coastal ecosystems.
- Erosion: Rising sea levels can accelerate coastal erosion, damaging infrastructure and displacing communities.
- Loss of habitats: Sea level rise can destroy coastal wetlands, mangroves, and other habitats that are crucial for marine life.

Causes of Sea Level Rise:

Q: What are the primary factors contributing to rising sea levels?

A: The primary factors contributing to rising sea levels are

- Thermal expansion: As the ocean absorbs heat from the atmosphere due to climate change, the water expands, causing sea levels to rise.
- Melting glaciers and ice sheets: Warming temperatures are causing glaciers and ice sheets to melt, adding water to the oceans.

Future Projections:

Q: Research and share information on scientific projections for future sea level rise under different climate change scenarios.

A: Scientific projections from the Intergovernmental Panel on Climate Change (IPCC) indicate that sea levels could rise by several feet by the end of this century, depending on the pathway of greenhouse gas emissions. These projections highlight the urgency of mitigating climate change to minimize the most severe impacts of rising sea levels.

Q: Which regions of the world are most vulnerable to the impacts of rising sea levels? Why?

A: Several regions around the world are particularly vulnerable to rising sea levels:

- Low-lying island nations: Island nations with limited land area are at high risk of inundation and displacement due to rising seas.

- Densely populated coastal areas: Coastal megacities and regions with high population densities face significant challenges from flooding, erosion, and infrastructure damage.

- Small island developing states (SIDS): These nations often lack the resources to adapt to rising sea levels and face threats to their economies, infrastructure, and food security.

Adaptation Strategies:

Q: Explore potential adaptation strategies that coastal communities can implement to address the challenges of rising sea levels.

A: Several adaptation strategies can help coastal communities cope with rising sea levels:

- moving infrastructure inland (coastal retreat)

- elevating structures to enhance resilience

- restoring wetlands and dunes as natural buffers

- managing stormwater with green infrastructure

- building seawalls and barriers for protection

- relocating at-risk populations (managed retreat)

- utilizing natural protection methods

- establishing insurance and financial strategies to promote resilience

- investing in monitoring and research to guide future adaptation efforts

- implementing policy and zoning changes to limit development in high-risk areas

- educating and engaging the community about climate risks

Data tables can also display written text in an organized manner, which can be easier to understand than paragraph form. Data Table 3.2 is another example of how credible sources can be prominently displayed. It showcases various categories of climate change impacts, exposing students to the breadth and complexity of climate change and demonstrating its wide-ranging effects on different aspects of Earth's system.

TABLE 3.2 • Global Impacts of Climate Change

Impact Category	Description	Example	Source
Temperature Change	Average global temperatures are rising, primarily due to greenhouse gas emissions.	The average global temperature in 2024 was 1.54°C warmer than the pre-industrial period (1850–1900).	National Aeronautics and Space Administration (NASA): https://climate.nasa.gov/)
Sea Level Rise	Melting glaciers and thermal expansion of oceans are causing sea levels to rise.	Sea levels have risen about 8–10 millimeters since 1880, threatening coastal communities, island nations, and ecosystems.	NOAA: https://qrs.ly/exg37ar/
Extreme Weather Events	Climate change increases the frequency and intensity of extreme weather events like heatwaves, droughts, floods, and wildfires.	In June 2024, 1,400 global temperature records were broken with heat waves spreading across the northern hemisphere (Anders, 2024).	IPCC Sixth Assessment Report: https://qrs.ly/g9g37at
Ocean Acidification	Increased atmospheric CO_2 dissolves in the oceans, making them more acidic.	Ocean acidity has increased by 30% since the pre-industrial era, harming marine life. For example, acidification makes it harder for coral to build their exoskeletons and for shellfish to develop shells.	National Oceanic and Atmospheric Administration (NOAA) Ocean Acidification Program: https://qrs.ly/ygg37aw
Changes in Precipitation Patterns	Rainfall patterns are changing, with some areas experiencing more droughts and others experiencing more intense precipitation events.	The summer of 2024 saw historic flooding across the midwestern United States.	IPCC Sixth Assessment Report: https://qrs.ly/g9g37at

Ask students the following questions about Table 3.2.

Q: How does the rising global temperature in 2024 compare to past decades?

A: The average global temperature in 2024 (1.54°C warmer than pre-industrial) was the highest ever recorded. This signifies a continued warming trend compared to past decades.

Q: How much sea level rise has occurred since 1880?

A: Sea levels have risen about 8–10 millimeters since 1880.

Q: What specific coastal communities and ecosystems are most at risk from rising sea levels?

A: Low-lying coastal areas, island nations, and wetlands are most at risk. Rising sea levels can inundate land, and saltwater intrusion can contaminate freshwater supplies and disrupt coastal ecosystems.

Extreme Weather Events:

Q: According to the IPCC report, how has the frequency and intensity of extreme weather events changed in recent decades?

A: The IPCC report indicates an increase in the frequency and intensity of extreme weather events like heatwaves, droughts, floods, and wildfires.

Q: By what percentage has ocean acidity increased since the pre-industrial era?

A: Ocean acidity has increased by 30% since the pre-industrial era, signifying a significant change in ocean chemistry.

Q: How does ocean acidification harm marine life? Can you find specific examples?

A: Ocean acidification makes it harder for some shellfish and corals to build their shells and skeletons. This can harm entire ecosystems that depend on these organisms.

Changes in Precipitation Patterns:

Q: According to the IPCC report, how are precipitation patterns changing globally?

A: The IPCC report suggests changes in precipitation patterns, with some areas experiencing more frequent droughts and others seeing more intense rainfall events.

Extension Activities:

1. For each impact category in Table 3.2, explain how climate change (specifically greenhouse gas emissions) is causing that impact.

2. Real-World Examples: Research a specific example of how one of these climate change impacts is affecting a particular region or ecosystem. Share your findings with the class.

3. Uneven Impacts: Discuss how climate change impacts are not evenly distributed around the world. Which regions or populations might be more vulnerable? Why?

4. Long-Term Consequences: Consider the long-term consequences of these climate change impacts. How might they affect human societies, economies, and natural ecosystems in the future?

5. Solutions and Mitigation: Explore potential solutions or mitigation strategies to address climate change and its impacts. What role can individuals, communities, and governments play?

6. Data Analysis: Imagine you are a climate scientist. How could you use data tables like this one, along with other forms of data, to study climate change and its impacts?

TIPS TO MAKE A DIFFERENCE: Recycling Ideas
Loretta Rowland-Kitley, Guilford Technical Community College, Greensboro, NC

1. Work with custodians to make recycling a priority with students and staff.

2. Start a recycling club.[1]

---

[1]Students may ask about reports that what we put in our recycling bins does not always get recycled. The answer is different from region to region, municipality to municipality. It's best to check locally before addressing the question. Recycling's effectiveness relies on overcoming collection challenges, sorting efficiently, market demand for recycled materials, and informed consumer participation to maximize environmental benefits (Clark, 2023).

Success Story: Human Activity and the Effect on the Planet

Jamie Ashburn, Heritage Hall Middle School, Oklahoma City, OK

As a middle school teacher (Figure 3.6), each year I have an "Earth and Human Activity" unit in which students learn about how various human behaviors have impacted our natural environment. We focus on understanding the factors that have caused the rise in global temperatures over the past century and methods for mitigating human impact on the environment (NGSS standards ESS3-3 and ESS3-5). Our unit ends with a group project in which students decide how to responsibly manage a 100-acre parcel of forested land. Students are given a grid with 100 squares and are told that they must create a land-use plan that is environmentally responsible in order to inherit the land from their relatives. Students have to support all of their needs by either using or selling resources from the land. As a teacher, I have fun watching the students collaborate and debate how best to use their land without hurting the environment. After groups have completed their plans, each group presents their plan to their classmates, who then role-play as the relatives and vote on whether the plan is environmentally friendly enough to inherit. If students do not get their plan approved, their classmates must explain what aspects of the plan were not environmentally sustainable and how they could be improved.

FIGURE 3.6 • Jamie Ashburn believes lessons with real-life scenarios are an effective tool for teaching about climate change.

Source: Jamie Ashburn

Reading Infographics

A well-designed infographic can be visually engaging and spark curiosity in students. Basic science content is essential for climate literacy. Heat energy transfer and its role in the Earth's climate and local weather patterns are basic concepts that can be reviewed with infographics. Figure 3.7 is an excellent infographic for this discussion.

FIGURE 3.7 • Land Breeze vs. Sea Breeze

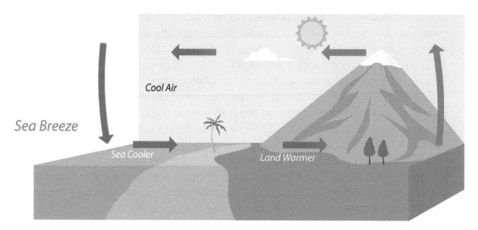

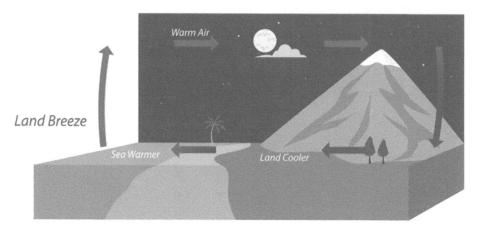

Source: istock.com/agung fatria

Ask the following questions about the infographic in Figure 3.7:

Q: What does the infographic show?

A: The infographic depicts a coastal landscape with arrows representing wind circulation patterns. One pattern (sea breeze) shows winds blowing from the water toward the land, while the other (land breeze) shows the opposite direction.

Q: Can you identify any key features in the infographic, like temperature variations?

A: The infographic shows cooler temperatures over water bodies compared to warmer temperatures over land during the daytime (for sea breezes). At night, it is the opposite.

Q: Based on the infographic and your understanding, how do you think sea and land breezes form?

A: Students might explain that sea breezes develop during the day because land heats up and cools down faster than water. During the day, the land warms up faster, making the air above the land warmer. Warmer air is less dense, causing it to rise. This creates a low-pressure zone over land, and cooler air from over the water moves in to fill the gap, resulting in a sea breeze. At night, the land cools faster than water, making it more dense, creating a high-pressure zone over land and causing a reversal of the wind direction (land breeze) as cooler air moves from land toward the warmer water. Because water does not change temperature as quickly as land, the temperature of the water stays more consistent throughout the day and night, but the land temperature is warmer during the day and cooler at night.

Q: Can you think of any implications of these sea and land breeze patterns for coastal areas?

A: Students might mention that sea breezes can bring cooler air and relief from hot temperatures in coastal areas during the day. They might also connect sea breezes to the movement of sailboats or windsurfing activities.

Q: With climate change leading to rising global temperatures, do you think sea and land breeze patterns might be affected in the future? How?

A: This is a more open-ended question encouraging discussion and critical thinking. Students might propose that if the overall temperature difference between land and water bodies lessens due to global warming, sea and land breezes could become weaker. They might also consider how changes in regional weather patterns could influence these local wind systems.

(NOAA National Centers for Environmental information, 2024)

The Earth's natural greenhouse effect is another important concept that can be introduced using an infographic.

Ask the following questions about the infographic in Figure 3.8:

FIGURE 3.8 • Earth's Greenhouse Effect

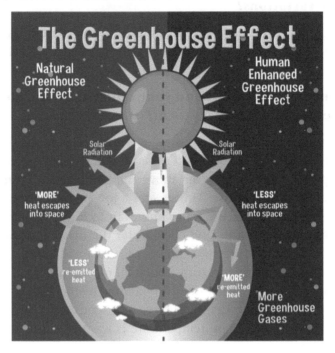

Source: istock.com/colematt

Q: Take a moment to look at this infographic. What do you see?

A: Sun, Earth, arrows, atmosphere, gas molecules.

Q: What do the two sides of the graphic represent?

A: The left shows the natural greenhouse effect of the Earth and the right shows how human activity has enhanced the greenhouse effect by adding more greenhouse gases to the atmosphere (Be sure to point out that the sides do NOT mean that one hemisphere is experiencing more greenhouse effect that the other).

Q: Can anyone explain what the arrows represent?

A: Arrows show the movement of energy from the Sun to Earth.

Q: What happens to this energy, according to the infographic?

A: Some energy is reflected back to space, and some is absorbed by Earth.

Q: The infographic shows certain gases in the atmosphere. These are greenhouse gases. They act like a blanket, trapping some of the Sun's heat energy that would normally escape back into space. This phenomenon is called the greenhouse effect, and the left side of the infographic shows that it is a natural

effect that keeps Earth habitable for life. The right side of the infographic shows how human activities are increasing the amount of greenhouse gases in the atmosphere. This can trap more heat, leading to a gradual warming of the planet, which we call climate change. What human activities are increasing greenhouse gases in the atmosphere?

How do *you* teach the difference between the natural greenhouse effect and anthropogenic climate change?

A: Burning fossil fuels for energy, transportation, and industrial processes is a major human activity increasing greenhouse gases.

The sources of greenhouse gas emissions produced by humans can be introduced as a list, but a visually appealing infographic like Figure 3.9 will be more eye-catching for students. It also provides them with visual clues for each source if they are not familiar with the terms or are multilingual learners.

FIGURE 3.9 • Greenhouse gas emissions come from a variety of sources.

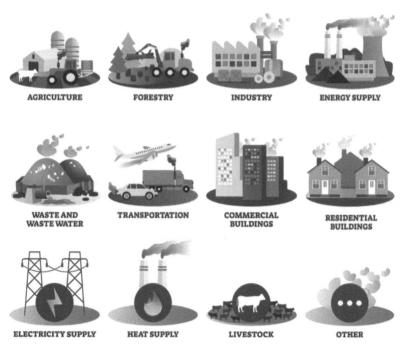

Source: istock.com/VectorMine

Ask the following questions about the infographic in Figure 3.9:

Q: **Can you name some ways humans might contribute to greenhouse gas emissions?**

A: Agriculture, forestry, energy production, transportation, commercial buildings, residential buildings, heat supply, livestock, etc.

Q: **The infographic shows various sources, like factories (industry), farms (agriculture), and power plants (where energy is transformed into electricity). How do you think these contribute to emissions?**

A: Factories might release gases when they make things. Industrial processes can involve burning fuels or releasing chemicals.

Q: **How do livestock cause an increase in greenhouse gas emissions?**

A: Livestock, especially cows, release methane through digestion. Bacteria in the cow's guts give off the methane when they aid in the cow's digestion process.

Q: **How do most power plants make electricity?**

A: They burn fossil fuels like coal or gas to heat water, which releases steam. The steam is directed through a turbine, where it turns the blades of the turbine and generates electricity

Q: **The infographic also includes buildings and heating sources. How might these contribute?**

A: Buildings use energy for lights and heating, maybe from burning something? Burning fuels for heating or using electricity from power plants contributes to emissions in both commercial and residential buildings.

Q: **What about transportation?**

A: Vehicles powered by gasoline or diesel contribute significantly to greenhouse gas emissions through exhaust.

Q: **We've seen how many activities contribute to greenhouse gas emissions. While some sources have a bigger impact, even our daily choices can play a role. Can you think of ways we, as individuals, can be more mindful of our impact?**

A: We contribute to greenhouse gas emissions through our daily choices, such as using cars, consuming electricity from fossil fuel sources, heating and cooling homes, and purchasing goods produced by industries. Electric vehicles can also indirectly contribute when fossil fuels are burned to produce electric power.

(EPA, 2020)

Q: There are dissenting views about climate change; what is the evidence that indicates that climate change is NOT happening?

Robert E. Tufts, Cranberry Middle School, Elk Park, NC

A: There is no evidence to indicate that climate change is not happening. There is, however, plenty of evidence that misleading studies purposely cherry-pick or misinterpret. If somebody asks for evidence that climate change is not happening, you can first *acknowledge the misconception.* You can say, "That's an interesting point. There can be a lot of noise around climate change, and it's good to be curious about the evidence."

Remember that facts alone can't always overcome strong beliefs and ideologies. Keep these factors in mind:

- Confirmation bias: People tend to seek out information that confirms their existing beliefs and ignore evidence that contradicts them.
- Emotional attachment: Beliefs can be tied to identity, values, or fear, making them hard to change.
- Social influence: People are influenced by their social circles, and some groups may promote specific ideologies.

Here are some strategies to consider when facts aren't enough:

- Focus on common ground: Find areas of agreement, like wanting a healthy planet for future generations.
- Appeal to values: Frame the issue in terms of values they might share, like protecting nature or economic opportunities.
- Tell stories: Stories and anecdotes can resonate more than just facts.
- Ask open-ended questions: Encourage people to think critically about their beliefs by asking open-ended questions.

It takes time to break through long-held biases. Be patient, respectful, and focus on building understanding.

Infographics can also act as springboards for exploring specific climate topics or diving into the scientific evidence behind climate change. Project Drawdown (https://drawdown.org/) serves as a valuable resource for anyone interested in understanding existing solutions to climate change and taking action to address this global challenge. They have many infographics available for classroom use. Two of the most popular ones follow in Figures 3.10 and 3.11.

FIGURE 3.10 • Project Drawdown Infographic #1: Drawdown Framework for Climate Solutions

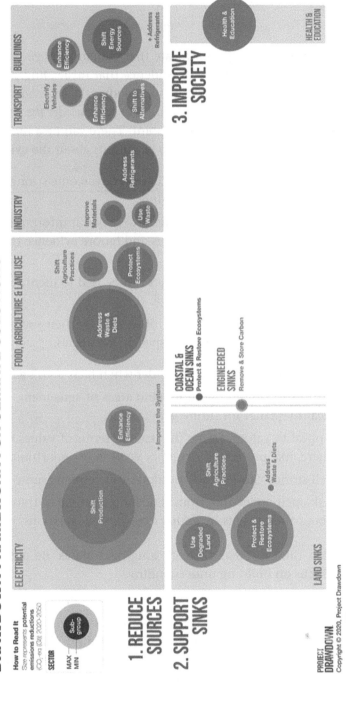

Source: Project Drawdown, drawdown.org

This infographic is a great resource for getting a broad overview of the diverse "solutionscape" for addressing climate change. Using circles of varying sizes, which correspond to the relative importance of the information depicted, it showcases solutions to climate change across various sectors like energy, food and land use, buildings, and materials. Each solution segment displays its estimated potential impact on reducing greenhouse gas emissions by 2050. It accompanies Project Drawdown's much more comprehensive list of 80 researched and ranked solutions (qrs.ly/8bg3gkx).

Ask the following questions about the infographic in Figure 3.10:

Q: What solutions are highlighted in this infographic?

A: It highlights solutions in seven categories:

- Energy: Shifting production to energy sources like solar, wind, geothermal, and energy efficiency improvements.
- Food & Land Use: Includes solutions like reducing food waste, protecting ecosystems, and improved agricultural practices.
- Industry: Highlights solutions for addressing refrigerants and using sustainable materials in construction and manufacturing.
- Transportation: Focuses on electric vehicles and improved vehicle efficiency.
- Buildings: Highlights solutions for energy-efficient buildings.
- Land Use: Includes solutions like protecting forests, restoring grasslands, and promoting regenerative agriculture.
- Improve Society: Improving health and education worldwide

Q: How do these solutions work to reduce emissions?

A: They reduce emissions in several ways:

- Renewable Energy: Replacing fossil fuels with increasingly affordable renewable sources like solar, wind, geothermal, and hydropower can reduce greenhouse gas emissions.
- Energy Efficiency: Buildings and appliances that consume less energy require less power plant output, resulting in lower overall emissions. Utilizing energy-efficient technologies like LED lighting, smart thermostats, and high-performance insulation can reduce our carbon footprint.
- Electric Vehicles and Public Transportation: Transportation is a major source of emissions. Shifting toward electric vehicles (EVs) powered by renewable energy sources drastically cuts emissions compared to gasoline-powered cars. Additionally, promoting public

transportation options like buses, trains, and subways can also reduce reliance on personal vehicles and associated emissions.

- Forest Protection and Restoration: Forests play a vital role in absorbing carbon dioxide from the atmosphere. Protecting existing forests and restoring degraded ones create natural carbon sinks that help mitigate climate change. Planting trees and promoting sustainable forest management practices can be powerful tools in the fight against climate change.

Q: Are there any surprises in terms of the solutions or their potential impact?

A: Health and education is an unexpected solution. Educating girls in developing countries, for example, can significantly reduce population growth, ultimately leading to lower emissions.

Q: Can you think of any challenges or limitations associated with these solutions?

A: Scaling up renewable energy infrastructure might require grid upgrades. Technological advancements might be needed for some solutions to become more cost-effective.

(Project Drawdown, 2023)

Figure 3.11 is an infographic on emissions and natural sinks (a molecule or group of molecules that are able to accept energy from another part of the system).

Ask the following questions about the infographic in Figure 3.11:

Q: According to the infographic, what are the main human activities that contribute to greenhouse gas emissions?

A: The infographic highlights activities like energy production that burns fossil fuels for energy (coal, oil, gas), food and agricultural land use, industrial processes, etc.

Q: What natural systems act as carbon sinks, absorbing some of the greenhouse gases emitted by human activities?

A: The infographic showcases oceans and land. Students can be encouraged to research these, with photosynthesis in mind.

Q: How does the infographic portray the balance between emissions and natural absorption? Is there an equilibrium, or is one side outweighing the other?

A: The infographic shows that natural sinks are currently overwhelmed by human-caused emissions, leading to a net increase in greenhouse gases in the atmosphere.

Q: **Considering the emission sources highlighted, can you propose some strategies to reduce greenhouse gas emissions?**

A: Students might suggest transitioning to renewable energy sources, improving energy efficiency, adopting sustainable agricultural practices, reducing deforestation, and managing waste more effectively.

Q: **What actions can we take as individuals and communities to address the issue of greenhouse gas emissions and support natural sinks like those shown in the infographic?**

A: Students can brainstorm actions like reducing energy consumption, adopting sustainable consumption habits, supporting responsible businesses, and advocating for policies that promote clean energy and conservation.

 TIPS TO MAKE A DIFFERENCE: Small Changes, Big Impact

Katie Smith, Westside Elementary, Valdosta, GA

1. Ensure that the corporations you support are environmentally aware.

2. Bathe or shower with cooler water instead of more energy-intensive hot water.

3. Turn gaming systems/computers/electronics OFF (not just on rest mode) when not in use.

4. Keep domestic pets (cats and dogs) indoors so they do not disrupt the local ecosystem.

Understanding Models

Climate models are sophisticated computer simulations that act as the Earth's virtual laboratory, enabling scientists to understand how human activities like greenhouse gas emissions impact the interactions between the atmosphere, oceans, land, and ice. Scientists use historical climate data to fine-tune these models, ensuring they accurately reflect past trends.

When they are fed different scenarios of future emissions, these models act like time machines, projecting potential climate changes on a regional and

FIGURE 3.11 • Project Drawdown Infographic #2: Emission Sources and Natural Sinks

EMISSIONS SOURCES & NATURAL SINKS

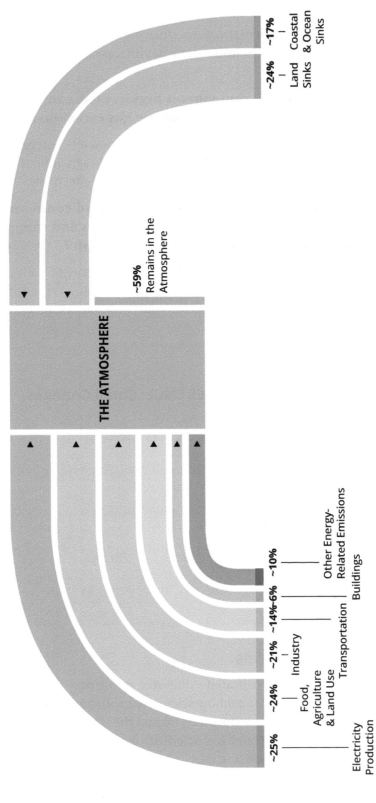

CURRENT SINKS

~17% Coastal & Ocean Sinks

~24% Land Sinks

~59% Remains in the Atmosphere

THE ATMOSPHERE

~25% Electricity Production

~24% Food, Agriculture & Land Use

~21% Industry

~14% Transportation

~6% Buildings

~10% Other Energy-Related Emissions

CURRENT SOURCES

Source: Project Drawdown, drawdown.org

global scale. This invaluable information helps us assess uncertainties, gain regional insights, and continuously improve our information.

The accuracy of past climate simulations serves as a crucial validation tool. If a model can faithfully recreate past trends, it lends greater confidence to its projections of future changes.

Models also help scientists separate the natural climate changes from the human-made ones. Like deciphering a complex musical score, scientists analyze past and present fluctuations to distinguish the natural "notes" from the human-caused ones. Armed with this knowledge, they can fine-tune their climate models and predictions for the future, giving us a clearer picture of what lies ahead.

Here are two examples of climate models:

1. The National Center for Atmospheric Research (NCAR) Community Earth System Model (CESM) is a widely used complex computer program that considers various factors that influence the Earth's climate system. The model is continuously being improved by incorporating the latest scientific understanding and observations. (www.cesm.ucar.edu)

2. The Hadley Centre Global Environment Model (HadGEM) is developed by the Met Office Hadley Centre in the United Kingdom. HadGEM is a sophisticated computer model used extensively for climate research and projections. (www.researchgate.net)

Ask the following questions about the models discussed above:

Q: How can scientists predict future weather patterns and climate changes?

A: Climate models help scientists predict future weather patterns and overall changes in temperature, air pressure, ocean currents, etc.

Q: How do you think climate models might be helpful?

A: Predicting future weather patterns, understanding climate change.

Q: How do the two models mentioned differ?

A: Imagine CESM and HadGEM are like different recipes for a big cake (representing the Earth's climate). They might use some similar ingredients (data) but have slightly different ways of mixing them together.

Scientific models are used in many science courses. What are other notable models used in your science class?

Q: **Why do you think scientists use more than one climate model?**

A: To get a more complete picture.

Q: **Climate models are powerful tools, but what are some limitations we should remember?**

A: Climate is a complex system; it's hard to factor everything in.

- -

Q: Where can I access good models that are appropriate for high school kids and use real data?

Veranda Johnson, Cherokee Community School, Cherokee, IA

A: Both of the models mentioned in this section, CESM and HadGEM, are Earth System Models (ESMs). For more classroom-friendly models, try the University of Washington's College of the Environment, which has a free, excellent lesson that can be found at https://pcc.uw.edu/education/k-12-educator-resources/classroom-resources/uwhs-atms-211-climate-model/

Another excellent site with information and simulations can be found at UCAR's Center for Science Education: https://scied.ucar.edu/learning-zone/how-climate-works/climate-modeling

- -

Success Story: Sustainable Building Practices

Kristina Klammer, Beaver Country Day School, Chestnut Hill, MA

I taught a unit on climate change to my eighth graders last year. As a culminating assessment, we did a project where they learned about sustainable building practices, and they designed their own eco-friendly, sustainable houses (Figure 3.12). We learned about Earthships, LEED-certified buildings, and other models of sustainable buildings. The week-long project follows a 5-E inquiry-based approach, starting with exploring sustainability, different building types, and the engineering design process. Students work in teams, brainstorming, designing,

FIGURE 3.12 • A Student's Design for an Eco-Friendly House

The Eco-House Project is an opportunity to help students make authentic connections to the work of actual engineers and building designers.

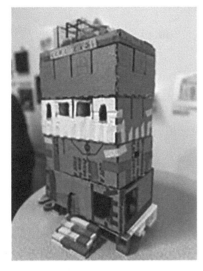

Photo Credit: Kristina Klammer

receiving feedback, and refining their plans. The highlight is the Eco-House Planning Game, where they use game cards to explore various sustainable options, considering budget and power limitations. In the next step, the student teams plan out their design while working within constraints such as a budget and how much energy they could use to power the things in their home. They considered factors such as water recycling, food, the location and climate of their house, sources of power, and more in their designs. In the end, the students presented their sustainable home models at a school "symposium." This project fosters deeper learning through interdisciplinarity, connecting building science, budgeting, and environmental impact. It encourages students to see the interconnectedness of concepts across disciplines and the value of iterative learning through creation and reflection. At the end of the year, many students cited the sustainable building project as the project that they were most proud of and the one that was their favorite activity that we did for the school year. My hope is that it will empower them to become the architects of a better tomorrow.

Q&A   Q: What are the best sources for students to use to look up current climate data, especially data for their area?

Shannon Rine, Tri-County Career Center, Nelsonville, OH

A: Government agencies such as NOAA and NASA Climate Change provide comprehensive resources with tools for visualizing and downloading data.

The U.S. Global Change Research Program has a guide titled "The Essential Principles of Climate Science" that provides crucial information to comprehend the Earth's climate, climate change impacts, and methods for adaption and mitigation.

- National Oceanic and Atmospheric Administration (NOAA) Climate Data Center: https://qrs.ly/4qg37b5
- NASA Climate Change: https://climate.nasa.gov/

The EPA Climate Change Indicators is a good resource for tracking national-level trends.

- EPA Climate Change: https://qrs.ly/n3g37b7

Educational and nonprofit organizations such as National Geographic and WWF offer educational resources and data visualizations on various climate indicators.

- National Geographic Climate Change Education: https://qrs.ly/byg37b8
- World Wildlife Fund (WWF) Climate Change: https://qrs.ly/hug3eo1

Climate Central (https://www.climatecentral.org/) is a website that focuses on climate change research and communication. They offer tools to understand the impacts of climate change, such as the Climate Shift Index (CSI), which helps quantify the daily influence of climate change on local weather. They also publish research on trends such as rising temperatures and longer allergy seasons.

When choosing a data source, students should consider the credibility, data availability, and usability of the website. Finally, it's important to guide students on how to interpret and analyze the data they find.

TEACHING STUDENTS HOW TO EVALUATE SOURCES AND IDENTIFY BIAS

Whenever I hear someone decrying the fact that we don't teach critical thinking in schools, I always defend my fellow science teachers. For decades, we have taken a hands-on approach to learning, allowing our students to design their own experiments and draw conclusions based on their data. "We do teach critical thinking!" I exclaim. "Haven't you read the Next Generation Science Standards?" It took a conversation with skeptics expert Melanie Trecek-King to help me see what we were missing. Trecek-King, creator of the website Thinking Is Power (https://thinkingispower.com/), explained that when students walked into my class, they assumed that what I taught them was based on credible sources. Since they were in kindergarten, the science experiments set up by their teachers were designed to find scientific truth. Students never consider questioning the process of photosynthesis or the electromagnetic spectrum. This is not representative of the real world, where online ads and social media influencers make extraordinary claims about everything, from the dubious origins of the Teletubbies to miraculous and inexpensive weight loss gummies. In addition to teaching students how science works, we must educate them about the existence of misinformation because they wade through almost limitless amounts of information daily.

As teachers we must perform this balancing act of teaching students to trust the process of science while encouraging healthy skepticism. An open mind and a pinch of humility are vital, but as Professor Walter Kotschnig told Holyoke College students way back in 1940, "Keep your minds open, but not so open that your brains fall out." The key is to teach young people how to identify credible from noncredible claims on their own.

Let's look at ways to accomplish this challenging task.

TIPS TO MAKE A DIFFERENCE: Be the Change You Wish to See

Teresa Madewell, South High School, Bakersfield, CA

1. Be a role model so that students emulate your acts.
2. Choose the "Ship Together" option if ordering multiple things online to reduce the number of materials used to ship and trips to your home to ship it.

The CRAAP Test

Created by Sarah Blakeslee, of the University of California at Chico's Meriam Library, the CRAAP test is a well-known method for evaluating the reliability and credibility of information sources. It was developed before the deluge of digital content and works best with print media. In today's digital world, many experts contend that the CRAAP test has some limitations (Fielding, 2019; Wineburg et al., 2020), which we will discuss later in this chapter. However, an in-depth look at this method is a good start.

The CRAAP test considers five key criteria: **C**urrency, **R**elevance, **A**uthority, **A**ccuracy, and **P**urpose. When checking a source to see if it is reliable, ask yourself the following questions:

•   Currency: How recent is the information? Check when the content was published or last updated. Some topics require the latest information, while others may not be as time sensitive.

- Relevance: Does the information meet your needs? Assess whether the content is appropriate and useful for your specific purpose. Consider the depth and specificity of the information.

- Authority: Who is the author, and are they credible? Investigate the author's qualifications, expertise, and credentials. Look for information about the author's background, education, or experience to determine whether they are considered an authority in the field.

- Accuracy: Is the information correct? Verify the accuracy of the information by cross-referencing it with other reliable sources. Check for supporting evidence, citations, or references. Be cautious of factual errors or misleading information.

- Purpose: Why was the information created? Understand the purpose of the information source. Determine whether it aims to inform, persuade, entertain, or sell a product. Be aware of potential biases or hidden agendas that may influence the content.

Let's compare two sources using the CRAAP test.

- **Article 1** is a recent journal article by a scientific researcher and renowned narwhal expert. The article contains data from credible sources such as peer-reviewed journals and government websites, painting a chilling picture of shrinking sea ice and struggling narwhal populations.

- **Article 2** is an online article that claims that the "narwhal panic" is overblown. It offers no sources and downplays the threat, even suggesting narwhals might enjoy habitats with less sea ice. The author does not provide any evidence of scientific credentials.

When we apply the CRAAP Test to these two sources, these are the results.

Currency:

A1: The article, published in 2022, discusses recent changes in narwhal habitats due to climate change.

A2: The article lacks a publication date, making it unclear how recent the information is.

Relevance:

A1: The article details information about how climate change is affecting narwhal habitats, including changes in ice patterns and vulnerability to predators.

A2: The article discusses general climate change impacts without specific information about narwhals, making it irrelevant to the user's needs.

Authority:

A1: The article is authored by a climate scientist with a Ph.D. in polar ecology and contains references to previous research, indicating expertise and boosting the author's credibility.

A2: The author is listed as an anonymous blogger with no credentials mentioned, raising concerns about authority.

Accuracy:

A1: The article references recent studies conducted by reputable scientific institutions such as NASA, NOAA, and the IPCC, and citations support the data. The reader can cross-check the information by reviewing these references.

A2: The article makes sweeping statements without citing any sources or providing verifiable data, raising questions about accuracy.

> **Practice makes perfect! In this lesson, students are given real sources to practice checking a source for currency, relevance, authority, accuracy, and purpose.**
>
> **Generation Skeptics' The CRAAP Test: https://qrs.ly/z4g37b9**

Purpose:

A1: The article aims to inform the public about the immediate threats climate change poses to narwhal populations, with the goal of promoting conservation efforts. While there is a clear goal, the information is presented objectively, and the author's intent is aligned with informing the public.

A2: The bottom of the article links to a think tank website that downplays the role of human activities in climate change, suggesting a biased purpose that may mislead readers.

TIPS TO MAKE A DIFFERENCE: Electricity Matters
Robert E. Tufts, Cranberry Middle School, Elk Park, NC

1. Turn off unused electronics in the classroom.

2. Lower the temperature on the thermostat in the winter.

3. Raise the temperature on the thermostat in the summer when the AC is running.

The Importance of Peer Review

The peer review process is an unknown concept to many students. Students should learn that not all published articles are created equal. Peer review acts as a quality control mechanism. In a peer-reviewed publication (which is considered the most authoritative in science), authors submit their work to the critical assessment of qualified peers within their field. These peers scrutinize the work against established standards and identify strengths, weaknesses, and potential flaws. This evaluation is meant to ensure that the final product meets certain benchmarks of accuracy, validity, and reliability. Peer review also helps identify potential biases, methodological errors, and logical inconsistencies, strengthening the work's overall rigor. Peer review helps combat misinformation and promotes reliable knowledge building. Of course, there are exceptions that prove the rule. We've all heard about peer-reviewed science that turns out to be falsified. It doesn't happen often—but it happens.

A simple YouTube search yields dozens of simple videos to introduce students to the basics of peer review. When using actual online resources as examples, pointing out certain components can help students recognize reliable sources:

- Author Credentials: Who wrote the information? Are they experts in the field with relevant qualifications?

- Methodology: Does the source explain how the information was gathered or researched? A transparent methodology builds trust.

- References: Does the source cite credible sources to support its claims? References allow for further investigation.

- Editorial Oversight: Was the information reviewed by editors or fact checkers to ensure accuracy? This indicates a commitment to quality.

. . . .

Q&A   **A:** Where's a good place to find age-appropriate data/curricula to share with students?

Megan Fullerton, Schoenbar Middle School, Ketchikan, AK

There are several great places to find age-appropriate data and curricula about climate change to share with students:

- The IPCC for Kids: https://qrs.ly/5kg37ba
- NASA Kids' Club: https://qrs.ly/qmg3eo3
- NASA Climate Kids: https://qrs.ly/wgg3ep3

- EPA Climate Change for Kids: https://qrs.ly/mqg37bg
- National Geographic Education: https://qrs.ly/vbg37bi

Limitations of the CRAAP Test

Critics argue that the CRAAP test's binary "true/false" approach to accuracy oversimplifies the process of evaluating sources (Bruce & Edwards, 2018). Critics add that it fails to consider the ever-changing digital landscape. The CRAAP test prioritizes traditional website features like author credentials and publication dates, so it may not work for social media, blogs, and user-generated content (Leitch, 2012). Examining only a single source without cross-checking with other sources might not reveal its true origin, biases, or potential manipulation (Caulfield, 2019). This could lead to the acceptance of misinformation as fact, especially as the dissemination of false information has become more sophisticated.

Lateral Reading

Our fact-checking methods need to become more sophisticated as misinformation and its more dangerous counterpart, disinformation, become more widespread in our increasingly polarized society. The ability of bad actors to generate large amounts of questionable content with generative artificial intelligence (GenAI) will only continue to worsen. Jennifer Fielding, the library services coordinator at Northern Essex Community College in Massachusetts, recommends a different method for evaluating the reliability of content, which is called "lateral reading." Lateral reading involves finding and comparing multiple sources of information on the same topic or event. Reading across different sources helps the reader assess their consistency and identify potential biases or conflicting viewpoints, an essential skill in today's media-driven world (Fielding, 2019). Lateral reading involves using search engines to look for reviews, fact-checks, or analyses of the website from credible sources like scientific organizations, media outlets, or fact-checking websites. Reputable climate scientists or experts might have already publicly addressed the website's misinformation.

Let's apply lateral reading to compare climate misinformation and climate fact.

- **Climate Misinformation:** "The recent rise in global temperatures is just a natural cycle. There's no evidence humans are causing climate change."

- **Climate Fact:** "The vast majority of scientists agree that human activities, primarily the burning of fossil fuels, are causing global temperatures to rise at an unprecedented rate."

Lateral Reading for Climate Misinformation:

1. **Source:** Identify the source of the climate misinformation claim. Often, these claims originate from nonscientific websites, social media posts, or fringe news outlets.

2. **Search online:** Look for the exact quote or similar claims with keywords like "natural cycle, global warming hoax."

3. **Fact-Checking Websites:** Use credible fact-checking websites like Climate Feedback (https://climatefeedback.org/) to see if the claim has been debunked.

4. **Scientific Consensus:** Search for reports by reputable scientific organizations like the Intergovernmental Panel on Climate Change (IPCC; https://www.ipcc.ch/) on the consensus among scientists about human-caused climate change.

Lateral Reading for the Climate Fact:

1. **Source:** The source itself might be a clue. Look for reputable scientific organizations, news outlets with science reporting teams, or government agencies focused on climate change.

2. **Evidence Cited:** Does the climate fact mention any evidence? Look for references to scientific studies, data analysis, or reports from scientific bodies.

3. **Further Reading:** Credible sources often offer links to further reading or research. See if they link to peer-reviewed scientific articles or reports.

Expected Results:

- The lateral reading for climate misinformation will likely reveal a lack of scientific backing and might even expose it as a known misconception.

- The lateral reading for the climate fact should lead you to credible sources and established scientific evidence supporting the claim.

TIPS TO MAKE A DIFFERENCE: Bee Friendly

Karen Nichols, Oakwood Friends School, Poughkeepsie, NY, and Mount Saint Mary College, Newburgh, NY

1. Unplug empty classroom refrigerators in science labs.

2. Do not kill insects because they are on the decline and are critical for biodiversity.

3. Foster pollinators on campus with flower gardens planted with native species.

CUTTING THROUGH THE MISINFORMATION MAZE: RELIABLE FACT-CHECKING SITES

Students can learn more about climate change through activities comparing information sources, discussions about the importance of reliable information, and access to reputable websites and resources dedicated to debunking climate myths. Here are some fact-checking websites to help your students discern fact from fiction:

For climate-related fact-checking:

* **Climate Feedback:** A global network of scientists meticulously analyzing climate change coverage in the media, separating fact from fiction with expert evaluation. https://climatefeedback.org/

For general fact-checking:

* **Fact Checker**: This award-winning fact-checking team dives deep into various topics, holding powerful figures accountable with rigorous research and clear explanations. https://qrs.ly/cjg37bl

* **Snopes.com:** One of the oldest and most comprehensive fact-checking sites, Snopes debunks rumors, urban legends, and misinformation across subject areas. https://www.snopes.com/

Generation Skeptics is an education program that promotes critical thinking. Their lesson "What's Your AI IQ?" is a time-saver for teachers; they've searched for the best online resources for teaching media literacy and put them all in one asynchronous lesson with discussion questions, teacher notes, and answer key. https://qrs.ly/rag37bm

- **Lead Stories**: Co-founded by individuals from different political backgrounds that aim for balanced reporting and fact-checking. https://leadstories.com/

Sharing Credible Sources

You do not need to look too far to discover comprehensive, credible online resources on climate literacy:

- **Climate Literacy and Energy Awareness Network (CLEAN):** CLEAN offers an excellent collection of peer-reviewed resources for climate change education. Educators can find resources by grade level, topic, and type. https://cleanet.org/about/

- **Teaching Climate:** This website offers a collection of educational resources to enhance climate literacy in K–12 classrooms. https://www.teachingclimate.org/

- **Climate Change: Science, Communication, and Action MOOC:** Offered by the University of Michigan on the Coursera platform, this Massive Open Online Course (MOOC) provides an overview of climate change science, communication strategies, and actions. qrs.ly/8zg3gky

- **The Climate Reality Project:** "Climate Change 101" provides an introductory guide to climate change science, impacts, and solutions. It is designed to help individuals take action in their communities. https://www.climaterealityproject.org/climate-101

- **The National Center for Science Education's Teaching Climate Change: Lessons, Tips, and Tools:** This resource offers guidance for teaching about climate change and professional development opportunities for educators. qrs.ly/t3g3eo4

Knowledge is power. But today, knowledge is a mouse click away. Perhaps we should replace this popular adage with a new one: Thinking Is Power.

—*Melanie Trecek-King*

☀ LEARNING FROM OUR COLLEAGUES
Scrutinizing Sources

Ms. Thakrar held a complex graph (see Figure 3.13). "This is from the Environmental Protection Agency, and it shows how different factors influence the Earth's temperature. What can you tell me about these lines, class?"

FIGURE 3.13 • Separating Human and Natural Influences on Climate

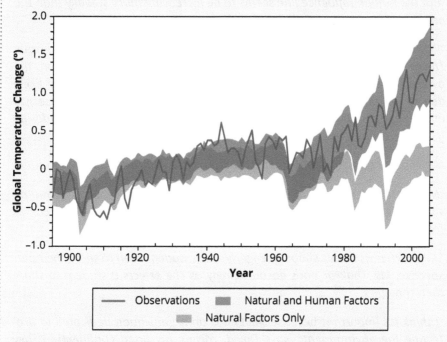

Source: EPA (2021).

A hand shot up. "This thin, dark green line," Sarah said, pointing, "It says 'Observations.' That must be the temperature anomalies, or how far off the average the temperature is each year, right?"

Ms. Thakrar beamed. "Exactly, Sarah! Now, look at the other thicker lines. Can anyone tell me what the thick, lighter green line represents, the one that stays closest to the x-axis?"

Daniel spoke up. "That one says 'Natural Factors,' so I guess it's showing how volcanoes, the sun, and the Earth's orbit affect the temperature."

"Perfect," Ms. Thakrar said. "And the thick, darker green line closest to the top right of the graph?"

"That's 'Natural and Human Factors,'" offered Emily. "Like greenhouse gases."

(Continued)

(Continued)

"Great," Ms. Thakrar said. "Now, what do you notice about the overall trend over time?"

Johanna raises her hand, "These natural ones can have a warming or cooling effect, but they tend to even out over time."

"But the human influence line seems to be increasing more steadily than the natural influence line," Emily observed.

"Right," Ms. Thakrar said. "That's the key point to take away from this graph. The EPA is saying that while natural factors can cause some variation, the overall increase in global temperature we're observing is much more likely due to the ongoing rise in human influences, particularly greenhouse gas emissions. I am showing you this graph because some of you were wondering if climate change was caused by natural causes."

Ms. Thakrar pauses for a moment to let the students process the information.

"Now that we've delved into the details of this graph, I want to ask you all something important. Why do you think it's significant that this graph comes from a credible source like the EPA?"

She watches as hands shoot up eagerly, each student keen to share their perspective. Ms. Thakrar nods encouragingly as she selects a student to share their thoughts.

"I think it's important because the EPA is an organization dedicated to protecting the environment," says David, raising his hand confidently. "They have scientists and experts who study these things, so the information on the graph is likely based on solid research and data."

"Exactly," Ms. Thakrar affirms. "The EPA is a government agency tasked with safeguarding public health and the environment. Their findings are backed by rigorous scientific research, peer-reviewed studies, and data analysis."

She scans the room, inviting more responses from her students. Another hand goes up, and a girl named Maya offers her thoughts.

"Using information from a credible source like the EPA helps us trust the information more," Maya explains. "It's not just some random website or social media post. It's from a reliable authority, so we know we can rely on it."

"Absolutely," Ms. Thakrar acknowledges, pleased with the depth of understanding her students are demonstrating. "Remember, when we discuss complex issues like climate change, it's crucial to rely on credible sources. They provide accurate information based on scientific evidence, helping us make informed decisions and understand the world around us."

Reflection Questions

1. What types of data are used to study climate change?

2. What resources can you utilize to improve your data literacy skills?

3. How has your understanding of climate change evolved after engaging with various sources?

4. Evaluate the credibility of the sources you used to gather information about climate change. How did you determine their reliability?

5. Analyze a climate-related news article or video using the CRAAP test. How does the media frame the issue, and what biases or perspectives might be present? Now analyze the same article using lateral reading. Did any additional biases emerge?

6. What role does fact-checking play in ensuring the accuracy of climate-related information?

7. In what ways does data literacy in science contribute to a deeper understanding of climate change?

For Further Reading

FOR TEACHERS

Rogow, F. (2022). *Media literacy for young children: Teaching beyond the screen time debates*. National Association for the Education of Young Children.

Scheibe, C., & Rogow, F. (2012). *The teacher's guide to media literacy: Critical thinking in a multimedia world*. Corwin.

Trecek-King, M. (n.d.). *Foundations in critical thinking*. https://thinkingispower.com/foundations-in-critical-thinking/ (This is a "mini course" in critical thinking, information literacy, and science literacy.)

FOR STUDENTS
Preschool–Age 7

Applegate, K., & Santoso, C. (2021). *Willodeen*. Feiwel and Friends.

Ages 10–14

Cherry, L., & Braasch, G. (2018). *How we know what we know about Our changing climate: Scientists and kids explore global warming*. Dawn.

Seuss, Dr. (2021). *The Lorax*. Beulah Reimer Legacy.

. . . .

CHAPTER FOUR

NAVIGATING THE POLITICS OF CLIMATE CHANGE

The first principle is that you must not fool yourself, and you are the easiest person to fool.

—*Richard Feynman*

THIS CHAPTER WILL DISCUSS

- Why we believe what we believe
- What to do about pushback
- Why science standards around teaching climate change are important; and
- Enlisting your allies: parents and administrators

I am proposing in this chapter that we add a very important component to how we teach the process of science in general and climate change in particular: the vulnerability of the human thought process. This essential component will influence how we speak with students, parents, and administrators. It begins with a simple question: What if facts aren't the problem?

WHAT IF FACTS AREN'T THE PROBLEM?

For more than 20 years, I taught with an outstanding teacher named Ana. Ana is passionate about climate science. In her wonderful classroom, students learn the science of climate change and develop an understanding of the process of science through experimentation, data collection, analysis, and communication. Many of her students go on to adopt the positive behaviors that lead to a more sustainable future.

However, Ana is not as successful when she encounters climate change denial. I have observed many of her conversations with skeptical students, colleagues, and parents. It's obvious that she knows *a lot* about climate change and can cite all sorts of data in an effort to show each person "the validity of the science." But here's the rub: Ana doesn't actually convince the skeptics most of the time. The reason, I think, is that Ana is operating under what is known as the Information Deficit Model (Reincke et al., 2020). This model holds that the reason a person does not accept the truth about a topic is they lack information about the topic. Ana thinks, "Oh, I see, you don't accept climate change, so that means you don't truly understand, so let me give you the facts behind climate change."

But what if facts aren't the problem? The best indicator of a person's acceptance of anthropogenic climate change is not their knowledge of the topic but their political affiliation (Furnham & Robinson, 2022). In fact, *many* of the things we each believe are tied more closely to our identities than to facts. Our beliefs, biases, and identities play a huge role in how we process information and knowledge. This reality—that our worldview affects how we process new information, and that science is the best way to put guardrails in place so we can seek the truth in the most objective way possible—should be an ongoing theme in our classrooms.

Why Do We Believe What We Believe?

I propose we introduce two ideas when we teach students how science works. These components should be introduced early and mentioned often throughout the school year.

1. Everyone, including ourselves, is a victim of flawed thinking, clouded by our biases, perceptions, and identities. The scientific method aims to eliminate these factors when seeking the truth.

2. Science denial and pseudoscience often find their way into the news, social media, and our own classrooms.

These ideas are crucial for students to understand because many will be exposed to science denial and pseudoscience—and we all bring our own biases into the classroom. These two ideas are important for all of us to consider when dealing with any topic.

Consider the vast amounts of information available to an individual with internet access. There's simply too much to know. Here's the key: One of the most important types of knowledge is knowing where to find knowledge. Some of the most important aspects of critical thinking are the dispositions around critical thinking, like recognizing the limitations of our knowledge and knowing when to consult with experts. And where to find such experts.

Chapter 3 discussed data literacy and source credibility. When teaching how to find credible sources of information, we should include how our own beliefs, biases, and identities play a role in this information-gathering process. Melanie Trecek-King of Thinking Is Power says it best,

> If I go to Google and I type something in, it's going to take me where I've asked it to go. The reasons that we fall for misinformation is because it confirms our biases and it triggers us emotionally, and we hear it repeatedly. We will usually find ourselves in a closed community of people who agree with what it is that we agree with, and all of that just builds up this worldview in our heads. And then when I see misinformation, if it supports what I think is true, then I am just going to accept it.

Teachers teach critical thinking. We teach that science is falsifiable and that it requires repeatedly tested hypotheses, multiple lines of evidence, and scientific consensus. We encourage our students to go through the process themselves. Wonderful science teachers all over the country are implementing NGSS practices such as asking questions, planning and carrying out investigations, and engaging in arguments stemming from evidence (NGSS Lead States, 2013). Many teachers incorporate project-based learning into their curriculum, which promotes critical thinking in creative ways that are grounded in real-life scenarios.

Now, here is what we do *not* teach: We don't teach the science of why we believe what we believe and how that can get in the way of accepting facts. We don't tell our students that their own perceptions and life experiences will affect how they process information. I propose that science education should include teaching students about their own flawed thinking and perceptions. Post Richard Feynman's quote (from the top of the chapter) on your classroom door. Tell them, "You are the easiest person to fool, and in this class, we learn about science, the best method we have to avoid fooling ourselves." Scientists purposely design experiments to rigorously prove themselves wrong, not right.

Have you ever caught your own biases affecting your conclusion about a news story or new piece of information?

Students mistakenly think that science provides absolute and unchanging truths. This overlooks the crucial aspects of scientific knowledge, like the need for continuous learning; the distinction between facts, theories, and laws; the role of consensus; and the inherent dynamism of knowledge. This limited understanding can hinder students' ability to critically evaluate information and adapt to new discoveries, such as readily processing the development of vaccines for new viruses. We saw science at work in real time during the COVID-19 pandemic. Many people were confused by the fact the CDC changed their position on masks and boosters. But that's science: With new evidence, conclusions are modified. For example, for centuries, the prevailing theory about stomach ulcers was that stress and spicy food caused them. However, in the early 1980s, Australian doctors Barry Marshall and Robin Warren discovered bacteria living in the stomachs of ulcer patients. This was a radical idea at the time, but they conducted experiments and gathered evidence to support their hypothesis. Eventually, further research confirmed their findings, and today we understand that peptic ulcers are primarily caused by *Helicobacter pylori* infection. This discovery revolutionized ulcer treatment, replacing dietary restrictions with antibiotics (Abbott, 2005).

If we incorporate how science seeks to reduce our biases through several tried-and-true methods like adding control groups, double-blind protocols, the peer review process, and replicability, students will understand why the science facts they are taught are credible and reliable.

Q: Will the science tell the truth?

Terry Neal Purvis, Hunter Huss High School, Gastonia, NC

A: Science is not about picking teams or promoting ideology. Science is an objective, self-correcting process. All students learn the humble scientific method by heart in elementary school, and most complete an annual science fair project to put the scientific method into practice. The usual steps of the science fair project look something like this:

1. State the problem
2. Gather information
3. Develop a hypothesis
4. Plan a procedure
5. Experiment
6. Collect and analyze data
7. Accept or reject your hypothesis
8. Draw a conclusion
9. Identify applications

But if you stop and think about this often-dreaded rite of passage, you realize it's much more profound than figuring out which laundry detergent works best. The scientific method is a beautiful blend of curiosity, logic, rigor, objectivity, universality, elegance, simplicity, self-correction, and progress.

Observations guide the formulation of questions, hypotheses provide tentative explanations, and experiments act as rigorous tests to validate or falsify those explanations. This cycle of observation, questioning, testing, and refining embodies the spirit of intellectual honesty and the pursuit of truth.

Unlike narratives based on subjective interpretations, the scientific method strives for objectivity. Findings are based on evidence acquired through rigorous experimentation and open to scrutiny by the scientific community.

Perhaps the most profound aspect of the scientific method is its inherent ability to correct itself. Theories are constantly tested, refined, and even discarded when new evidence emerges. This self-correcting mechanism ensures that scientific knowledge continuously evolves, reflecting our ever-deepening understanding of the world.

Success Story: Hands-On Ecology

Graeme Marcoux, Salem High School, Salem, MA

In Fall 2023, my Ecology students began what we hope will be a long-term ecological study in Salem Woods, our local forest. The primary goal of this study is for students to explore the potential relationships between climate trends, oak tree (*Quercus* sp.) health, acorn production, white-footed mouse (*Peromyscus leucopus*) activity, and black-legged tick (*Ixodes scapularis*) abundance. Students analyzed and will continue to monitor oak trees for signs of ill health, measured annual acorn abundance and mass, used tracking tunnels (a tracking tunnel is a small, enclosed passage with openings at each end. Inside the tunnel, there is usually an ink pad or other tracking surface in the middle. A lure, like peanut butter, is placed near the ink pad. As the curious animal walks through the tunnel, it steps on the ink pad, leaving its footprints on a piece of paper or card placed at the opposite end; Figure 4.1) and wildlife cameras (Figure 4.2) to monitor the activities of white-footed mice, and conducted tick drags to measure the abundance of black-legged ticks. Students learned about the relationships between these variables and began piecing together a timeline of how each variable might produce changes to others. Over time and multiple years of data collection, future students will be able to analyze the data and determine whether any of the variables could be used to predict future outbreaks of Lyme disease and identify any potential trends that may be associated with a changing global climate. In the short term, students use their own research to develop predictions about how each variable might change in the coming years based on the data collected during their recent field season.

FIGURE 4.1 • The inked footprints from a tracking tunnel.

FIGURE 4.2 • A mouse photo captured by a wildlife camera.

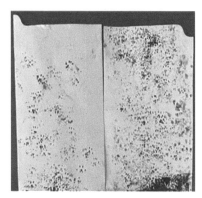

Source: Graeme Marcoux

Source: Graeme Marcoux

To increase their global worldview, students reflected on how the fate of other zoonotic diseases may change under the conditions of a changing climate. As a follow-up unit to our fieldwork, students researched potential solutions that could be implemented to manage Lyme disease outbreaks through the management of wildlife populations. Students enjoyed the hands-on nature of these units as well as the authenticity of the work they were doing. They truly felt like they were producing something that could provide a valuable service to their community.

How Do We Acknowledge Biases and Make Sense of Information?

Here are eight recommendations on how to acknowledge our own inherent biases and help students make sense of the deluge of information to which they are exposed every day.

1. Introduce the concept of flawed thinking early in the school year when the process of science is introduced. After all, it's why the process of science is so powerful; it minimizes the influence of our flawed thinking! None of us is immune to flawed thinking. For example, all of us favor information that confirms our existing beliefs or expectations, while ignoring or downplaying information that contradicts them. This is known as confirmation bias.

2. Remind students about their own biases; we all have them. Jonathan Haidt (2006) uses the analogy of a person riding an elephant to depict the complex dance between our emotions and reason in shaping our decisions and behavior. Imagine the rider perched atop the elephant. The powerful elephant represents our emotional core. It's driven by our emotions, biases, and identities. This emotional elephant is responsible for our gut feelings, immediate reactions, and primal urges. The rider symbolizes our rational side. Though smaller and weaker than the elephant, the rider possesses the crucial ability to reason, plan, and make conscious choices. The rider tries to guide the elephant toward a specific path, but the elephant's sheer power often prevails (Figure 4.3). This reflects how emotions frequently overpower our logic, leading us toward choices and opinions that might not be the most rational in the long run. Posting a photo similar to Figure 4.3 with a student on the back of an elephant can be a constant reminder to keep our biases in check as we encounter new information.

FIGURE 4.3 • Building on the work of social psychologist Jonathan Haidt, the "elephant and rider" analogy offers a way to understand our internal struggle when encountering new information.

Source: istock/BsWei

Ask yourself: What do I want to believe or don't want to believe, and why? Critical thinking involves understanding your emotions and your motivations for believing what you believe. Encourage your students to do the same.

3. It's OK to be wrong: Stress the importance of intellectual humility.

Here are some key practices to promote intellectual humility:

- **Self-reflection:** Ask yourself "How do I know this?" and, more importantly, "How would I know if I were wrong?" This encourages you to critically examine the foundations of your knowledge and identify potential biases.

- **Evidence evaluation:** Be honest and thorough in your evaluation of evidence. Consider whether you have the necessary expertise to effectively assess the information at hand.

- **Curiosity about the unknown:** Embrace your knowledge gaps and actively seek out areas where your understanding is limited. This openness to learning fosters intellectual growth.

- **Seeking expert feedback:** Do not shy away from seeking insights from individuals with deeper knowledge in relevant areas. Be receptive to their feedback and suggestions, even if they point out errors or oversights on your part.

- **Embracing uncertainty:** Accept that complexity and nuance are inherent in many issues. Acknowledge that complete certainty is often unattainable, and strive to navigate uncertainties with a growth mindset.

- **Be humble:** We gravitate toward conclusions that match our ideology or beliefs. Do not hold your beliefs too tightly to yourself so that you're able to be more objective about them. This is easier said than done, but as with anything, practice will increase our skills of objectivity (see Figure 4.4).

FIGURE 4.4 • Words to live by.

Aspire to be
less wrong.

Picture frame source: istock.com/Recebin

 TIPS TO MAKE A DIFFERENCE: Close to Nature
Janet Villas, New Garden Friends School, Greensboro, NC

1. Compost your food waste.
2. Plant a garden.
3. Use natural light as much as possible.
4. Have plants in your room.
5. Use bamboo cutlery.

4. Teach the difference between reasoning and rationalizing. We all like to rationalize—and we may mistake this for reasoning (see Figure 4.5). Reasoning requires you to look at all the evidence before drawing a conclusion. When you rationalize, on the other hand, you are selecting evidence that will lead you to a desired conclusion. You seek out and use information that confirms your existing beliefs and dismiss information that contradicts them.

FIGURE 4.5 • Reasoning vs. Rationalizing

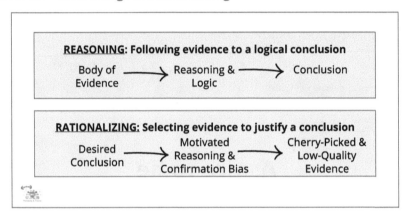

Source: Melanie Trecek-King

Reasoning about climate change means looking at scientific studies, global temperature data, and reports from credible organizations. If I were to rationalize about climate change, for example, I might downplay the evidence. I might seek to fortify my position by focusing on isolated data points or cherry-picking information that aligns with my existing beliefs. I might try to dismiss scientific consensus or discredit expert opinions. This would allow me to avoid actions that might seem inconvenient.

5. Stress that the process of science has been, time and time again, the best possible way of arriving at valid understanding. For example, explain that before the rise of modern germ theory in the 19th century, several different explanations dominated beliefs about what caused disease. Ancient Greeks held that imbalances in bodily fluids (humors) like blood, yellow bile, black bile, and phlegm led to illness. Others believed that diseases arose from bad air, called miasma. Some cultures attributed diseases to the position of stars and planets, which

could influence a person's health and susceptibility to disease. The notion that disease was caused by microscopic life-forms wasn't a sudden discovery, but a gradual shift in understanding fueled by scientific observations. Early advancements in microscopy revealed a hidden world of tiny organisms, and scientists noticed a correlation between these microbes and spoiled food or diseased tissue. These observations, combined with increasingly powerful microscopes and ongoing research, eventually led to the widely accepted germ theory of disease, revolutionizing medicine and public health practices.

Unlike beliefs, which stem from personal convictions or trust in authority, scientific evidence rests on a foundation of hard-won observations, measurements, and data. It isn't about blind acceptance; it's about subjecting ideas to rigorous testing through experiments, studies, and analysis. These processes are not one-offs: Rigorous research involves peer review by other scientists, ensuring objectivity and the ability to reproduce findings, minimizing the influence of bias. The aim is to uncover universal truths, not personal truths, by striving for objectivity and repeatability. While not infallible, science is a self-correcting system—new findings update our understanding, ensuring we constantly revise and refine our picture of the world.

6. Introduce and define the terms *science denial* and *pseudoscience*. Science denial rejects well-established scientific theories, even when supported by strong evidence. It often involves setting unreasonably high standards for proof, making it nearly impossible for science to disprove the denier's claims—for example, climate science deals with complex systems and therefore involves some small degree of uncertainty. Insisting on a 100% guarantee of every specific future impact of climate change is unreasonable. This can lead to a disregard for established scientific knowledge. Pseudoscience, on the other hand, offers alternative explanations that lack scientific rigor and credibility. It may accept weak evidence or rely on appeals to emotion or personal beliefs—for example, taking short-term fluctuations in temperature data and presenting them as evidence that global warming isn't happening. Focusing on a single cold winter as proof that Earth isn't warming ignores the long-term trends that show a clear warming pattern. Both approaches can negatively impact public understanding of science and lead people and governments to make poor decisions that have lasting real-world consequences.

Science denial can result from misinformation researchers call vested interests or solution aversion. Certain industries, like fossil fuel companies, have a significant financial stake in maintaining the status quo. Climate action that promotes renewable energy or stricter regulations on emissions threaten their profits. Because of these vested interests, these companies might fund lobbyists and campaigns that downplay the severity of climate change or cast doubt on scientific evidence.

We can teach our students to spot both science denial and pseudoscience using the acronym FLICC, developed by John Cook and the Skeptical Science team at the University of Queensland, Australia. Cook introduced the initial framework for FLICC in his 2010 blog post titled "The Five Techniques of Denialism," outlining the five core tactics employed by those who deny established scientific findings. He later elaborated on this concept in his book *Cranky Uncle vs. Climate Change: How to Understand and Respond to Climate Science Deniers* (Cook, 2020; see Figure 4.6). FLICC stands for

F: Fake Experts. This tactic relies on presenting unqualified or irrelevant individuals as credible authorities to mislead the public, for example, a celebrity with no scientific background who promotes alternative explanations for climate change, like increased solar activity being the sole cause.

L: Logical Fallacy. This tactic involves using flawed reasoning or manipulative logic to mislead the audience. It could involve faulty cause-and-effect relationships, strawman arguments, or ad hominem attacks. Using the argument "climate has always changed" to dismiss the unprecedented rate and human influence on current climate change is a logical fallacy. Citing a fringe scientist who denies climate change while ignoring the overwhelming scientific consensus falls under the "appeal to authority" fallacy. Fringe scientists often lack strong supporting evidence for their claims or rely on anecdotal accounts rather than rigorous research methods. Their results may be difficult for other scientists to replicate and do not pass peer review, which is a crucial part of scientific validation.

I: Impossible Expectations: This tactic involves setting unreasonably high standards for scientific evidence, making it virtually impossible for established science to disprove their claims. For example, demanding absolute certainty from climate models and ignoring the inherent uncertainties and limitations of any complex predictive system are impossible expectations. Claiming that scientists can never "prove" climate change is caused by humans, despite the overwhelming evidence already established, is another example.

C: Cherry-picking: This tactic involves selectively using data or evidence that supports the desired conclusion while ignoring or downplaying contradictory information. Focusing on isolated weather events like cold snaps to discredit the long-term trends of global warming is cherry-picking and leads to several of the misconceptions described in Chapter 2.

C: Conspiracy: This tactic attributes the cause of an event or phenomenon to a hidden conspiracy, often involving powerful groups or individuals, without providing credible evidence. One common conspiracy theory is attributing climate change to a secret plot by foreign powers to weaken the economy of specific countries.

FIGURE 4.6 • Climate denial is not about facts or lack thereof.

Source: John Cook

TIPS TO MAKE A DIFFERENCE: Every Little Bit Helps

Jacki Grady, Mount Hermon School, Mt. Hermon, LA

1. Plant trees.
2. Reuse copies as scratch paper.
3. Properly seal windows, doors, outlets, etc.
4. Collect rainwater for house plants.
5. Check and change oil filters regularly.

Science denial has many root causes but one of the most common ones is solution aversion. Solution aversion stems from several factors, such as a fear of change. Shifting away from a fossil fuel–based economy can be disruptive and require significant changes to infrastructure and lifestyles. Some people might resist these changes due to fear of the unknown, potential economic disruptions, or concerns about job security in certain industries.

Inconvenience can also lead to solution aversion. Implementing solutions to climate change might require personal sacrifices, such as biking to work or riding the bus instead of driving a car or paying a premium for cleaner energy sources like solar panels. People might resist these changes and cling to the convenience of the current system, even if they acknowledge the problems associated with it, because making the change is expensive or time-consuming or otherwise inconvenient.

Although the issue of climate change is very serious, humor can be a useful tool to combat climate misinformation. Playful approaches like games can be effective. "Cranky Uncle" teaches students how to recognize misinformation through humor, critical thinking exercises, and cartoons (Cook, 2024). https://crankyuncle.com/

Solution aversion is sometimes only indirectly linked to actual climate change. Many people are against too much government regulation, and government regulation is a necessary component to address climate change. For example, a person who believes in individual responsibility and free markets might support actions like personal energy conservation or switching to electric vehicles. However, they might reject government regulations mandating energy efficiency standards for appliances or carbon pricing mechanisms because they see these regulations as an infringement on individual freedom and market forces. Even if they acknowledge climate change is a problem, they might be averse to solutions that involve government intervention.

7. Finally, teach students that the process of science they've been learning since elementary school actively aims to minimize these natural human mental tendencies. Teach this idea early and reinforce it often. Developing a healthy skepticism of the information we encounter and of our own tendency to rationalize over our ability to think logically should apply to all the new information we encounter. Important: This does not mean students should question everything in their science textbooks. It's equally important to stress repeatedly that the scientific process, with its emphasis on peer review, objectivity, reproducibility, and open data, actively fights against inherent human biases to ensure the most reliable understanding of the world.

If these seven recommendations become the underlying theme of our science classes and we constantly focus on how science knows what it knows, students will have a very different mindset when climate change is introduced. Compare this approach to a teacher saying, "I know you don't believe in climate change, but science says it's happening. And that's it."

> **How does the double-blind protocol reduce researcher bias? In a double-blind protocol, neither the participants nor the researchers initially know who is receiving the experimental treatment or control.**

So now, let's go back to focus specifically on climate change. How do we talk to somebody who does not accept the science behind climate change? Most people will be receptive and welcome learning about climate change. That's the good news we will address in the latter part of this chapter. But first, we'll consider possible conflicts.

Q&A   **Q:** Can you offer tips for teaching climate change to skeptical students?

Jennifer Skrobisz, Harlem High School, Harlem, GA

A: Read this chapter! But the most important advice we can offer is to *not* wait until you start your climate unit to teach students that we should consider how our biases and identities filter all the information we encounter in our lives. Teach intellectual humility from the first day of school. One simple way is to model the strategy known as SIFT (Figure 4.7) often in your classrooms:

- **Stop**: Identify the information source and its claims. Check your own emotional reaction to the information.

- **Investigate the Source**: Take a few seconds to find out the expertise and agenda of the source, so you can decide whether it's worth your time and trust.

- **Find Other Coverage**: Practice the lateral reading strategy featured in Chapter 3—figure out what others have said and whether those sources agree or disagree with the original information resource.

- **Trace Ideas Back to the Source**: Track the claims, quotes, and media sources back to their original context. Are they being taken out of context? (Caulfield, 2019)

FIGURE 4.7 • SIFT stands for Stop, Investigate the source, Find other coverage, Trace claims. It's a framework for evaluating the credibility of information you find online, particularly on websites and social media.

SIFT Approach
A CRITICAL THINKING APPROACH

STOP
Check your emotion. Strong reaction? Be careful. Also, check what biases you may have allowed in, such as confirmation bias (favoring information that confirms what your believe ture).

QUESTIONS TO ASK
- What is my initial reaction to the headline?
- What do I already know about the topic?
- What do I know about the source?

INVESTIGATE
Look into the author of the claims, the publisher or information source. Assess what bioses they may have to get a better understanding of their creadibility.

QUESTIONS TO ASK
- Who is the author?
- What is the mission of the source?
- Are there any potential biases?

FIND
Look around and find other corroborating or contradicting reports from other sources, such as websites, recognized experts in the field, and more. Consider using AI to assist with finding other controdictory sources.

QUESTIONS TO ASK
- Are other reputable sources reporting on this?
- Do fact-checkers support the claims made?

TRACE
Track claims, quotes, and media to their original context. Have they been taken out of context in some way? Were they really meant to apply to this claim?

QUESTIONS TO ASK
- Can the original studies or announcement be found?
- Is the information presented in its true context?

Adopted from Kaitlyn Van Kampen's work at The University of Chicago Library. Leam more about TCEA's application of SIFT to K–12 education at **https://blog.tcea.org**

Source: Miguel Guhlin

TIPS TO MAKE A DIFFERENCE: Go Paperless!
Morgan Massey, Sheffield High School, Sheffield, AL

1. To save paper, have students submit assignments electronically.

WHAT DO I DO IF I GET PUSHBACK?

Our students are with us for nine months. We can weave the new approach proposed in the first half of this chapter into many of our lessons, encouraging our students to think about how science works and how our perceptions play a role in what we believe. With our students, we have the luxury of time.

This is not the case with parents. Our conversations with parents might occur in a brief hallway exchange. Handling the issue of science denial in much more time-constrained situations, such as in an email to an angry parent or conflict-avoiding administrator, poses a different set of challenges.

How Do I Talk to People Who Disagree?

Our job as educators is not to change anyone's worldview. But when teaching a topic that can be as emotional and partisan as climate change, we will sometimes have to have difficult discussions with people who disagree with us. It should go without saying that when approaching someone with a different opinion, it is always best to do so with respect. It's important to avoid getting into a debate in which the aim is to win. Instead, aim for a respectful conversation in which both parties can understand each other's perspective. Acknowledging each other's concerns is crucial, and it is important to validate everyone's right to have a different opinion and acknowledge any sources of information that they might be relying on. Listening actively is also important, as it can help in understanding the root of the disagreement. We all know well that mocking somebody or dismissing them for their beliefs will only make them adhere even tighter to those beliefs.

It's important to focus on common ground. One way to do this is by finding shared values, such as the need for environmental protection or a clean future for generations to come. Starting with local impacts can also help because it can make the topic more relatable. Discussing potential local effects of climate change, like extreme weather events or rising sea levels, can be a good way to start the conversation.

Instead of dwelling on the negative aspects of climate change, discuss potential solutions and innovations related to climate change. We all want to build the economy of the 21st century. Renewable energy can do for this era what the internal combustion engine and the light bulb did for the United States 100 years ago. Imagine if the blacksmiths, horse breeders, and candle makers stopped the rise of the automobile and the incandescent bulb. Think about what those two inventions did for the U.S. economy. Glass, steel, rubber—U.S. industry took off, and the nation prospered. The same can happen now with innovations in solar, wind, and other alternative energy technologies.

> **Take a moment to consider the last time you changed your mind about a closely held belief. Did it happen gradually or did you have a eureka moment?**

Leading by example can also be effective; demonstrate your own commitment to sustainability through your actions and choices. Be patient and persistent in your approach, and remember that change is a gradual process.

Q&A   Q: What is the most effective way to talk to someone who denies climate change?

Katherine Korn, Williamsville East High School, East Amherst, NY

A: Try street epistemology. Co-founded by Anthony Magnabosco, Street Epistemology International is a nonprofit organization that encourages critical thinking and skepticism. Practitioners of street epistemology use fair, open-ended questions to help people examine and critically reflect on the foundations of their beliefs in a collaborative manner. Street Epistemology offers a free, self-paced course at https://qrs.ly/dcg37bv that aims to help people become more confident and thoughtful communicators capable of tackling complex conversations about beliefs.

The Importance of Good Curriculum Standards

Good curriculum standards on climate science will minimize the possibility of pushback. As an advocate also for evolution education, I am often asked by teachers, "What do I do if a parent or administrator tells me I must teach creationism or intelligent design alongside the well-established science of evolutionary biology?" My answer is to respond, "Thanks for your suggestion, but the curriculum for the class is set by the district in conformity with the state's science education standards."

This honest response makes three things clear: it's not going to happen, it's not within the teacher's control anyhow, and the teacher isn't going to address (or argue about) the actual content of the suggestion. This response takes the teacher out of the picture.

Although there are places in the science curriculum where climate change can be taught (see Q&A on p. 229 and Chapter 7), the reality is that most states do not have climate change curriculum standards. Yet. (See Chapter 8 for more on the work being done in New Jersey, Connecticut, California, and elsewhere.) For now, most teachers cannot fall back on the strategy of answering climate critics by stating that the class content is based on the state standards. However, standardized learning objectives (e.g., those built into the NGSS; see Chapter 7) guarantee that students will encounter core concepts like the greenhouse effect, human impact on the climate system, and potential consequences of climate change. Strong standards promote consistency and coherence in climate change education across different schools and districts. This prevents a situation where some students receive in-depth climate education while others have limited exposure (Worth, 2021)—which just makes the problem of bias even worse. Finally, by establishing a foundation in climate science, standards can create a springboard for students to engage with solutions, mitigation strategies, and the societal and ethical implications of climate change.

It's worth mentioning that good curriculum standards also help teachers address so-called academic freedom bills. These are legislative initiatives that seek to limit or remove the requirements for teaching climate change in schools. Supporters portray these bills as safeguarding academic freedom and argue that schools should have the discretion to determine whether to teach climate change. In reality, these bills are efforts to undercut the scientific consensus on climate change and advance climate change denial in education. In states without clear climate standards, several strategies addressed in this book can be implemented to work around legislative restrictions on teaching climate change. For example, educators can integrate related concepts into existing curriculum areas such as biology and geography, emphasize scientific processes and critical thinking, address local environmental issues, promote independent student research, collaborate with parents and communities, and highlight climate literacy as part of broader scientific education efforts.

Success Story: From Birds to Blossoms

Kathleen Small, Hartshorn Elementary, Short Hills, NJ

Our community garden has blossomed over the past 20 years. What began as a bird study with Cornell's Ornithology Lab, with feeders in an unused corner of the schoolyard, has grown into a vibrant space for learning and sustainability.

Students now have an outdoor classroom where they get their hands dirty—literally. They learn valuable gardening and composting skills, using leftover classroom snacks to create nutrient-rich compost for the garden beds. Plus, they have a fun "pizza garden" where they grow fresh ingredients for delicious pizzas: tomatoes, basil, and oregano (Figure 4.8). Through these experiences, students develop a deeper understanding of the importance of plants and trees in a healthy environment.

FIGURE 4.8 • School gardens offer students hands-on learning in science, nutrition, and environmental responsibility.

Source: istock.com/BsWei

TIPS TO MAKE A DIFFERENCE: Keep It Simple

Liam Plybon, Longview High School, Longview, TX

1. Reduce paper consumption by always printing worksheets on the front and back!

How Do I Escalate the Situation If Needed?

It's important to know our limits as teachers, and it's OK to walk away from a conversation if it becomes disrespectful or unproductive. We should choose our battles. Focus on conversations where we feel there's a chance to make a difference. Focus on positive outcomes. Even if we don't see eye to eye, we can still have a successful conversation by fostering understanding and respectful communication.

If a parent or student escalates an argument regarding climate denial in the classroom, teachers can use the following resources and strategies. First, de-escalation techniques should be used, which include maintaining calm and avoiding getting drawn into a heated argument, acknowledging the parent or student's concerns and validating their right to have an opinion, reframing the conversation to focus on learning objectives or the specific activity at hand, and politely but firmly setting boundaries regarding disruptive behavior and disrespectful communication. If the situation becomes difficult to manage, teachers can seek support from their department chair, principal, school counselor, or district science coordinator. Teachers should encourage open discussions in the classroom, but we also have a responsibility to maintain a safe and respectful learning environment for all students. In the worst-case scenario, when a parent or student loses control, teachers should involve their school administration or security personnel immediately.

There are several resources available for teachers that offer guidance and professional development opportunities for navigating challenging conversations about climate change in the classroom. Take a look:

- National Science Teaching Association (NSTA): The NSTA offers resources and professional development opportunities for teachers on climate change education, including strategies for navigating challenging conversations. (https://www.nsta.org/)

- Yale Climate Connections: This website by Yale University provides science-based communication resources for educators, including tips on talking about climate change with students and parents. (https://climatecommunication.yale.edu/)

- National Center for Science Education (NCSE): The NCSE provides resources and support for educators facing challenges related to teaching evolution and climate change. (https://ncse.ngo/)

Dealing with climate-denying students and parents was a recurring theme among teachers who sent us their questions. The following question was submitted by two different educators.

Q: How do we discuss studies that deny climate change with parents and students?

John Winkler, Mt. Pleasant Schools, Mt. Pleasant, MI, and Ellen Andrews, St. Joseph High School, South Bend, IN

A: Don't get bogged down in debates—the bigger picture involves established evidence like rising temperatures and melting ice. Instead, frame a productive discussion that encourages critical thinking about the studies and how they fit within the broader scientific understanding. You can also discuss tactics used to spread misinformation, such as cherry-picking data. Finally, offer credible resources like NASA, NOAA, and IPCC reports for further exploration. By equipping parents and students with these tools, you can empower them to have informed and productive conversations about climate change.

NOW FOR THE GOOD NEWS

It's safe to say that teachers want to avoid conflict with their students and students' parents. Teaching about climate change can lead to anxiety among educators because we know we may receive pushback. Therefore, it will be comforting to hear that a majority of adults in the United States express support for the inclusion of climate change education in schools. This support comes from more than 80% of parents, including 2 out of 3 Republicans and 9 out of 10 Democrats (Kwauk & Winthrop, 2020).

A Yale study on American views of global warming shows a significant shift in public opinion over the past decade (Figure 4.9). They grouped Americans based on their views on climate change as follows:

• Alarmed: Very concerned, believe it's human-caused and urgent, but unsure of solutions.

• Concerned: Believe it's happening and serious, but not a pressing issue.

- Cautious: Undecided about the cause, seriousness, or urgency.

- Disengaged: Unaware or uninterested in the issue.

- Doubtful: Don't believe it's happening or see it as natural.

- Dismissive: Deny it's happening, human-caused, or a threat.

The study found that the "Alarmed" group, most worried about climate change, nearly doubled in size from 15% in 2013 to 28% in 2023. The "Cautious" group, once the largest, has shrunk considerably, from 27% in 2013 to 15% in 2023, moving into the "Concerned" and "Alarmed" groups. The combined percentage of "Alarmed" and "Concerned" Americans has risen from 40% to 57%, reflecting a growing national concern. The "Disengaged" and "Dismissive" groups haven't changed much in size. Perhaps that's because these two positions are most rooted in identity and, as explained, the facts don't matter.

FIGURE 4.9 • Comparing the two pie graphs shows the shift in American views on climate change.

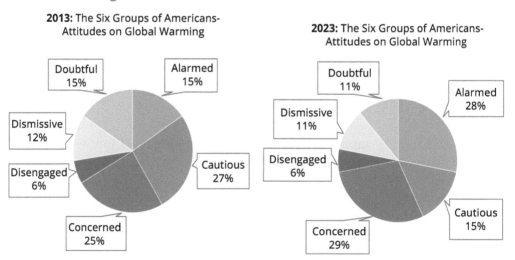

2013: The Six Groups of Americans-Attitudes on Global Warming

2023: The Six Groups of Americans-Attitudes on Global Warming

Source: Leiserowitz et al. (2024).

· ·

 Q: How do you focus on climate change without bringing politics into the classroom?

Todd Bloch, Warren Woods Middle School, Warren, MI

A: Teachers can dispel the myth that one's thinking about climate change should be based on political ideology in the following ways:

- Encourage students to analyze data and evidence, which is more effective than simply asking students to accept information.

- Focus on how action on climate change can positively impact our national economy and personal bank accounts.

· ·

Talking With Students

Students need to know you care before they care what you know. Climate science and data literacy are essential components when teaching about climate change, but making real-life connections using personal stories and project-based learning can go a long way in fostering not just informed students but also environmentally conscious young citizens. When students feel a connection to the issue on a personal level, the dry facts and figures of climate science become tools they can wield to understand the challenges and contribute to solutions.

PERSONAL STORIES

Personal stories are powerful tools for enriching climate education. Helping our students connect with the struggles and experiences of individuals facing extreme weather events, rising sea levels, or changes in their local environment can make the issue feel closer to home.

In addition, by immersing themselves in someone else's journey, students develop a sense of empathy for those affected by climate change. This emotional connection creates a deeper understanding of the issue and motivates students to take action. Stories don't have to paint a picture of despair. Highlighting individuals and communities finding solutions and adapting to climate change shows students there's hope and demonstrates the power of collective action (Figure 4.10).

FIGURE 4.10 • Anya: Now a Scientist at the Woodwell Climate Research Center

In one of the *Young Voices for the Planet* films, Anya, an Indigenous Siberian girl, joins Arctic scientist Max Holmes's research team to learn, and teach her schoolmates about, global warming. Now grown up, she is a scientist at the Woodwell Climate Research Center in Woods Hall, Massachusetts (https://www.youtube.com/watch?v=eJGp16Va-m0).

Source: Max Holmes

PROJECT-BASED LEARNING

Climate change can be a complex and sometimes overwhelming topic. By actively participating in experiments, simulations, or projects, students become more invested in their learning (Freeman et al., 2014). Students can see how their actions can make a difference and are more likely to adopt sustainable practices and advocate for climate action. What's more, hands-on activities that involve nature, like community and citizen science projects or studying local environmental changes, can cultivate a sense of connection with the natural world, inspiring students to take action to protect the environment.

> The *Young Voices for the Planet* films are a collection of short documentaries showcasing the inspiring stories of young people taking action on climate change. https://celfeducation.org/yvfp/

Here are some hands-on lessons that can help students engage with climate change:

1. Model Greenhouse: Creating a mini greenhouse using a clear container, soil, a plant, and thermometers is a simple class project. Place one thermometer inside the container and another outside and observe temperature changes to understand how greenhouse gases trap heat. (https://qrs.ly/3kg3dgw)

2. **Carbon Footprint Assessment:** Calculating your own carbon footprint and identifying areas where you can reduce it involves measuring energy consumption, transportation habits, and lifestyle choices. Use online calculators or DIY methods to assess your carbon footprint. (https://qrs.ly/8cg37bx)

3. **Community Garden or Urban Farming:** Starting a community garden or getting involved in urban farming initiatives can help students understand several key issues: the role of agriculture in climate change, the importance of local food production (reducing food miles), and carbon sequestration in the soil. (https://qrs.ly/qkg37by)

4. **Energy Efficiency Audit:** Conducting a classroom or home energy audit to identify areas where energy consumption can be reduced could involve turning off lights, unplugging unused electronics, and brainstorming alternative solutions. Many power companies offer customers the option to complete an energy audit on their websites. As a teacher, I assigned a home energy audit every year. Some parents even went above and beyond, adding energy-efficient appliances, insulation, or solar panels to their homes in response (Our Testing: Dangerous Dirt, 2014). (https://qrs.ly/sqg37c0)

> Citizen and community science projects can be a great way to learn about science, contribute to research, and connect with nature. National Geographic has citizen and community science projects for any age group: https://qrs.ly/hsg37c4

5. **Citizen and Community Science Projects:** Participating in citizen and community science projects where students collect and upload temperature data to monitor local climate trends is an example of an engaging, real-life research opportunity. You can also measure temperatures in different parts of the schoolyard (pavement vs. grassy areas) to understand the urban heat island effect.

Talking With Parents

Although it's not a traditional academic paper, HP's *Sustainable Impact Report* provides valuable insights into how our students' parents feel about climate change. It found that 91% of parents express worry regarding climate change, with many stating that this concern has influenced their views on expanding their families. The study also highlights that a significant portion of parents expect companies to address climate change actively and are placing emphasis on sustainable behaviors and purchases (HP, 2022).

Q: How influential are parents regarding students' opinions on climate change?

Harvey Norris, Marshall High School, Marshall, IL

A: Parents play a significant role in developing the environmental perceptions of their children. Family discussions about climate change have been identified as one of the most important factors influencing children's perceptions and behaviors (Mead et al., 2012).

INDIRECT COMMUNICATION WITH PARENTS

A study conducted in North Carolina researched how children influenced their parents' feelings about climate change. Researchers surveyed more than 1,000 families and found that children who expressed concern about climate change increased their parents' level of concern by 22%. This was especially true for conservative parents, whose concern rose by 28%, showing that kids can be powerful messengers on this issue, even in politically divided contexts (Lawson et al., 2019).

Children can act as climate change messengers within their families, raising awareness, challenging perspectives, and inspiring action through their enthusiasm, knowledge, and, sometimes, gentle nudges. They might bring home projects, ask questions, or simply talk about what they learned. This exposure can spark curiosity and raise awareness among parents who might not have previously considered the issue in depth.

In addition, when children express concern about climate change, it can challenge parents' existing beliefs or lack of awareness. Seeing their children worried might motivate parents to learn more about the issue and prioritize it more immediately. This could involve things like reducing energy consumption, recycling more diligently, changing to more energy efficient lightbulbs, or participating in environmentally friendly activities (Kiest, 2023).

Many parents want to talk to their kids about climate change but often struggle with how to approach it. Parents want to support their children's learning. Therefore, activities that get both parents and kids involved in climate action, such as a home energy audit, could be very beneficial and an opportunity to engage the entire family (Dayton et al., 2023).

DIRECT COMMUNICATION WITH PARENTS

Focusing on student learning and shared concern will send the message that teachers and parents have the same goals for the students. A good starting point is to highlight how climate change education aligns with science standards and equips students with valuable life skills like critical thinking and problem solving. Discussing how climate change can impact their children's futures will appeal to parents' desire to prepare their kids for the world they'll inherit.

When parents speak, actively listen to them. Acknowledge their concerns and validate their feelings before presenting information or resources. Once the initial communication has been established in a respectful manner, consider showcasing examples of how climate change education is presented in your class, emphasizing age-appropriate content and activities. You can also provide parents with reliable resources about climate change that they can explore with their children at home.

Time-permitting, try these recommendations:

- Focus on how understanding climate change empowers students to make informed choices and take action, fostering a sense of agency.

- Showcase ways students are learning about solutions and innovations related to climate change, fostering hope and optimism.

- Offer opportunities for parents to participate in climate change discussions or activities alongside their children.

- Explore possibilities for connecting parents with local environmental organizations or climate action initiatives.

. . . .

 Q: How are parents impacting the teaching of climate change at our schools?

Natalye James, Breck School, Golden Valley, MN

A: Approximately 30% of all teachers are concerned that parents may complain if their children are learning about climate change at school, negatively impacting the teaching of climate change in our schools. This concern may be unfounded. In a study mentioned earlier in this chapter, 80% of adults think climate change should be taught (Kwauk & Winthrop, 2020).

Consider that parents can be powerful allies in climate change education by advocating for its inclusion in curricula and supporting teachers with projects and resources. For example, thanks to the efforts of students and parents in Miami-Dade County, their school board adopted the goal to transition their school district to 100% clean energy by 2030. One of the parents involved, Michele Drucker, became the Environmental Chair for the Florida PTA and played a key role in drafting the resolution (Generation180, 2023). Reach out to your students' parents; you may be pleasantly surprised.

. . . .

Talking to Your Administration About Climate Change Education

A teacher's role may include speaking with school and district administrators on behalf of your students about the importance of climate education.

For example, students may want to start a recycling club or raise climate change awareness at their school through a series of informative pieces featured on the school's morning announcements. Students may inquire about spearheading schoolwide initiatives such as systematically turning off classroom lights at the end of the day.

Here are some things to consider when speaking to school leaders on behalf of students:

1. Be prepared.
   - Collect data on student interest in climate change at your school. Studies show that young people are interested in the subject. A recent survey found that only 4% of students feel they know a lot about climate change; sadly, 42% feel they have learned next to nothing about it at school; and 57% of students want to learn more (Kwauk & Winthrop, 2020).
   - Become familiar with the national science standards that emphasize climate education (see Chapter 7).
   - Showcase studies demonstrating the effectiveness of climate education, such as the Lawson study mentioned earlier (Lawson et al., 2019).
   - When considering asking your administrator to do a schoolwide climate project, tailor your proposal to highlight how climate change impacts your local community. This can make the issue more relevant and impactful for both students and administrators.

2. Know your audience.
   - Research your school district's curriculum guidelines and any existing policies on climate change education.
   - Tailor your approach to address potential concerns of administrators, such as time constraints or curriculum overload.

3. Be positive.
   - Emphasize the importance of climate change education in preparing students for the future.
   - Highlight how understanding climate science helps students develop critical thinking, problem-solving, and decision-making skills—all valuable life skills.

4. Offer solutions.
   - Present specific ideas for integrating climate change education into the curriculum.
   - Express your willingness to collaborate with other teachers and administrators to develop a curriculum that aligns with existing standards and addresses potential concerns.

5. Be respectful and persistent.
   - Request a meeting with your principal or curriculum director to discuss incorporating climate change education.
   - Be open to discussing any concerns they might have, and offer to address them constructively.
   - If the initial meeting doesn't lead to immediate change, don't be discouraged. Follow up with additional information or explore the possibility of piloting a climate change unit with your class to showcase its effectiveness.

6. You are not alone.
   - Connect with other science teachers and faculty members who share your interest in teaching climate education, creating a united front. Other teachers are likely to have strengths to complement your own.
   - Consider engaging parents; they can be powerful allies.

. . . .

 Q: Will parents find the topic of teaching climate change controversial?

Janett Akerman, Cypress-Fairbanks Independent School District, Cypress, TX

A: Because climate change has become a partisan issue, teachers may encounter some parents who find the topic controversial. However, many teachers will be surprised to learn that the opposite is more likely to happen; many parents want to see more climate change education. The statistics differ slightly across studies, but not significantly. A study by Will and Prothero in 2022 showed parental support for climate change education hovering around 80%. An NPR/Ipsos poll shows an even greater majority of U.S. teachers (86%) and parents (84%) in favor of adding climate change education to school curriculums (Kamenetz, 2019). What about globally? According to a recent survey from the United Nations Development Programme, roughly the same average of 80% of the respondents are in favor of schools in their country teaching more about climate change, whereas only 6% believe that schools should teach less about climate change. However, in the United States, the number was lower than the previous studies cited: 66% of respondents preferred "more," while 29% preferred "less." Interestingly, the report highlighted that the proportion of individuals wanting more climate education was highest in least-developed countries at 93% (Flynn et al., 2024).

* * *

The perspective introduced in this chapter will help teachers navigate the politics of climate change. Adding how our minds work to our usual lessons on the process of science will equip our students with new tools to recognize bias when presented with new information, not just bias from the source but from within our own minds. This, in turn, will improve climate education, and the impact of effective climate education is significant. If climate change education were to be provided to only 16% of high school students in high- and middle-income countries, it could result in a reduction of nearly 19 gigatons of carbon dioxide by 2050 (Cordero et al., 2020). Such education can be particularly impactful when it helps students develop a personal connection to climate solutions and empowers them to make a difference through their daily behaviors and decision making. Just imagine the potential impact if every student in the world were to receive such an education.

LEARNING FROM OUR COLLEAGUES
Look in the Mirror

Ms. Garcia wasn't just showing a graph today. Today, she was challenging mindsets. "Alright, class," she began, "we've been delving deep into climate change, and today, I want to talk about something a little different: ourselves."

(Continued)

(Continued)

A murmur rippled through the room. "What do you mean, Ms. Garcia?" Paulina asked.

"How about this," Ms. Garcia said, drawing a thought bubble on the board with "Climate Change" written inside. "Imagine this bubble represents our understanding of climate change. Now, what might influence what goes inside that bubble?"

Colin raised his hand. "The information we learn, right? Like the science we've been studying."

Ms. Garcia nodded. "Absolutely, science is crucial. But there's more. We all have . . . " she paused, searching for the right word, ". . . biases."

A beat of silence followed. "Biases?" Jackson echoed, a flicker of confusion in his eyes.

"Yes," Ms. Garcia explained. "Unconscious beliefs or preferences that can shape how we interpret information. For instance, someone who loves to drive might (consciously or unconsciously) downplay the impact of cars on climate change. See how that could work?"

"So, our biases can mess up our understanding?" Olivia asked, furrowing her brow.

"Exactly," Ms. Garcia said. "That's why it's important to be aware of them. Maybe we tend to focus on information that confirms what we already believe, or maybe we dismiss opposing viewpoints too quickly."

"So, how do we fix this?" Paulina inquired.

"The first step is acknowledging that those biases exist," Ms. Garcia said. "Then, we can actively seek out diverse viewpoints and information—studies from different countries and perspectives from people impacted by climate change. The broader our understanding, the less likely our biases are to distort reality."

"That makes sense," Colin said. "Like wearing different colored glasses when you study the same thing."

Ms. Garcia chuckled. "Exactly, Colin! By recognizing our biases, we can remove those colored glasses and see climate change for what it truly is: a complex issue with real consequences."

The students nodded with newfound awareness. It wasn't just about data and graphs anymore. It was about critical thinking, open-mindedness, and the responsibility they all held to understand the world around them—biases and all.

Reflection Questions

1. What are your personal experiences with climate change (e.g., witnessing extreme weather events, living in an area affected by rising sea levels)? How might these experiences influence your perspective?

2. Do you hold any beliefs or values that could color your views on climate change (e.g., skepticism about science, strong economic ties to certain industries)? How might these beliefs impact your teaching?

3. Have you ever felt uncomfortable discussing climate change due to potential controversy? Why or why not? How can you address these concerns in the classroom?

4. How do you currently present information about climate change in your classroom?

5. How do you encourage critical thinking and discussion about climate change in your classroom?

6. Do you create a safe space for students to ask questions and express concerns?

7. How do you think your students' current perceptions might influence their understanding of climate change?

For Further Reading

FOR TEACHERS

Caulfield, M., & Wineberg, S. (2023). *Verified: How to think straight, get duped less, and make better decisions about what to believe online*. The University of Chicago Press.

Conway, E. M., & Oreskes, N. (2014). *Merchants of doubt*. Bloomsbury.

Cook, J. (2020). *Cranky Uncle vs. climate change: How to understand and respond to climate science deniers*. Citadel Press.

Damico, J. S., & Baildon, M. (2022). *How to confront climate denial: Literacy, social studies, and climate change*. Teachers College Press.

Gilovich, T. (2008). *How we know what isn't so: The fallibility of human reason in everyday life*. Free Press.

Grant, A. M. (2021). *Think again: The power of knowing what you don't know*. Viking.

Harrison, G. P. (2015). *Good thinking: What you need to know to be smarter, safer, wealthier, and wiser*. Prometheus Books.

FOR STUDENTS

Ages 3–7

Kamkwamba, W., & Mealer, B. (2023). *The boy who harnessed the wind* (Young readers ed.). Ernst Klett Sprachen.

Ages 3–12

Harris, D. (2023). *Don't be mean to 13: A triskaidekaphobia story*. Label Free Publishing.

Ages 5–10

Pakman, D. (2023). *Think like a scientist: A kid's guide to scientific thinking.*

Ages 6–9

Reynolds, P. A., & Reynolds, P. H. (2015). *Go green!* Charlesbridge.

Ages 8–11

Applegate, K., & Santoso, C. (2021). *Willodeen* (Nebraska Golden Sower Nominee 2023–2024). Feiwel and Friends.

Ages 9–12

Klass, P. J. (1997). *Bringing UFOs down to Earth*. Prometheus Books.

All Ages

Hupp, S. (2021). *Superhuman abilities: Game book for skeptical folk*. Malarkey World.

PART III

HOW DO I AVOID ANXIETY AND ENCOURAGE HEALTHY ENGAGEMENT IN MY STUDENTS?

Source: Istock.com/Jiri Hrebicek

CHAPTER FIVE

CLIMATE INJUSTICE AND THE NEW NARRATIVE OF ACTIVISM

Those least responsible for climate change are worst affected by it.

—*Vandana Shiva*

THIS CHAPTER WILL DISCUSS

- Environmental justice as an interdisciplinary topic
- System inequalities that lead one group or population to be more adversely affected by climate change than others
- The need to teach climate justice, and
- BIPOC youth activists working for change

WHAT ARE ENVIRONMENTAL JUSTICE AND CLIMATE JUSTICE?

Robert Bullard, a leader in the environmental justice movement, defines environmental justice as the principle that "all people and communities are entitled to equal protection from environmental and public health laws and regulations" (Bullard, 1993). The U.S. Environmental Protection Agency (EPA) adds that environmental justice must also include the "meaningful involvement of all people regardless of race, color, national origin or income with respect to the development, implementation, and enforcement of environmental laws, regulations, and policies" (Bryant, 1995).

You can help your students understand environmental justice by looking at it as a combination of issues related to the environment, social justice, health, race, and economics. The First and Second National People of Color Environmental Leadership Summits in 1991 and 2002 found that environmental justice has been largely absent in environmental education. At the Second Summit, Running Grass and Julian Agyeman (2002) indicated that many mainstream environmental education programs "reflect ecosystem-based concerns, e.g., a focus on natural resources and wildlife generally without consideration of cultural or social justice issues." Similarly, elsewhere I (Kimi) have maintained that teaching about environmental hazards without addressing the related social, economic, and political forces will make environmental education programs irrelevant for students from frontline communities, who are disproportionately students of color (Waite, 2024). Teaching for environmental justice requires an interdisciplinary perspective and approach because connecting the dots between disciplines and subjects is necessary. Teaching for climate justice requires the same, and teachers of all grades and subject areas can help.

· ·

 Q: I would like more activities for high school teaching on climate change.

Christine Briske, Ronan High School, Ronan, MT

A: Some great resources for secondary students can be found in *A People's Curriculum for the Earth: Teaching Climate Change and the Environmental Crisis,* edited by Bill Bigelow and Tim Swinehart. It also features interdisciplinary lessons that can be used across content areas.

· ·

According to researchers Schlosberg and Collins (2014), climate justice connects the goals of the decades-long environmental justice and climate change movements to address how climate change disproportionately harms people who are already more vulnerable to its impacts. This vulnerability can be due to personal factors at the individual level (e.g., age, income, or disability) and/or social factors at the larger systemic level (e.g., racism and other forms of oppression). The Intergovernmental Panel on Climate Change (IPCC, 2022) maintains that the goals of climate justice include reducing the unequal harms of climate change, providing equitable benefits from climate solutions, and involving affected communities in decision making. The United States has recently included climate justice in federal climate policy with the Justice40 Initiative (2022), and the White House Environmental Justice Advisory Council (EPA, 2024) intends to increase federal funding to historically underserved communities. The United Nations Framework Convention on Climate Change (UNFCCC, 2020) maintains this would ensure that no one is left behind in transitioning from fossil fuels to clean and renewable energy. With this in mind, it's important that we incorporate this perspective into our teaching of climate change.

TIPS TO MAKE A DIFFERENCE: Use Less Energy at Home
Jamie Bothwell, Freedom High School, Bethlehem, PA

1. Turn your heat down at night.
2. Avoid air conditioning use.

What Are Americans' Beliefs About Climate Justice?

Let's take a step back and consider how Americans look at climate justice. According to *Climate Change in the American Mind: Climate Justice* (Carman et al., 2023), from the Yale Program on Climate Change Communication and George Mason University Center for Climate Change Communication, about half of Americans (49%) agree that global climate change harms some groups in the United States more than others. When asked to elaborate, the most common response was "people with lower incomes" (22%). When probed further, nearly half of Americans (48%) think global warming harms lower-income people more than wealthier people. Even fewer Americans think global climate change harms people of color more than it harms white people (32%) or that global climate change harms everyone equally. Additionally, about one in three Americans (34%) agree that a history of racist policies makes people of color more likely than white people to be harmed by global climate change.

About one in three Americans (34%) have heard a little about climate justice. After learning more explicitly about the goals of climate justice, about half of Americans (53%) say that they support its goals.

TIPS TO MAKE A DIFFERENCE: Empowering Students With Information Literacy Tools

Incorporating current events and news stories in your classroom curriculum is an excellent way to promote information and media literacy. It can also help students connect the dots between equity and the environment and can help them determine whose story is being told and whose story is not being told. Here are some questions and resources to consider:

1. In cases of extreme weather, are there certain populations that we don't hear about?

2. Which populations receive resources more quickly in natural disasters?

3. Useful sources to examine include *Time for Kids* or *Newsela* to get grade-level-appropriate articles for your class.

4. Having students examine community news outlets, such as Spanish-language news outlets, to gain perspectives about what's happening in the community is another useful strategy.

Education Focused on How Climate Change Disproportionately Impacts People

The data in the Carman et al. (2023) report clearly tells us as educators and education collaborators that there needs to be more explicit education about how climate change disproportionately impacts people at the individual level (such as age, gender, income, or disability) and at the larger systemic level (such as racism and other forms of oppression).

A common misconception among teachers is that certain topics are confined to specific disciplines. However, climate justice is a complex topic that transcends the individual disciplines. What other curricular entry points can you think of?

This need for education also demonstrates the urgency for teaching climate justice across content areas and at all grade levels across the TK–12 system. In addition, the 2023 report by Carman et al. found that a large majority of registered voters support policies that promote climate justice goals that have cross-curricular content entry points for teachers (see Table 5.1).

TABLE 5.1 • Cross-Curricular Content Entry Points for Teachers

Climate Justice Goals (Carman et al., 2023)	Curricular Entry Points and Connections
• Creating more parks and green spaces in low-income communities and communities of color	• Environmental education • Geography • History • Social Studies • Economics
• Strengthening the enforcement of industrial pollution limits in low-income communities and communities consisting of people of color that are disproportionately impacted by air and water pollution	• Environmental Education • Environmental Science • Economics • Geography • Math
• Increasing federal funding to low-income communities and communities consisting of people of color who are disproportionately impacted by air and water pollution	• Environmental Education • Geography • Economics • Social studies
• Transitioning the U.S. economy from fossil fuels to 100% clean energy by 2050	• Economics • History • Social Studies • Environmental Science • Math

Now that we know what Americans think about climate justice, let's dig deeper into why different groups of people disproportionately experience climate change.

TIPS TO MAKE A DIFFERENCE: Focus on the Why!

Anthony Tournis, Mary Gage Peterson Elementary, Chicago, IL

1. Focus on carbon-neutral products.
2. Explore the reason why climate change is such an issue and how our climate will change without intervention. We all know it is happening, but students do not really understand the ramifications of climate change.
3. Use project-based learning to create solutions to climate change and its impacts.

CLIMATE CHANGE AND GENDER

It is important for students to understand that climate change has dispro-portionately impacted girls and women around the world. The IPCC found that climate-related hazards further exaggerate existing gender inequalities. According to Verona Callantes, an intergovernmental specialist with UN Women, climate-related hazards result in "higher workloads for women, occupational hazards indoors and outdoors, psychological and emotional stress, and higher mortality compared to men" (McCarthy, 2020).

For example, Hurricane Maria hit Puerto Rico in 2017. A report from Oxfam (2018) found that nearly 3,000 people were killed by the storm, and tens of thousands of people across the island were displaced. Women were hit the hardest. The report states,

> *Women were usually the ones who spent hours wringing sodden towels by hand and hanging them to dry, carrying containers of water into the kitchen, bathing children in buckets, or washing floors with rainwater collected in cans. It was exhausting and demoralizing. (Oxfam, 2018, para. 3)*

TIPS TO MAKE A DIFFERENCE: Do It the Old-Fashioned Way

Kylie Currie, Classical Preparatory School, Springhill, FL

1. Air dry clothes when possible to reduce electricity usage.

Water and Farming

In rural communities worldwide, women and girls overwhelmingly take on the labor of gathering food, water, and household energy resources (Figure 5.1). According to a UNICEF (2021) report, as climate conditions like droughts and fires increase, it becomes harder to manage domestic chores like gathering resources, cooking, cleaning, and caring for children. Additionally, natural disasters and the effects of rising sea levels can tar-nish water quality—which affects women and girls especially because in many cultures they are responsible for securing the family's water that is necessary for household and personal needs, like cooking and bathing. As the rivers become saltier, women must travel longer distances, often in unsafe conditions, to obtain clean and safe water. In addition, women in Bangladesh (one of the countries most vulnerable to climate change in the world—by 2050 it is expected that one in seven people in Bangladesh will be displaced by climate change) have experienced health consequences as rivers become saltier (Climate Reality Project, 2021). A study in the *American Journal of Environmental Protection* by Khan et al. (2016) found higher rates of (pre)eclampsia and gestational hypertension in pregnant women in coastal Bangladesh, compared with noncoastal pregnant women, which is hypothesized to be caused by saline-contaminated drinking water.

FIGURE 5.1 • Girl in India collecting water from a lake.

Istock.com/hadynyah

Flooding also causes areas around bodies of water to erode, which can result in siltation, which is a process in which minerals enter the water. Journalist Mahbubur Rahman Khan (2016) reported in *The Daily Star* that siltation significantly contributed to the disappearance of 32 fish species from Hakaluki Haor, Bangladesh's largest body of water. Here we see the interrelation of environmental deterioration and women in Bangladesh. Thus, as the fish disappear, so does their economic livelihood.

As droughts and extreme temperatures from a warming planet dry up water sources, women have to travel longer distances to collect water for cleaning, growing food, and cooking. For example, in Senegal, women have to travel farther to retrieve water for their everyday use, limiting their ability to be independent farmers and preventing them from being economically independent (Rojo, 2019). According to Lei Win (2019), women make up nearly half the global workforce in farming, but many say their contribution has long gone unrecognized, particularly in developing countries. Women are denied property rights in half of the countries around the world and are often barred from borrowing money for fertilizer and tools, which prevents them from successfully growing crops to sell. As soil quality worsens and water becomes more scarce due to climate change, women will be less likely to find financial means to adapt to changing conditions. This is problematic because, in much of the world, the face of farming is female, and according to the United Nations Food and Agriculture Organization (2024), most economically active women in the least-developed countries work in agriculture (Figures 5.2, 5.3, and 5.4).

FIGURE 5.2 • Agriculture in Turkey

Source: Istock.com/uchar

FIGURE 5.3 • Cultivating Coffee in Ethiopia

Source: Istock.com/Bartosz Hadyniak

FIGURE 5.4 • Latin American Woman Harvesting Onions at a Farm With the Help of Her Daughter

Source: istock.com/andreser

Highlighting true stories and lived experiences when we teach about climate change and climate justice is essential. Storytelling is an excellent strategy to facilitate climate communications and to plant the seeds to take action. Here are some prompts that you can use with your students to amplify their climate stories:

- Think of a memory from your local community that gave you great joy or made you smile. When you close your eyes, what do you see? What do you smell? What do you hear? What do you feel?

- What are your experiences with climate change? This can be personal experiences with extreme weather such as wildfires, air quality, drought, heat, and pollution.

- What do you dream and imagine is possible for the future?

According to the International Union for the Conservation of Nature (IUCN, 2020), gender-based violence and exploitation increase as resources diminish. Consequently, these environmental degradation stressors have fueled the creation of organizations that engage in human trafficking and extreme labor exploitation. For example, in Northeastern Nigeria, the country's most prominent insurgent sect fighting for Islamic rule, Boko Haram, has targeted populations, particularly women, who have been displaced from their land by drought. Drought is one of the consequences of our warming planet. Consequently, we can see that "climate change is a multiplicator of the many threats" (Prager & Samson, 2019). Yale Climate Connections (2021) reported on the link between climate change and terrorism and found that extreme weather worsens social tensions, poverty, and hunger. In turn, "this makes those societies vulnerable to recruitment by terrorist groups."

Women and girls worldwide may face disproportionate impacts of climate change, but they are still actively fighting for a more equitable Earth and environment. SubjectToClimate is a great organization with resources to bring the stories of women's participation in the climate and environmental movement into your classroom. Check out the selection of lessons, unit plans, resources, blogs, news, and articles here: https://qrs.ly/clg37c5

Climate change also worsens gender-based violence. Prolonged drought around the world increases the amount of time that women and girls need to gather water and food. According to the Global Network of Women Peacebuilders, the long and often unaccompanied journeys leaves women and girls vulnerable to physical attack, sexual exploitation, and violence. Sexual exploitation and violence against women and girls can also be a way to gain control over natural resources and land.

Taking Back the Narrative

These are difficult topics to discuss with students of any age, especially with young children. But there's good news to share as well: Although climate change disproportionately impacts women and girls, it has also enabled women to take back the narrative and write their own rules. For example, female youth climate activists like Ugandan Vanessa Nakate and Greta Thunberg of Sweden have helped launch a global climate movement and have garnered worldwide attention.

Women worldwide are also working to create solutions to the pressing issues created by our warming planet. For example, Kotchakorn Varaakham designs urban parks to absorb and reuse excess water in Thailand, to prevent flooding. Jennifer Holmgren has pioneered a carbon recycling company that converts carbon monoxide and carbon dioxide into ethanol, a usable fuel. Nemonte Nenquimo, an indigenous Waorani woman, cofounded the Ceibo Alliance to fight against planned oil concessions in Ecuador.

WHAT CAN WE DO? ADVANCING STUDENT AGENCY

Share with your students the female-led initiatives and organizations that follow, and encourage them to find examples of their own. Think about writing assignments, oral presentations, or other lessons that could be built around the stories of these women creating change.

- Mukuru Clean Stoves (MCS): Through her company, Charlot Magayi supplies people in Kenya with affordable cook stoves that reduce toxic emissions by up to 90%, use up to 60% less fuel, and decrease the risk of burns. This will improve community health outcomes and reduce greenhouse gas emissions. (https://mukurustoves.org/)

- Solar Sister: A woman-led African initiative that helps communities build small-scale solar grids to become energy independent. The grids reduce greenhouse gas emissions and air pollution. (https://solarsister.org/)

- Barefoot College: Trains women to be solar engineers and install clean energy sources in their communities. Their mission is to provide pathways to self-reliant solutions for village communities and pathways to boost income and create employment. (https://www.barefootcollege.org)

- Jo-Jikum: Jo-Jikum means "your home" or "your place" in Marshallese. This organization's mission is to support the next generation of Marshallese in navigating and developing solutions to environmental issues that impact their islands, such as climate change and pollution. Kathy Jetnil-Kijiner, an internationally acclaimed poet, co-founded Jo-Jikum along with her cousins. (https://www.instagram.com/jo_jikum/?hl=en)

- People Not Pozos: *Pozo* means *well* in Spanish. People Not Pozos is a grassroots environmental justice campaign founded by youth activist Nalleli Cobo-Uriarte, which aims to secure a safe and healthy neighborhood and end toxic oil wells and drilling in South Los Angeles. (https://x.com/peoplenotpozos?lang=en)

- We Act for Environmental Justice: An environmental justice organization co-founded by Peggy Shepard in New York City, We Act's mission is to build healthy communities by ensuring that people of color and low-income community members participate meaningfully in creating sound and fair environmental health and protection policies and practices. (https://www.weact.org/)

- Re-Earth Initiative: Co-founded by youth climate activist from Mexico Xiye Bastida, Re-Earth Initiative aims to make the climate movement accessible to everyone. They organize global digital protests for youth and host informational webinars and writing toolkits. (https://reearthin.org/)

It's important for students to take on authentic roles as they take action for climate justice, especially because each discipline has an entry point in the issue of climate change. To illustrate, how can students use these female-led organizations and initiatives as a starting point to take this further? For example,

- How can they take on the role of a historian in a history class?

- How can they take on the role of an artist in art class?

- How can they take on an activist role in social studies, history, or political science class?

When students take on the authentic roles of experts, they're given the tools to answer and explore global issues in real and impactful ways. This is a fundamental component of taking climate action.

Q: What laboratory activities do you recommend that are centered on climate change?

Jamie Bothwell, Freedom High School, Bethlehem, PA

A: SubjectToClimate.org offers a collection of 10 climate change lab activities designed for middle and high school students. These activities are hands-on and engaging, helping students learn about the science behind climate change through experimentation and analysis.

https://qrs.ly/23g37c8

CLIMATE CHANGE AND RACIAL DISPARITIES

According to the EPA, the most severe harm from climate change in the United States is experienced disproportionately by underserved communities. The EPA's 2021 report, *Climate Change and Social Vulnerability in the United States,* outlines the degree to which four socially vulnerable groups (based on income, educational attainment, race and ethnicity, and age) are more exposed to the highest impacts of climate change. The populations and definitions of populations used in the report are explained in Table 5.2.

TABLE 5.2 • Social Groups Most Vulnerable to Climate Change

Category	Definition
Low income	Individuals living in households with income that is at or below 200% of the poverty line established by the federal government.
Minoritized populations	Individuals identifying as Black; American Indian; Alaska Native; Asian American; Pacific Islander; or Latin or Hispanic.
No high school diploma	Individuals aged 25 and older with a maximum educational attainment of less than a high school diploma equivalent
65 and older	Individuals aged 65 and older

The report analyzed primary climate change impacts, which are as follows:

- Air quality and its health impacts

istock.com/Максим Шмаков

- Flooding and impacts on property and traffic

Source: Istock.com/ANATOLIY Arkhipenko

- Extreme temperature and its effect on health and labor

*Source:*istock.com/Liudmila Chernetska

TIPS TO MAKE A DIFFERENCE: Keep It Clean Outdoors

Brittany Crawley, Vestavia Hills High School, Vestavia Hills, AL

1. Do not use pesticides or herbicides.

2. Don't burn wood in fire pits outside.

The key findings in the EPA report are as follows:

- Black and African American individuals in the United States are projected to face higher impacts of climate change for all six impacts analyzed in this report, compared to all other demographic groups. For example, with 2°C (3.6°F) of global warming, Black and African American individuals are

  ○ 34% more likely to currently live in areas with the highest projected increases in childhood asthma diagnosis due to climate changes in particulate air production.

  ○ 40% more likely to currently live in areas with the highest projected increases in extreme temperature–related deaths. This rises to 59% under 4°C of global warming.

- Latin and Hispanic individuals have high participation in weather-exposed industries, such as construction and agriculture, which are especially vulnerable to the effects of extreme temperatures.

  ○ With 2°C (3.6°F) of global warming, Latin and Hispanic individuals are 43% more likely to live in areas with the highest projected labor-hour reductions due to extreme temperatures.

  ○ Latin and Hispanic individuals are about 50% more likely to live in areas with the highest estimated increases in traffic delays due to increased coastal flooding.

- American Indian and Alaskan Natives are 48% more likely than other individuals to live in areas where the highest percentage of land is projected to be inundated due to rising sea levels.

To unpack this information and to incorporate it into your curriculum, suggest to your students that they apply this question to your local city or county: How are the differences in air quality across our city or county related to the socioeconomic status of different neighborhoods and their residents? Here are some tools that you can use to get these data:

- **California Communities Environmental Health Screening Tool—CalEnviroScreen 4.0: qrs.ly/ukgh6z1**

- **EPA's Environmental Justice Screening and Mapping Tool: https://www.epa.gov/ejscreen**

MOST VULNERABLE AREAS IN THE WORLD

According to the International Rescue Committee (2023), the climate crisis is creating a humanitarian crisis around the world. The 10 countries most at risk for climate disaster are as follows: Somalia, Syria, Democratic Republic of the Congo, Afghanistan, Yemen, Chad, South Sudan, Central African Republic, Nigeria, and Ethiopia. These are also countries that are most likely to experience a humanitarian crisis; thus, taking a people-first approach to addressing climate change is crucial, which means incorporating lived experiences, untold narratives, and personal stories into your curriculum. This also makes a case for teaching about climate change through the lenses of geography, history, economics, and social studies. Of these 10 countries most impacted worldwide, let's take a closer look at the top five most impacted.

- Somalia: Somalia is already vulnerable to climate change due to food insecurity and drought challenges. Political instability makes adaptation and mitigation strategies difficult to address. In addition, the flash flooding experienced in March 2023 affected 460,000 people and displaced tens of thousands.

- Syria: More than a decade of war coupled with intense economic crises have forced 90% of Syrians below the poverty line. The February 2023 earthquake near the Syrian-Turkish border affected hundreds of thousands and magnified challenges in emergency response.

Source: Istock.com/Siraj Albasha

- Democratic Republic of the Congo (DRC): Economic challenges and conflict have substantially weakened the country's ability to prepare for climate disaster. More than 100 armed groups fight for control in Eastern Congo and often target civilians. In addition, disease outbreaks such as Ebola, malaria, and measles pose a consistent threat to an already weakened healthcare system. The frequency of rainfall in DRC has increased substantially over the last 10 years. In May 2023, extreme flooding in South Kivu destroyed villages and affected more than 15,000 people.

Supporting vulnerable communities worldwide in the face of climate change is imperative. As a result, students must learn about the United Nations Sustainable Development Goals (SDGs) and why having a global perspective is more important now than ever. Do you know about the SDGs?

- Afghanistan: The Taliban rule in Afghanistan has resulted in an increased fragility with breakdowns in the country receiving foreign aid. Afghanistan is currently experiencing the worst drought in 27 years, with intense flooding that has reduced food production and has caused people to leave their homes.

- Yemen: At the end of 2022, 17 million people in Yemen required food assistance, and 2.2 million children and 1.3 million pregnant or breastfeeding women required treatment for malnutrition. Climate change has also worsened drought in the country.

TIPS TO MAKE A DIFFERENCE: Actions Big and Small

Kim Decker, Dyersburg City Schools, Dyersburg, TN

1. Install motion sensor lights to cut down on electricity use.
2. Use solar energy.
3. Ban Styrofoam in school.
4. Lead systemic change to rethink starting school (typically in August) during the hottest days of summer to avoid the need for excessive air conditioning use.

Ideas for the Classroom Across Content Areas: UN Sustainable Development Goals

The 2030 Agenda for Sustainable Development was adopted by all United Nations members in 2015 and provides a blueprint of peace for people and the planet (United Nations, n.d.) The member states recognize that ending poverty and other humanitarian issues must go together with improving health and education, economic growth, and education inequity, all while addressing climate change and working to preserve resources like the ocean and forests.

SUSTAINABLE DEVELOPMENT GOALS

	PARTNERSHIP FOR THE GOALS
	NO POVERTY
	ZERO HUNGER
	GOOD HEALTH AND WELL-BEING
	QUALITY EDUCATION
	GENDER EQUALITY
	CLEAN WATER AND SANITATION
	AFFORDABLE AND CLEAN ENERGY
	DECENT WORK AND ECONOMIC GROWTH
	INDUSTRY, INNOVATION AND INFRASTRUCTURE
	REDUCED INEQUALITY
	SUSTAINABLE CITIES AND COMMUNITIES
	RESPONSIBLE CONSUMPTION AND PRODUCTION
	CLIMATE ACTION
	LIFE BELOW WATER
	LIFE ON LAND
	PEACE, JUSTICE AND STRONG INSTITUTIONS

Source: istock.com/Hanna Siamashka

Here are some resources to help you teach about the Climate Action Sustainable Development Goal 13:

- https://qrs.ly/rwg37cc

- https://qrs.ly/e3g37gh

- https://qrs.ly/wog37ci

How can you infuse this global perspective and the SDGs into your curriculum? What entry points and curricular connections do you see? Think about each of the SDGs, like gender equality, life on land, no poverty, etc. How does climate change impact these SDGs? Why is it important to address each of these SDGs when addressing our changing climate?

Are your students living in areas that are indicated as most at risk? Some tips and strategies to implement in the classroom to continue this learning are listed in this chapter.

United States

In the United States, areas are vulnerable to climate change because of their location's predisposition to drought (and seasonal flooding), risk of high heat, and risk of flooding because of sea-level rise. New research from Virginia Tech using satellites found that "one in 50 people living in coastal cities are at risk of significant flooding by 2050" (White, 2024, para. 1). The U.S. cities most at risk:

- Miami, Florida;

- New Orleans, Louisiana;

- Port Arthur, Texas;

- Foster City, California; and

- Savannah, Georgia.

The researchers maintain that the consequences and impact will be devastating if effective flooding prevention structures are not implemented in time.

Table 5.3 provides some ideas for teaching climate change from a local perspective across the curriculum.

TABLE 5.3 • Ideas for the Classroom Across Content Areas

Content Area/ Subject	Curricular Ideas
Math	• Climate Central is an organization of scientists and journalists who focus on studying climate change and its impacts. The Coastal Risk Screening Tool is an interactive Climate Central map showing the areas threatened by sea level rise and coastal flooding. You and your students can explore the map to research vulnerable areas in the United States and near your local community: https://coastal.climatecentral.org/ • To integrate math, students can look at precipitation data in their state or local community over the past 100 years. Students can then take a 50- or 25-year span of the data and use math standards to plot the data, draw a line of best fit, and write it in slope-intercept form.
Social Studies and Economics	• Climate Central's Coastal Risk Screening Tool: Affordable Housing Map enables students to explore the intersections between affordable housing in the United States and the impacts of sea level rise and coastal flooding in the coming decades, combined with multiple pollution scenarios. Using the map, students can analyze affordable housing at risk by state, city, county, congressional district, legislative district, or zip code: qrs.ly/wzg3dhc • What connections do your students see between sea level rise, coastal flooding, and socioeconomic status? What does this mean for the most vulnerable residents in your local community? After researching, students can present this information to the school board, superintendent, mayor, city council, etc.
English/ Language Arts	• Students can practice informative or persuasive writing and write about the data that they gathered from the math and/ or social studies and economic lessons. • Students can learn about creating more just futures by exploring the "climate fiction" stories in *Grist's Imagine 2200* project: qrs.ly/ulg3eot

YOUTH ACTIVISM AND CLIMATE ACTIVISM

It's not unusual to hear people complain that "young people" have no interest in global politics. Direct action by students challenges this outdated myth. Campbell et al. (2022) found that millennials and younger adults are more likely to support organizations that engage in nonviolent civil disobedience for the planet than older generations. A Pew Research Center Report found that 32% of Gen Z and 28% of millennials say they've done something in the past year to address climate change, such as "donating money, volunteering, contacting an elected official or attending a rally or protest" (Funk, 2021, p. 1).

There's a long history of this activism. The student-led climate activist movement began in Australia as early as 1991 with the Students of Sustainability. Other efforts include the Student Environmental Network in 1997, the Australian Youth Climate Coalition in 2006, and the Indigenous Youth Climate Network Seed Mob in 2014. Since 2014, similar youth-led climate coalitions have been established in other countries, such as the UK Youth Climate Coalition, the Canadian Youth Climate Coalition, and the Indian Youth Climate Coalition. In the United States, the Rethinking Schools student movement launched its own climate activist school-based organizing toolkit in 2016 in Portland, Oregon.

In 2018, the world turned to Greta Thunberg, the 15-year-old Swedish student activist who was protesting on the steps of her country's parliament for hours with a *Skolstrejk för klimatet* (School Strike for Climate) sign instead of going to school. Today's students are literally walking away from a form of schooling and politics that has failed to address and respond to their concerns. As educators, we owe it to our students to help.

 KIMI: THIS IS MY STORY

My orientation to activism is through teaching. I became a public school teacher because I am an activist for educational, environmental, and racial justice. I believe these issues are fundamentally inseparable from the teacher's role in the classroom. Teaching is a political act and an act of resistance. As someone who was recognized by the North American Association for Environmental Education in 2019 as one of the "Environmental Education 30 Under 30," my environmental activism has centered on mobilizing California's teachers and students to take environmental civic action for local and global change.

Since 2019, I've been a steering committee member for California's state-wide climate change initiative, the UC-CSU Environmental and Climate Change Literacy Projects (ECCLPs). As a former kindergarten teacher in South LA, mobilizing young learners to take action for environmental justice through GIS and mapping helped me to find my purpose. Kindergarteners have such a strong sense of equality and fairness, and they are natural scientists with plenty of observations about our world. In addition, serving as a STEM & Innovation Curriculum Specialist in Compton helped me to refine my passion for using project-based learning in environmental education.

Now as a professor and researcher (assistant professor of Child & Family Studies), I teach future early childhood educators and future elementary school teachers who also dream of teaching for social and environmental justice.

 Q: How do we explain that doing one small act—like not using plastic straws—slows down climate change?

Ebony Jamison, Humanities II Charter, Bronx, NY

A: 1. Focus on the bigger picture:

- Plastic production relies heavily on fossil fuels, and its manufacturing process releases greenhouse gases that contribute to climate change.

- Every small reduction in plastic use translates to a decrease in the demand for its production, ultimately leading to less reliance on fossil fuels and fewer greenhouse gas emissions.

2. Emphasize collective impact:

- A single person avoiding straws might seem insignificant, but imagine the impact if millions of people did the same. This collective action can significantly reduce plastic production and its environmental footprint.

You might explain by saying something like this:

"Plastic straws might seem like a small thing, but they contribute to a larger problem. Making plastic uses a lot of energy and creates pollution. If everyone used fewer straws, or switched to reusable ones, it would add up to a big difference. It's like a million tiny drops making a big wave. Plus, if we think about avoiding straws, that effort can be a reminder to look for other ways to be more eco-friendly in our daily lives."

ELEVATING BIPOC YOUTH CLIMATE ACTIVISTS

Researchers Berberian et al. (2022) found that the children of Black, Indigenous, and people of color (BIPOC) from frontline communities, those that are disproportionately impacted by the climate crisis, are particularly vulnerable to the health impacts of climate change, and infants and children of color have experienced adverse perinatal outcomes, occupational heat stress, and increases in emergency department visits associated with extreme weather. Additionally, youth from frontline communities are also underrepresented within the environmental movement. To protect our planet, the input and contributions of as many people as possible must be incorporated. Greta Thunberg may be the most recognizable youth climate activist, but there are other BIPOC youth climate activists who are directly from frontline communities impacted by climate change. The next time you want to introduce students to a youth climate activist, consider incorporating these young people and their stories into your lessons. Students can also research these youth climate activists for lessons incorporating biographies, writing, or English/Language Arts. Learn more about them and their stories below.

What other ways might you incorporate these young activists into your curriculum?

More Young Activists to Share With Your Students

- Aletta Brady: A queer writer, organizer, and strategist from Minneapolis, Minnesota; the founder and executive director of Our Climate Voices; a member of the U.S. National Commission for UNESCO's Youth Working Group; and a former Fulbright research fellow in Jordan.

- Isaias Hernandez: An environmentalist and eco-educator. Through social platforms such as Instagram, Twitter, and X, Isaias shares accessible content under his brand Queer Brown Vegan to educate people on various topics related to environmental justice and green living.

- Kathy Jetñil-Kijiner: A Marshallese writer, poet, journalist, and climate change activist, Kathy co-founded the nonprofit Jo-Jikum, dedicated to empowering Marshallese youth to seek solutions to climate change and other environmental impacts.

- Thomas Tonatiuh Lopez, Jr.: Thomas is a descendant of the Otomi, Diné, Apache, and Lakota people. He spent months working with the

International Indigenous Youth Council (IIYC) on the ground at Standing Rock to stop the construction of the Dakota Access Pipeline.

- Autumn Peltier: An Indigenous rights activist and designated "water protector," Autumn Peltier empowers young people with the tools they need to protect the environment. As the chief water commissioner for the Anishinabek Nation, she has spent nearly half her life speaking about the importance of clean water to organizations, including the United Nations and the World Economic Forum.

- Rebeca Sabnam: A Bangladeshi American teen activist highlighting risks Bangladeshi women and Rohingya face due to climate change.

More Ways to Get Your Students Involved

There are countless ways students can get involved as climate change activists that are linked to existing curriculum. For example, they can create a book of young climate activists to practice research skills and information literacy. When finished with their books, students can also engage in "buddy reading" with students who are older or younger at their school to spread awareness about notable climate activists. Additionally, students might consider contacting one or more of the youth activists they know of through social media.

Children have specific rights that are laid out in the UN Convention on the Rights of the Child. Knowing their rights can help students advocate for climate actions across multiple curricular levels and entry points. Older students can engage in a research project and read the Articles of the Convention to see which ones apply to climate justice and which Articles the youth climate activists advocate for.

Inside the Movement has campaigns and direct actions that students can use for more inspiration for how to get involved. Check out their website for ideas: https://itm.earth/

TIPS TO MAKE A DIFFERENCE: Shop Smart
Katie O'Connor, King School, Stamford, CT

1. Make meal plans before you grocery shop to reduce food waste.

TOOLS FOR SUCCESS: USING THE LEARNING FOR JUSTICE SOCIAL JUSTICE STANDARDS TO TEACH CLIMATE CHANGE

Teaching Tolerance is now known as "Learning for Justice" and is an initiative of the Southern Poverty Law Center. The social justice standards represent an approach to learning that is grounded in social justice, with the aim to reduce prejudice and bring about collective action for positive change. The standards are written for K–12 audiences. The four domains in the standards are Identity, Diversity, Justice, and Action. Using these domains provides a powerful pathway to center students' lived experiences, personal stories, and family histories as they relate to the environment and our changing climate.

Domain 1: Identity

In the Identity Domain, teachers provide students with opportunities to learn about who they are and where they are from. This aims to reduce bias as children learn about their identities, responsibilities, and privileges. The goal is to develop positive social identities and to understand that multiple identities intersect and create unique and complex individuals. A child's sense of self is important to learning about the environment and climate change, as everyone has a climate change story. Not all students' environmental knowledge is seen as valuable in the dominant education systems, as the environmental movement has been historically white. As teachers, we can engage students in honoring and respecting identities by drawing on students' lived experiences. Table 5.4 outlines what teachers and students can do to further their understanding of identity in the context of climate change teaching.

TABLE 5.4 • Identity Domain in the Context of Climate Change Teaching and Learning

Identity
Teachers
• Elevate and recenter the knowledge traditions, identities, and perspectives about the environment that have historically been silenced.
• Honor and acknowledge students' multiple social identities in the design and implementation of curriculum.

Identity
• View students as competent and ensure their lived experiences and community and cultural ways of knowledge are elevated, acknowledged, and leveraged in the teaching of climate justice. • Deconstruct negative stereotypes about children's environmental identities and negative stereotypes about who can and cannot learn about climate justice. **Students** • Develop historical and cultural knowledge to affirm and describe membership in multiple identity groups and their contributions to the environmental movement. • Express pride, confidence, self-love, and healthy self-esteem about themselves and their community as climate change thinkers and learners. • Recognize the traits of the dominant culture, their own culture, and other cultures and understand how to negotiate their own identity in multiple spaces. • Recognize that people's multiple identities interact and create unique and complex individuals that contribute to the environmental movement and climate activism.

Source: Learning for Justice (2022).

Domain 2: Diversity

To achieve a culture of respect for diversity in our classrooms, it is important for educators to recognize that all children have distinct differences in cultures, backgrounds, and ways of thinking about the environment. These differences can be assets and leveraged to strengthen student learning and create a dynamic classroom (see Table 5.5).

TABLE 5.5 • Diversity Domain in the Context of Climate Change Teaching and Learning

Diversity
Teachers • Implement and design curriculum that honors diversity and equity in climate change education, where diversity is positioned as a strength. This means centering the stories and lived experiences of frontline communities and valuing different forms of climate change expertise (e.g., storytelling, generational knowledge, cultural knowledge). • Create multidimensional classrooms where students are expected to equally contribute in different ways.

(Continued)

(Continued)

> ### Diversity
>
> - Deconstruct stereotypes about who can and cannot participate in the environmental movement and take climate action (e.g., feature a youth climate activist whose stories are typically not heard, bring intersectional experiences into the classroom, and bring different abilities into the classroom and climate change conversation).
>
> **Students**
>
> - Express comfort in working and learning with people who are both similar and different from them and engage respectfully in discussion and collaborative work.
>
> - Express curiosity about contributions to climate change and the experiences of others and share perspectives and ideas in an open-minded way.
>
> - Respond to diversity by building connections, respect, understanding, and empathy for different ways of knowing and being in the classroom as it relates to scientific knowledge or knowledge of climate solutions.

Source: Learning for Justice (2022).

 Q: Is there a good (and recent) documentary about climate change that will keep the attention of a middle schooler?

Michael Winship, Pattonville Heights Middle School, Maryland Heights, MO

A: The documentary film *The Race to Save the World* (2021) focuses on climate change activists and their fight for a better future. It highlights the passion and dedication of these individuals who are working tirelessly to combat the climate crisis.

Slightly older but still well worth the time is *This Changes Everything* (2015), which explores the connection between climate change and our economic system. It argues that tackling the climate crisis presents an opportunity to transform our economic and social structures for a better future.

Domain 3: Justice

The Justice Domain focuses on the root causes of inequalities. As teachers attending to the Justice Domain, we are called to reflect on how inequities in the larger society are replicated in everyday practices and structures that perpetuate the disproportionate impacts of climate change based on gender, race, socioeconomic status, etc. We need to provide students with multiple learning activities and pathways to recognize that power and privilege impact relationships at intergroup, interpersonal, and institutional levels. Paying attention to justice prepares students to understand how oppression in the environmental space operates at the individual level and systemic level, so they will be better equipped with an understanding of their own lived experiences and can develop strategic climate solutions based on historical and scientific facts (see Table 5.6).

TABLE 5.6 • Justice Domain in the Context of Climate Change Teaching and Learning

Justice
Teachers
• Locate the root causes of inequalities in social conditions rather than believe conditions are inherent within individuals.
• Recognize that inequities of the larger society are replicated in common structures and practices that perpetuate disparities in how climate change is experienced based on race, class, gender, etc.
• Explicitly shift the power dynamic between teacher-and-student and student-and-student by positioning the perspectives, identities, and knowledge traditions that have been historically silenced.
Students
• Recognize that stereotypes impact who is considered to be good at science and capable of working toward climate change mitigations and solutions.
• Recognize that privilege and power influence relationships on interpersonal, intergroup, and institutional levels and consider how they would have been affected by those dynamics as it relates to climate change.
• Use climate change education and climate justice as a tool to identify the inequitable impacts of climate change that occur at the systemic level.

Source: Learning for Justice (2022).

Domain 4: Action

Within the Action Domain, students can think about social movements for climate change (or other related movements throughout history) and work to take action to address it. Students can identify issues of climate change that they are passionate about and impacts of climate change in their local communities or at the state and/or regional level. They can learn how to do research, analyze who has the power to change situations, and engage in civic action and learning projects to address the impacts of climate change (Table 5.7).

TABLE 5.7 • Action Domain in the Context of Climate Teaching and Learning

Action
Teachers
• Engage in community- and place-based pedagogies and experiences that bridge all classrooms with social movements and community movements for climate change and climate justice.
• Understand that learning can occur from a problem-posing pedagogy, designed around doubt, fear, ideas, hopes, and questions that occur when students think about climate change.
• Provide students with constant opportunity to recognize their own responsibility to stand up to climate injustices.
Students
• Understand the nature and creation of social oppression as it relates to climate change and feel empowered to make change and take action.
• Make informed decisions about how and when to take a stand against bias and status differences within the environmental movement and in their communities.
• Plan and carry out collective action using climate change as a tool to address injustice in the world.

Source: Learning for Justice (2022).

Success Story: Teaching About Environmental Racism

Joan Gillman, The Browning School, New York City, NY

In my sixth-grade science class, we have a unit that I have developed on climate change and environmental racism. To begin this unit, we first look at the mission statement from our own school to see whether the institution is actually following what they preach. This usually leads to a good discussion on what our school is doing well and what needs to be improved. Once the children comprehend the purpose of mission statements, we are now ready to tackle the mission statements from three different relief organizations to see whether they actually follow what they say they do. Recently we looked at FEMA, the American Red Cross, and Habitat for Humanity. The sixth-grade students recorded the information in their lab notebooks so that they had the information at their fingertips and ready to use when we started analyzing the type of help these organizations provided for the survivors of six different hurricanes. The students were then asked to evaluate whether or not the organizations followed what they claimed to do in their mission statements. If the answer was no, the students then had to come up with ways for the organizations to improve their practice. To complete this study, the sixth-grade students developed slideshow presentations, videos, or television interview shows where they presented their findings.

My students have responded positively to this unit. They have become quite shocked when they discover that some of these organizations have failed in their missions. The unit makes the students more aware of the difficulties people experience due to the effects of climate change on hurricane development and strength. It also empowers them to find ways to help the survivors of these disasters.

In addition to being a lower and middle school science teacher, I am one of two teachers leading our school's Green Team. This is a K–12th-grade club that works to bring positive changes in our school and community by emphasizing environmentally friendly practices. Each Monday morning, the students all gather in my science lab where we first compose the "Green Action of the Week." Selections could include making sure that all paper products are placed in the correct bin, pencils are not wasted by cracking them in half, or even reminding everyone to only take as much food as they can consume in the cafeteria. The students all play a role in deciding what should be posted on the signs. Once we are all in agreement, the students write the message on the eight signs we have and then post them around the school. Not only do we have a "Green Action of the Week" posted in the school for everyone to follow, but we also do periodic park cleanups in Central Park. The team would gather at 7:30 AM in the school's lobby. Cleanup tools would be distributed to each child, and then we would head for the park. Along the way, we would clean up any garbage that was left on the sidewalk as well as in the park. Even though this involves a great deal of work so early in the morning, the students come back feeling as though they have accomplished something really important for their community. They cannot wait for me to schedule another outing.

The Green Team also holds fundraisers to help the survivors of natural disasters. A few years ago, my science class was focusing on the topic of water. We were looking at who in the world had access to clean drinking water and who did not. One of my students did not just want to learn about this topic. He wanted to come up with a solution to remedy this problem. After doing some research, my student decided to make a presentation to the rest of the Green Team to encourage the possibility of holding a fundraiser for Water.org. He felt that this organization lived up to its mission statement and helped the people around the world who most needed clean water. As a result of my student's enthusiasm for this endeavor, the team held a fundraiser for two weeks and raised more than a thousand dollars.

If you like this success story, here are some additional resources to teach about environmental racism:

Reporting on Environmental Racism lesson from Learning for Justice: https://qrs.ly/7ag37cl

Teaching About Environmental Racism: Four Domains from The Institute for Humane Education: https://qrs.ly/3xg37d0

The Red Dot of Environmental Racism from the Zinn Education Project: https://qrs.ly/52g37d8

Through Study, Art, Action: Raising Awareness of Environmental Racism from the Pulitzer Center: https://qrs.ly/bqg37d9

 Q: How do I find materials on urban sprawl (deforestation, heat islands, less permeable surfaces for water) and the impact it has on our environment?

Debbie Bond, PACE Academy, Columbia, SC

A: NASA has some amazing resources for teaching about urban heat islands. There's a plethora of lesson plans, activities, and resources on this website: https://qrs.ly/kng37dc

Additionally, if you'd like to expand your own knowledge and learning, the U.S. EPA has some resources as well: https://qrs.ly/gcg37dd

LEARNING FROM OUR COLLEAGUES
Kindergarten Environmental Justice Activists

As the kindergarten students did their morning routine of unloading backpacks and putting folders into cubbies, Timmy and Mateo talked about their morning walk to school.

"There was so much trash in the street, the garbage man didn't come yet," Timmy said.

"That's nothing," said Mateo. "You shoulda smelled the gasoline on Harris Boulevard! Pee-ewww! I felt like choking!"

Ms. W 's five- and six-year-old kindergarten students, who are all Black, Latin, and Hispanic, quickly recognized the inequities related to the environment in their community in South Los Angeles. Her students were particularly full of anecdotes in the morning and had plenty of stories to tell about their walks to school. The sun was particularly brutal at the beginning of the school year, with temperatures in the high nineties.

"It's too hot today!" said Yessica, her tongue sticking out, mimicking a dog panting. "I just want a tree to sit under," she said.

Ms. W's students were also quick to recognize that there aren't a lot of green spaces where they live. Several students compared schools on TV where students play in the park and schools where there are a lot of trees near the playground. Her students wanted to know if other neighborhoods and cities have problems with no parks and trees and why that is.

Ms. W wanted to capitalize on her students' curiosity and told the class to "ask the computer."

The first step was to look at Google Maps to see where the parks and green spaces are in the community surrounding the school and how far away they are from the school.

Ms. W projected Google Maps onto the whiteboard. Students had been learning to read maps as part of the social studies curriculum. She showed the features of the map: streets, buildings, and green space.

Lucas said, "I see our school!" Ms. W encouraged him to come up to the whiteboard and point to the school to show the class.

De'Shawn said, "We don't see green for plants or brown for Earth or blue for water! It's all grey around there (pointing to the area around the school)."

Ms. W showed the students how to count city blocks on the map. She asked, "OK class, let's count the number of blocks to the nearest park. We know this is a park over here because it's green. But I want to know how many blocks away from the school it is and how long it will take me to get there."

The students counted in unison together: "One, two, three, four, five, six, seven, eight, nine, ten, eleven, twelve, thirteen, fourteen...." A collective gasp filled the room.

"Oh my gosh, Ms. W, that's so far," Hector said.

"What about some of those schools you see on TV," Ms. W said. "Let's look and see how close a park is to the schools in Beverly Hills. That is probably what you see on TV."

Ms. W changed the Google Maps city and typed in Beverly Hills. A collective gasp filled the room again and students said, "Whoa, look at all that green."

Ms. W found a school on the map and told students to count. Jamal interjected and said, "Hey Ms. W, I don't need to count, I see a bunch of green right there, right next to the school."

(Continued)

(Continued)

"Excellent, Jamal," Ms. W said. "OK, class, let's take out our scientist notebooks. Remember we're practicing making bar charts in math. Let's make a bar chart of our school and the school we see in Beverly Hills."

"How many blocks away from our school is the closest park?" Students began to write in their notebooks with enthusiasm.

"How many blocks away from this school in Beverly Hills is the closest park?" Students began to write again in their notebooks.

Ms. W then asked, "What is the difference in blocks?"

"THIRTEEN! THIRTEEN BLOCKS," the class shouted.

"That's crazy," said Lucas. "People need to know this."

"Not fair!" said Joanna.

"You're right, it's not fair," said Ms. W. "So who makes decisions in a city, and who is the leader? Should we tell them about this problem?"

"YEAH!" the kindergartners shouted with excitement. "That's the mayor," said Jose.

"Okay, excellent work, class. Yes, you're right, Jose, we should write to the mayor and tell him this is a problem. We'll do that for our writing assignment today. Then we can mail them to the mayor's office!"

Ms. W now has her next interdisciplinary lesson, which will feature civic engagement and activism for environmental justice. Students will write to the mayor and tell him about the issue related to the lack of green space in their city. Students will create an awareness campaign for how they can advocate for change in their school community and at home.

Reflection Questions

1. How do issues impacting women and girls worldwide demonstrate the need for teaching across the disciplines regarding climate change?

2. How do issues demonstrate why human-environment geography and social studies are necessary to teach climate change?

3. What other cross-disciplinary connections do you see?

4. How do the data on climate change and racial disparities demonstrate the need for teaching across the disciplines regarding climate change?

5. What larger social issues are apparent in the data from the EPA report? For example, environmental injustice, environmental racism, etc.

For Further Reading

FOR TEACHERS:

The All We Can Save Project. (2024). *Resources for teaching* All We Can Save. https://www.allwecansave.earth/for-educators

Bigelow, B., & Swinehart, T. (Eds.). (2014). *A people's curriculum for the Earth: Teaching climate change and the environmental crisis.* Rethinking Schools. https://qrs.ly/yqg37dm

Bullard, R. D. (Ed.). (2005). *The quest for environmental justice: Human rights and the politics of pollution* (Vol. 19, pp. 32–33). Sierra Club Books.

Climate Generation. (2024, Jan 18). *Decolonizing climate: Reimagining environmental justice and confronting imperial legacies in the Middle East* [Video]. YouTube. https://www.youtube.com/watch?v=wW177Tm-N-4

Gilio-Whitaker, D. (2019). *As long as grass grows: The indigenous fight for environmental justice, from colonization to standing rock.* Beacon Press.

Johnson, A. E., & Wilkinson, K. K. (Eds.). (2021). *All we can save: Truth, courage, and solutions for the climate crisis.* One World.

Méndez, M. (2020). *Climate change from the streets: How conflict and collaboration strengthen the environmental justice movement.* Yale University Press.

Siperstein, S., Hall, S., & LeMenager, S. (Eds.). (2016). *Teaching climate change in the humanities.* Taylor & Francis.

Thomas, L. (2022). *The intersectional environmentalist: How to dismantle systems of oppression to protect people + planet.* Souvenir Press.

Zinn Education Project. (2024). *Teach climate justice campaign.* https://qrs .ly/lfg37dj

FOR STUDENTS:

Ages 5–7

Ahuja, N., & Syed, A. (2021). *Rise up and write it: With real mail, posters, and more!* HarperFestival.

Barretta, G., & Morrison, F. (2020). *The secret garden of George Washington Carver.* Tegan Books.

Hillery. T., & Hartland, J. (2020). *Harlem grown: How one big idea transformed a neighborhood.* Simon & Schuster/Paula Wiseman Books.

Lindstrom, C., & Goade, M. (2020). *We are water protectors.* Roaring Brook Press.

Tyline King, H., & Holmes, E. (2021). *Saving American Beach: The biography of African American environmentalist MaVynee Betsch.* G.P Putnam's Sons Books for Young Readers.

Ages 8–10

Diavolo, L. (Ed.). (2021). *No planet B: The Teen Vogue guide to the climate crisis.* Haymarket Books.

Hudson, W., & Willis Hudson, C. (Eds.). (2019). *We rise, we resist, we raise our voices.* Yearling.

CHAPTER SIX

TACKLING CLIMATE ANXIETY BY PROMOTING STUDENT AGENCY

Activists need to be in the room where the decisions are being made. We need the people in power to listen to us— the generation that will inherit their decisions.

—Xiye Bastida

THIS CHAPTER WILL DISCUSS

- What climate anxiety looks and feels like
- Ideas and strategies for centering equity and justice in conversations about climate anxiety, and
- More student activists who can serve as inspiration for students

Climate anxiety is often cited as a reason why teachers are reluctant to teach climate change, especially to very young children. But even many young children are already aware of climate change, and attempting to "protect" them from the truth robs students of the opportunity to take action and help to control their own futures. As Tina Grotzer from Harvard Graduate School of Education has said,

> *We owe it to future generations to help them develop sustainable ways to live in the world. Life on Earth depends upon our making urgent and long-term changes for how we think about the planet and its resources. Besides that, kids are well aware of what is happening to the planet. They need teachers who can support their emotional development as well. (quoted in Hough, 2023)*

With this in mind, let's first take a look at what we mean by "climate anxiety."

WHAT IS CLIMATE ANXIETY?

Negative emotions about climate change are often referred to as "eco-anxiety," "climate grief," or "climate anxiety." Google searches for "climate anxiety" soared by 565% in 2021 (Moench, 2023). The two most typically Googled questions were "What is eco-anxiety?" and "How to deal with climate anxiety." Climate anxiety, or eco-anxiety, is "the distress caused by climate change where people are becoming anxious about their future" (Coffey et al., 2021, p. 1).

Data from the Yale Program on Climate Change Communication (Leiserowitz et al., 2021) found that 70% of Americans are now very or somewhat worried about climate change, with significant increases after summer 2023, in which the United States faced an onslaught of hurricanes, wildfires, floods, and heatwaves. Rising temperatures have been associated with increased emergency department visits for psychiatric reasons (Majeed & Lee, 2017). Anxiety may also impair cognitive development in adolescents and children (Porras-Salazar et al., 2018), and the food insecurity that may occur because of extreme climate-induced weather events is associated with depression, anxiety, and behavioral problems (Whitaker et al., 2006).

TIPS TO MAKE A DIFFERENCE: Pay Attention to the Details

Allyson Israel, Kinneret Day School, Riverdale, NY

1. Use energy-efficient LED bulbs for lighting.
2. Fix leaky faucets to conserve water and the energy to heat it.

Healthy Response to an Existential Threat

As humans we're programed evolutionarily to survive. When threatened by something that puts that survival at risk, we react in one of three ways. You've probably heard of the fight or flight reaction—which describes the urge to fight the threat or run away from it. There has been much attention in recent years to a third option: freeze. This describes how human beings can also become paralyzed by fear. When faced with a threat that we can't fight or run away from, it makes sense that such paralysis takes over, and the anxiety and stress that comes with worrying about the future is all but inevitable (Gray & McNaughton, 2000).

Source: istock.com/FG Trade Latin

When put into context, it is important to understand that climate anxiety is a healthy response to an existential threat and should not be dismissed as overreacting. Children may experience climate anxiety at a heightened level as they are more vulnerable to the direct experience of climate change. They have stronger responses to extreme weather events, such as PTSD, sleep disorders, and depression, due to their greater dependence on social support networks and adult family members that may be disrupted or impacted by the event (Bartlett, 2008). They are also more vulnerable to heat due to their bodies' incompletely developed ability to thermoregulate (Zivin & Shrader, 2016). This means that infants and young children are less able to regulate their body temperature and are more vulnerable during extreme heatwaves, such as the dangerously hot summers we've seen the past few years caused by climate change.

Early stress can also increase the risk of mental health issues later in life (Burke et al., 2018). Thus, the possibilities for long-term and permanent effects of trauma are concerning. With more people aware of the climate crisis, the need for support and resources, particularly those protective of mental health, is growing. Today's young people are keenly aware of the results of climate change and its subsequent impacts. At the same time, they are faced with navigating big developmental milestones such as puberty, school, finding employment, planning for their future, and creating supportive social systems and structures. Education is one of the supportive systems and structures that can be utilized to help prevent climate anxiety.

According to researcher Tina Grotzer, climate anxiety can vary by age. For example, older students in high school are more likely to be concerned due to a background in climate science and a greater awareness of the environmental impacts, as well as how extreme weather events have changed and increased over time. In contrast, younger children may not know what the world was like without these natural disasters. Grotzer argues that "we should emphasize helping the youngest children develop a relationship with the Earth—to become eco-centric instead of ego-centric, and to empower them to do things to support the health of planet Earth" (quoted in Hough, 2023, p. 1).

Climate activism has been shown to promote resilience, "especially when young people and children are emotionally engaged in the climate crisis; when mental health is systemically supported; and when climate change communication is transparent and comprehensive" (Godden et al., 2021, p. 1). For example, Emma Heyink, a youth activist from Australia states, "I'm involved in activism because it gives you a real sense of power, it feels like you are actually doing something that will help. It's so easy to feel powerless and overwhelmed by the many problems the world is facing and activism is kind of a relief for that" (Godden et al., 2021, p. 1).

Coping With Climate Anxiety

As we have argued throughout this book, education offers one way to cope with climate anxiety. Table 6.1 lists some other resources for coping with climate anxiety that everyone can benefit from.

TABLE 6.1 • Resources to Help Cope With Climate Anxiety

Resource Type	Resource
Climate-Aware Therapy In recent years, social workers, psychiatrists, psychotherapists, and psychologists have come together to help people live more comfortably with their climate awareness through various methods and practices. These therapists all specialize in eco- and climate anxiety and can provide perspectives, tools, and techniques for coping.	• Climate-aware therapist directory: https://qrs.ly/tsg3gm3 • Climate Psychology Alliance United Kingdom: https://qrs.ly/ohg3gm4 • Climate Psychology Alliance North America: https://www .climatepsychology.us/ • Climate Psychiatry Alliance: https://qrs.ly/v3g3gm6 • Psychologists For Future: https://qrs.ly/f5g3gmf
Climate Awakening A series of ongoing sharing and listening sessions that anyone can drop into virtually. Share your climate terror, grief, and rage with people who understand. Join a Climate Emotions Conversation—a small group sharing and listening session about the climate emergency.	• https://climateawakening.org/
Eco-Anxious Stories A welcoming and calming online realm, aimed at people who feel alone in their climate fears. It uses the power of story exchange to relieve that sense of loneliness and offers a suite of reflection guides and resources.	• https://qrs.ly/fhg3gmh

(Continued)

(Continued)

Resource Type	Resource
Gen Dread A newsletter that regularly explores tools for coping with eco-distress, the intersection of eco-anxiety and grief with social inequality, and new research and practices that are emerging from climate psychology and emotionally intelligent change-making.	• https://qrs.ly/6jg3gmi
The Good Grief Network The Good Grief Network (GGN) is an innovative peer support network for processing and integrating the uncertainty and grief that the climate and wider eco-crisis can awaken in people.	• https://www.goodgriefnetwork.org/

TIPS TO MAKE A DIFFERENCE: Bring It Along

Amber Pitts, New Kent Elementary School, Booneville, MS

1. Buy biodegradable items.
2. Take your own reusable bags to stores with you.

Combatting Hopelessness

For youth, climate anxiety is heightened due to the perception that adults, leaders, and policymakers are not doing enough to address the climate crisis and its impacts. According to a study by Blue California News Center (2022), a significant majority of Gen Z youth (approximately 75% nationwide) have experienced mental health–related issues like stress, anxiety, and feelings of being overwhelmed because of hearing, reading, or seeing news about climate change. Gen Z survey respondents mentioned the following areas of concern:

• Most of the youth (81% nationwide) agree that global leaders are not doing enough to address climate change.

- Three-quarters of youth (74% nationwide) agree that companies in the United States bear some responsibility to help people combat the impacts of climate change on their mental health.

- A majority (85% nationwide) believe it is important to support companies and brands that are sustainable and environmentally friendly.

One of the most powerful ways to combat hopelessness is by being involved alongside a larger group to foster community, understanding, and belonging. Sustained engagement and collective action can have various benefits, including social connectedness with people with similar goals and values. Social support is also one of the greatest predictors of mental well-being, and researchers have shown that collective action can be a buffer against climate anxiety for young adults. Schwartz et al. (2003) found that anxiety about climate change was linked to symptoms of depression only in those who were not engaged in group and collaborative activities to address climate change.

Source: Istock.com/LeoPatrizi

Among the efforts to hold global leaders accountable, there have been lawsuits in which young people have taken their governments to court over climate change, arguing that political leaders have failed miserably to protect their right to a healthy environment and a future. Offer their stories to your students, so that they may learn from these youth leaders around the world who are holding political systems accountable:

- Portugal: Young activists from Portugal filed the first climate change cause at the European Court of Human Rights in Strasbourg, demanding that 33 countries make more ambitious emissions cuts to safeguard their mental and physical well-being. The case was filed after Portugal recorded its hottest July in 90 years. The case was heard by 22 judges, with 86 government lawyers in attendance, proving that the youth captured the world's attention. Learn more about the case here, and meet the young people who are leading the charge by reading their profiles: https://youth4climatejustice.org/

· ·

 Q: What are some short lessons about teaching climate change that might have impressionable impacts on my students??

Joel Wickert, Hayes Middle School, Albuquerque, NM

A: Here are some organizations that provide online modules and lesson plans about teaching climate change:
- EcoRise: https://qrs.ly/hdg37dw
- Subject To Climate: https://qrs.ly/1pg3eos
- Stanford University Middle School Curriculum: https://qrs.ly/gpg37e1
- PBS Learning Media: https://qrs.ly/sig37e6
- The *New York Times*: https://qrs.ly/2sg3791
- Climate Generation: https://qrs.ly/1vg3eo9

· ·

- Peru: Saúl Amaru Álvarez Cantoral, age 15, is one of seven Peruvian children who filed a complaint against the Peruvian government for its alleged failure to adequately halt deforestation in the Amazon (see Figure 6.1). The youth activists argue that due to the climate crisis, their rights to enjoy a healthy environment and health, water, and life are compromised. They are seeking a plan for achieving net-zero deforestation in the Peruvian Amazon by 2025, climate adaptation and mitigation measures, for regional governments to form plans, and to halt deforestation on public lands. Learn more about these inspiring young people here: https://qrs.ly/8dg37ec

FIGURE 6.1 • Deforestation in the Peruvian Amazon

Source: Istock.com/Christian Mark Inga Osorio

 TIPS TO MAKE A DIFFERENCE: Take a Hike!
Mario Patino, The Preuss School-UCSD, San Diego, CA

1. Take public transit.
2. If you drive your own car, keep tires properly inflated (which will maximize fuel efficiency).

- United States: Our Children's Trust is a nonprofit public interest law firm that provides legal services to youth from diverse backgrounds to secure their legal rights to a safe climate. Our Children's Trust is celebrating its first major climate litigation victory in the United States. Over the past decade, it has launched youth-led climate lawsuits and legal actions in all 50 states. Legal actions are pending in five states, with several more cases in development. Visit their website to research active state legal actions: https://qrs.ly/xng37ee

- Germany: Youth activists in Germany saw success when the highest court ruled that parts of Germany's emissions reduction laws were unconstitutional because the goals offloaded the burden onto younger generations and were too vague (Figure 6.2). The case was brought by nine climate activists with the backing of environmental organizations. Germany's 2019 Change Act requires the country to reduce its greenhouse gas emissions by 55% by 2030. The youth plaintiffs filed complaints that argued that by not setting specific targets for the following years, the act violated their rights to a humane future. The court agreed. Learn more here: https://qrs.ly/64g37ef

FIGURE 6.2 • German students march in front of the Duesseldorf city hall as part of the #FridaysForFuture protests.

Source: istock.com/We-Ge

- Canada: Fifteen youth climate activists in Canada filed a lawsuit arguing that the federal government failed to protect Canadians against climate change, which is a violation of their right to life, liberty, and security of the person under the Canadian Charter of Rights and Freedoms. In 2019, at the time of the filing, the plaintiffs were 10 to 19 years old. The lawsuit was dismissed in 2020 by a federal court judge who ruled that the plaintiffs didn't have a reasonable cause of action because their claim was too broad; they didn't identify specific laws that violated the Charter, but argued that the government's conduct as a whole violated their rights. However, the plaintiffs appealed that decision and in December 2023, the Federal Court of Appeal ruled that the trial could proceed if the plaintiffs amended their claim to be more specific. The trial is expected to proceed in 2025. Meet the plaintiffs and learn their story here: https://qrs.ly/2rg37eg

- South Korea: Choi Heewoo is one of the youngest among the 250 plaintiffs in *Woodpecker et al. v. South Korea,* one of four petitions filed since 2020 that the South Korean court is considering in a landmark case. Woodpecker is a 17-month-old infant, and his legal representative and mother, Lee Donghyun, made him a plaintiff while he was still in the womb. This is likely to be the first climate change court case in Asia to have a public hearing, and the court's verdict will also be the first in Asia. The plaintiffs argue that by not addressing climate change, the government is violating the rights of the citizens. Read more about the landmark case here: https://climatecasechart.com/non-us-case/woodpecker-et-al-v-south-korea/

 Q: How can I teach the gravity of the situation without the students deciding that it would be too much work and giving up?

Preston Reeder, Dallas Independent School District, Dallas, TX

A: The Climate Psychology Alliance of North America Educators and School Counselors Committee came out with a publication for educators: "An Educator's Guide to Climate Emotions." This resource was written by a team of teachers, researchers, and mental health clinicians in consultation with youth climate leaders and climate psychology professionals to offer a variety of approaches to working with climate emotions in an educational setting. Check it out here: https://qrs.ly/ljg37ek

What Do I Do if I Sense My Students Are (or I Am) Feeling Anxious?

Larissa Dooley, a research psychologist who focuses on the mental health impacts of climate change in young people, offers these suggestions for youth, children, and families to help minimize stress surrounding the effects of our warming planet (Blue Shield of California, 2022, p. 1):

- Acknowledge your feelings: Take time to honor emotions and recognize your feelings.

- Use emotional coping tools: Start some daily practices like mindfulness and meditation or breathwork to avoid being overwhelmed by climate emotions.

- Connecting with others can foster a sense of community and show that you're not alone. This can be done through school clubs, support groups, or other resources.

- Engage in self-care: Fear or concern about climate change can lead to anxiety and stress if not balanced with self-care, such as walks, meditation, exercise, eating a good meal, and talking with friends.

- Connect with nature: Spending time outside can calm our nervous systems and reduce stress.

- Act: After holding space for processing and acknowledging emotions, taking meaningful action to combat climate change is one of the most powerful things to do: For your mental health, well-being, and the world.

- Become climate justice aware: Cultivate an awareness of how the burden of environmental disaster falls disproportionately on low-income communities, as well as other historically and contemporaneously marginalized communities. Many youths feel that climate anxiety, at the foundation, is a deep-seated feeling of betrayal due to their own government's inaction and failure to enact meaningful and actionable solutions. To truly address this root cause of the anxiety, students need justice, as not everyone experiences the impacts of climate change equally, and historically and contemporaneously marginalized groups experience disproportionate impacts of climate change.

TIPS TO MAKE A DIFFERENCE: Odorless Solutions

Aaron D. Sloboda, The Boy's Latin School of Maryland, Baltimore, MD

1.   Use Bokashi (odorless) composters in the classroom/dining hall.

CLIMATE ANXIETY AND THE EQUITY ISSUE

As discussed elsewhere in this book, communities of color disproportionately experience climate change (see Chapter 5). U.S. researchers with the Yale Program on Climate Change Communication (Ballew et al., 2020) assert that these communities are most concerned about climate change. However, those responding to the concept of "climate anxiety" are overwhelmingly white. Dr. Jaquette Ray wonders, "If people of color are more concerned about climate change than white people, why is the interest in climate anxiety so white?" (Jaquette Ray, 2021, p. 2).

Climate anxiety must be harnessed for climate justice. Jaquette maintains, "Climate anxiety must be directed towards addressing the ways that racism manifests as environmental trauma and vice versa—how environmentalism manifests as racialized violence. We must channel grief toward collective liberation" (Jaquette Ray, 2021, p. 1). This is essential because, due to systemic racism and the disproportionate impacts of climate change, the concept of an uncertain and even unlivable future has always shaped the emotional terrain for people of color.

Additionally, the claim that climate change is the greatest existential threat of our time is a fallacy because it ignores the lived experiences of people who have been experiencing existential threats for generations, including police brutality as well as slavery and colonialism. Climate justice writer Mary Annaïse Heglar deemed this "existential exceptionalism" (Heglar, 2019) when the privileged represent climate change as humanity's greatest existential crisis. This understanding can also be extended to the global south. Thus, it's imperative to not only teach climate change but to teach climate justice. This includes centering the stories and lived experiences of historically and contemporaneously marginalized communities and utilizing the teaching strategies and resources outlined in Chapter 7.

CLIMATE ANXIETY AND MENTAL HEALTH: A GLOBAL AND CULTURAL PERSPECTIVE

When young people worldwide were surveyed about climate anxiety, youth in the Philippines reported being the most worried about climate change, according to Hickman et al. (2021). Climate change has worsened the Philippines' typhoons and rising sea levels. However, there remains a stigma around seeking mental health care in some countries and cultures, especially in Asia; in addition, therapy or mental health professionals are a luxury and privilege not afforded to all. Although people can get excited about the novel thing that needs to be done for climate anxiety, having a well-functioning mental healthcare system must come first to address any root causes.

The global conversation about mental health is relatively new, and much of the early research has been focused on Europe and North America—as a result, the attention to climate anxiety has been similarly focused. In addition, certain groups dominate the conversation around climate anxiety because of language. For example, "climate anxiety" is a term that might have a different meaning to a white middle-class European compared to a poor farmer in Africa or the Philippines. The reasons for anxiety can also be cultural, as well as what words we are socialized to attribute to the meaning of anxiety and what we have the words for in each language. Words for trauma or even understandings of trauma are not the same in different cultures or languages and can vary by context.

For example, Mitzi Jonelle Tan, a climate justice activist in the Philippines, mentions that the back-to-back typhoons that struck the Philippines weren't discussed publicly, especially the mental health impacts of this event. Her organization, Youth Advocates for Climate Action Philippines, asked many people how they felt after the event. She states, "Not many people talked about the anxiety and the trauma that they experienced... [she thinks] it might be attributed in part to the idea of Filipino resilience, which can be a positive thing, but also to the fact that mental health is not talked about a lot in the Philippines" (Browne, 2022, p. 1).

 Q: Are there any working WebQuests to look at climate change data already made?

Lynn Connor, Old Rochester Regional High School, Mattapoisett, MA

A: Here are three free WebQuests on climate change:

- PolarTREC has the following WebQuests in its teacher resources section:
    - Impact of Climate Change on Ecosystems WebQuest: https://www.polartrec.com/resources/lesson/impact-of-climate-change-on-ecosystems-webquest
    - Why Can't I Eat This Fish? Bioaccumulation WebQuest: https://www.polartrec.com/resources/lesson/why-cant-i-eat-fish
- The EcoRise Introduction to Environmental Justice: Grades 9–12 lesson plan includes a WebQuest: https://www.ecorise.org/clean-ej/#high

CENTERING THE LIVED EXPERIENCES OF ALL STUDENTS

As we've been discussing, the climate emergency is far more than merely a "science issue." It's imperative for students to bring their whole selves into activism and problem solving, and activism and education promote resilience. As a result, students need a classroom environment where they can confidently and safely be their authentic selves. The first thing we can do as educators is create a safe and authentic learning community for our students, starting at the beginning of the school year. Table 6.2 lists some tips from Facing History and Ourselves (2023) for facilitating crucial conversations. This can be used as whole-class sentence starters or as sentence frames for partner talk. Both are great opportunities to set the tone in the classroom and promote civil dialogue, and this is a good Common Core connection to speaking and listening standards.

> **How might you use these tips and strategies to facilitate crucial conversations with your students?**

TABLE 6.2 • Facilitating Crucial Conversations

Step	Conversation Starters
• Affirm: Affirm and appreciate someone's willingness and openness to have a conversation.	• Thank you for bringing that up. • I'm happy to talk to you about that.
• Acknowledge: Acknowledge what someone is saying. You can paraphrase their words and feelings to make sure that they feel seen and understood.	• What I hear you saying is___. Is that correct? • It sounds like you feel___. • From your perspective and/or lived experience, ___.
• Ask: Asking questions can help you understand a person's thoughts, feelings, and motivations.	• What do you mean by that? I want to know more. • What life experiences have made you feel that way?
• Add: Relate and then offer additional information. To start, you should try to connect or empathize with what they're saying.	• I've had a similar experience; I can relate. • I can understand why you think/feel that way. • I've learned that ___.
• Address and Assess: Assess the person's response and notice their body language.	• What are you thinking and/or feeling right now? • Can you tell me more about that?
• Appreciate: Affirm their willingness to talk to you and listen to your perspective.	• Thank you for taking the time to meet with me. • Thank you for hearing my perspective. • Thank you for sharing your experiences and life story.

Source: istock.com/pixeluxe

To find ways that students can take action to help address the climate crisis while drawing on their lived experiences, we can start by thinking about how each student has a specific and unique skill set to tap into for climate action. Climate scientist and ocean justice expert Ayana Elizabeth Johnson offers inspiration by asking these three questions:

1. What brings you joy? What makes you feel alive, and what makes your heart truly happy?

2. What work needs doing? This can be system-level local, regional, or global change. Are there certain climate and justice solutions that are of interest? Like voting, composting, protecting forests?

> **There are some ideas about work that needs doing in the Project Drawdown Solutions Library: https://drawdown.org/solutions.**

3. What are you good at? This can be networks, resources, and skills. What are your areas of expertise? Who and what do you have access to? What do you bring to the table? What gives you the satisfaction of a job well done?

At the intersection of these three questions is your climate action. Here are some resources to prompt further learning:

Taking collective action is a great way to feel connected to others and can reduce feelings of hopelessness and isolation. Learning about the different people and players involved in the climate movement space can also be a great way to connect to social studies, history, and art. Drawing from Grassroots Economic Organizing's butterfly model of transformative social justice (Warfield & Kolhatkar, 2021), Soul Fire Farm co-founder Leah Penniman describes the four "wings" of the butterfly model (Figure 6.3):

- Resisters: The protestors engaging in nonviolent civil disobedience

- Reformers: The people trying to make change from within the system, like teachers, lawyers, and elected officials

- Builders: Those who create alternative institutions such as freedom schools, farms, health clinics, etc.

- Healers: The conflict mediators, the therapists, the singers, dancers, artists, etc.

FIGURE 6.3 • The Butterfly Model

Source: istock.com/golden_SUN

The climate crisis requires system changes that start with local actions. The following are questions to consider with your students to help them focus on things that they can do in their own community:

1. What is your climate action?

2. Which wing on the butterfly would your climate action fall under?

3. Which wings are missing and who can you ask for help? Who can you connect to and work with?

4. Who are your supporters to help you act? And who do you support (e.g., parents, friends, siblings, colleagues, teachers)?

Civic engagement is a key to managing climate anxiety. In this chapter's Success Story, learn about how one teacher connects civics and climate change.

Your class or whole school can make a giant butterfly out of butcher paper to model how individual people with unique talents and skill sets can come together to form a movement for social and environmental change. Another idea is to have students research youth activists, as shown throughout this book, and make a butterfly with all the youth activists' examples. This demonstrates the impacts of collective action and organizing and the ripple effect that climate actions can create in the community, nation, and the world.

Success Story: Exercise Your Right to Vote!

Kim Decker, Dyersburg City Schools, Dyersburg, TN

All my students are given information concerning voting rights and how to become a registered voter. We all must stay informed and vote for candidates who stand for strategies and policies that line up with our personal views of the climate. I consider it a success whenever my students become better informed about how climate change is affecting their world. I believe that most understand that adaptation will be significant to their generation to continue our way of life. Classes that were taught two and three years prior are seeing events unfold that were predicted.

Istock.com/shironosov

After engaging with the two previous activities, you and your students might also ponder these questions:

- How does climate justice impact people?
- What advantages or disadvantages do I notice because of identity groups?
- How is my life easier or more difficult based on who I am and where I was born?
- How can I use my unique interests and skillsets to make a difference?
- What careers related to climate change might interest me?

Green Careers

Your students might want to explore the different sectors of climate work. For example, according to the BBC, more than two-thirds of kids hope to have a career that helps the environment (BBC, 2020; see Table 6.3 for some ideas).

TABLE 6.3 • Green STEM Careers

City environmental planner	City environmental planners help manage the growth of cities while ensuring that the planning designs meet sustainability requirements.
Climate activist and/or community organizer	Activists are individuals or groups who advocate for environmental causes, such as climate change mitigation and adaptation efforts. Activists and community organizers both work to mobilize communities and create coalitions for change.
College professor	All education jobs can be powerful "green jobs." A university professor at a four-year institution or a community college can be in any field or specialization and advocate for climate change action (e.g., professors of science education, early childhood education, engineering, STEM, environmental studies and more). College professors require advanced degrees, most typically a Ph.D.
Environmental lawyer	Environmental lawyers are lawyers who specialize in the natural environment, human health, and natural resources. They are trained to use the law to advocate for a better environment.
Environmental engineer	An environmental engineer is an engineer who designs systems for the environment, such as cleaning municipal water supplies or finding engineering solutions to waste treatment or pollution.

(Continued)

(Continued)

Geoscientist	A geoscientist studies and works with soils, minerals, energy resources, fossils, oceans and freshwater, and the atmosphere. A geoscience job could be a meteorologist, volcanologist, seismologist, and more.
Green architect	Green architecture is a field of architecture that is focused on designing buildings to be environmentally friendly and have the lowest possible impact on their surrounding environment.
PreK–12 Teacher	All teachers, from preschool to twelfth grade, can be powerful allies for climate change education. They can be science teachers, the teachers reading this book, or teachers of any subject and content area. Environmental education and climate change education needs to be taught across all subjects and all content areas.
Sustainability social media influencer	A social media influencer is someone who has a platform on social media and uses their platform to advocate or speak out about certain issues. Social media influencers can be important voices in climate change communication.
Urban farmer	Urban farming in cities is a climate change adaptation effort and helps to enhance vegetation cover in cities and cut down on fuel needed for transportation.

What other green jobs can your students think of? Are there green jobs that don't exist yet but should? Discuss how students can share this information with the school or broader community. Can you hold a career fair on campus or invite green job experts to speak at your school? Does the school have classes that will prepare students for green jobs in the future?

Are There More Ideas for Green Careers?

- Check out NASA Climate Kids for more inspiration for green careers: https://qrs .ly/9ig37et (see also Figure 6.4).

- Check out Time for Kids Climate Jobs: qrs.ly/pmg3dhn

- The Biden-Harris Administration launched the American Climate Corps. It's a workforce training and service initiative that will ensure more young people have access to the skill-based training necessary for careers in the clean energy and climate resilience economy. The American Climate Corps will focus on equity and environmental justice.

FIGURE 6.4 • An engineer examining a solar panel

Source: istock.com/Alvarez

Success Story: Community-Based Climate Change Projects

Andrew McCullough, Brunswick High School, Brunswick, ME

In Fall 2023, our science department worked with our town's environmental planner on a project to get more students to share opinions regarding our town's new emissions reduction targets. Local collaborators, including businesses and town officials, entered our high school and set up stations in our theater with information regarding how the town might lower its carbon emissions to hit the new targets. Stations included poster presentations and mapping exercises where students learned about the town's new emissions targets, priority action areas, vulnerability assessments that had already been conducted, and more. High school students in their science classes came through and visited each station,

(Continued)

(Continued)

talking with collaborators and town officials about methods of carbon emission reduction. Students could fill out sticky notes at each station with further questions, thoughts, or ideas about what they saw and learned.

Additionally, they were asked about the effects of climate change they were already seeing in our community and what positive actions they might already be seeing in our town. This enabled our town environmental planner to collect much-needed information from students and younger community members about their thoughts and ideas on different strategies that will impact them in their lifetimes. It also allowed our high school students to have a voice and talk openly about what they are seeing and doing in our community about climate change. Students learned about efforts to reduce carbon emissions but also got to interview and talk with people from our community who are a part of this wide-reaching initiative to mitigate climate change in our area. Because students got to say what efforts for climate emission reduction they liked and which they thought could be improved, investment in later discussions in the classroom on climate change was greater. From conversations in class afterward, students reported a strong appreciation for being asked about their opinions and feelings and said that they were more connected to this problem than they had been. Students felt like they were part of the solution, not just the problem, and this went a long way toward helping our students connect and share ideas on this important issue.

 Q&A   **Q:** What can the public do to support better student learning about climate change in the classroom/school setting?

Morgan Massey, Sheffield High School, Sheffield, AL

A: The North American Association for Environmental Education's (NAAEE) Coalition for Climate Education Policy has some excellent resources for public advocacy for environmental education and climate change education at the local, state, and federal levels. Check out the resources to learn more: https://naaee.org/programs/coalition

 TIPS TO MAKE A DIFFERENCE: Daily Green Habit
Renee Pascale-Reynolds, Atlanta Jewish Academy, Atlanta, GA

1. Practice meatless Mondays.
2. Walk instead of driving, when possible.

STUDENT ACTIVIST STORIES AND STRATEGIES

Yale and Suffolk University faculty conducted a joint research study on climate change–related anxiety and depression in college students and examined how collective action can help prevent these symptoms. The researchers concluded that students with climate change anxiety who participated in collective activism tended to have significantly fewer depressive symptoms. Such collective actions might include going to events and protests, sending letters to policymakers, forming or joining a club, or becoming a member of an environmental organization.

Creating the Space for Communication About Feelings of Anxiety

Today's youth also tap into their feelings of climate anxiety to fuel their work. For example, Greta Thunberg used climate anxiety to motivate world leaders at the 2019 World Economic Forum, saying, "I want you to feel the fear I feel every day. And then I want you to act" (Thunberg, 2019, p. 1).

As educators, we have the chance to provide young people with opportunities to voice their concerns and priorities. In addition, students are mobilizing to take action. They are creating initiatives such as climate action groups, in-person and online, and student clubs to address climate change and provide platforms for youth leaders to demand action from world leaders.

Let's talk about some examples you might want to share with your students as inspiration. Climate Café LA (https://qrs.ly/fig37ex) was created by millennials who wanted to strengthen community systems as an alternative to therapy for climate anxiety. The founders state, "It's a thinking and feeling space…

> **How can students replicate this "café" model for creating climate change discussions in their school or local community?**

this is where people get together and get into our emotional responses to the climate crisis" (Agrawal, 2023, p. 1). A virtual café is hosted each month, and there are partnerships with universities and other public spaces like libraries to host climate discussions. This virtual café serves to facilitate informal conversations in a confidential space. It's intended to facilitate dialogue, reflection, and sharing of thoughts and experiences rather than "doing," so it's more reflection-based to discuss the emotional responses and reactions related to the climate emergency.

Inemesit Williams, a former co-leader of the social justice working group at Climate Action Network for International Educators (CANIE; https://canie.org/about-canie), recognized the historic lack of diversity among leadership in environmental organizations (Rapin, 2023) and saw the imperative to create spaces for climate conversations specifically for Black women and non-binary people. Williams identifies "as a queer, Black American descendant of chattel slavery . . . and the only participant in her Circle who identifies as Black...you can't engage in that kind of space if you don't feel like what you have to say is going to be welcome" (Rapin, 2023, p. 1).

How can you establish a safe space for climate conversations in your classroom and in your school so that all experiences are prioritized? Why are affinity groups also important for facilitating climate conversations?

Creating safe spaces for historically and contemporarily marginalized people is why psychotherapist Taryn Crosby, who is Black, co-organized We Outside, a climate conversation specifically for Black women and non-binary people. Crosby stated, "We want to create a space where our experiences are prioritized" (Rapin, 2023, p. 1), as systemic racism has historically excluded Black Americans from outdoor recreation and Black, Indigenous, and people of color (BIPOC) people haven't always felt welcomed or invited into other climate conversations. Crosby hopes initiatives like We Outside, an affinity space for climate change conversations to be more inclusive, will be a model for the goal to "hold space where people can be open and curious about the way that they are affected by their environment and nature, and [also] how *they* affect their environment and nature—ultimately encouraging them to move that into action" (Rapin, 2023, p. 1).

Strategies for Civic Engagement and Participation

Youth activists are creating radical change and are unapologetic in their approaches for bold pathways for civic engagement and participation. Activism can also help youth channel their climate anxiety into collective and collaborative action. As educators, providing students with tools that foster and encourage their self-efficacy and self-determination is important.

As discussed, cultivating community, connection, and activism are the building blocks for systemic change. Take a look at some examples and strategies for civic engagement from youth-led climate justice groups:

• The American Civil Liberties Union (ACLU) offers a guide on "Students' Rights: Speech, Walkouts, and Other Protests." Check out the guide here: https://qrs.ly/2zg37ey

• SustainUs brings youth to international negotiations to engage in protest and civil disobedience to demand stronger and more urgent climate action. Students must know their rights regarding free speech, walkouts, and other protests. https://sustainus.org/

- Sunrise is redefining youth activism in the United States with their movement's support of the Green New Deal and partnering with Rep. Alexandria Ocasio-Cortez. Sunrise has redefined climate politics in the United States. In 2017, the climate crisis was barely mentioned by politicians. In three years the organization grew exponentially and has helped to plan the global climate strikes and forced politicians to take the climate crisis seriously. Learn about the Green New Deal for Communities Campaign: qrs.ly/zeg3dhq Learn about Sunrise's Electoral Organizing Campaign: https://qrs.ly/uxg37ez

- Youth vs Apocalypse has an Education for Mobilization campaign where they engage in school organizing to support frontline youth leadership. They currently have clubs in 26 schools for climate and social justice, and the student club leaders have training and support from Youth vs Apocalypse's community education organizers. Learn about starting a club today: https://qrs.ly/6ag3di1

Avoiding Activist Burnout

Avoiding activist burnout is crucial for youth, students, and the public to sustain their commitment to community work. Let's look at a few strategies you can use to help your students to advocate for their community, themselves, and peers to avoid burnout:

1. Wellness Planning: The Audre Lorde Project has a framework for wellness planning that encourages you to assess your needs in four categories and to ask yourself what needs you might anticipate having during this time:

   > What strategies for avoiding burnout can you use in your teaching practice? What strategies for avoiding burnout can you use in your nonprofessional life?

   - Heart: Spiritual needs and motivational needs, which help keep you grounded

   - Body: Biological and physical needs

   - Mind: Emotional needs; thought process

   - Community: Need from social relationships and interpersonal needs

   You can find more information at https://qrs.ly/xxg37f0

2. Body Scan Meditation: Bring awareness into each part of your body and try this full-body meditation by Lesly University Professor Nancy Waring. Find information here: https://qrs.ly/uzg37f3

3. Action Hour: To avoid burnout and overloading your schedule with tasks or requests for action, like calling senators and legislators or phone banking, schedule an "action hour" to maintain a balance.

LEARNING FROM OUR COLLEAGUES
Finding Joy and Peace in the Classroom

Mr. Gomez instructed his students to come in quietly after recess and take out their pencils. "Okay, class," he said, "Today we're going to take out our writing notebooks, and your prompt for today is as follows."

When you think about the future of the planet, how do you feel?

"I want you to write down all the emotions and feelings that you experience. Remember to use adjectives and verbs. You can also draw emojis or pictures and use colors; all these tools help you express yourself."

The students eagerly got out their supplies, and the room was silent as pencils made scratching sounds on the pages of their open notebooks.

"Okay, excellent work," Mr. Gomez said after 10 minutes. "Next, we're going to practice a guided meditation to help us address all of those feelings and emotions you listed or represented in your notebook."

"Sit back in your chair and close your eyes. Relax your shoulders and feel your breathing travel into your arms as you exhale. Now relax your legs and your toes. Imagine something that gives you joy or peace. Keep that image in your mind, and we'll rest for 5 minutes."

After 5 minutes, students were instructed to open their eyes. "How do you feel, class?" Mr. Gomez asked. He saw slow smiles spread across his student's faces, and a sense of calm filled the classroom.

"Okay, now we're going to do a partner share. You will discuss with your partner how you felt during the meditation and what image you imagined that gave you joy and peace. After you finish talking, you will represent that image in your notebook."

Tomas tuned to Lupe and said, "I imagined going to the beach with my family and drinking horchata with my cousins when it's really hot outside."

Lupe said, "I imagined eating popsicles in the summer; I can feel the juice drip down my chin, it's so sweet and sticky."

Across the room, Peter and La'Bre got out their pencils and began to draw in their notebooks.

Mr. Gomez said, "Whenever you feel anxious about anything, you can try drawing, meditating, and talking to a friend to help you. Those are called coping strategies."

How might you use these strategies of drawing, meditation, and talking to a friend to help your students with climate change anxiety?

Reflection Questions

1. How might you use the strategies and resources for civic engagement and activism to help students cope with and process climate anxiety?

2. Are there particular climate anxiety initiatives and resources that would be a good fit for the needs of your community or your students?

3. Do you know anyone in the community with a green career? Can you arrange a "green careers panel" for your class?

4. How can you use the resources for climate anxiety to help students with general social and emotional skills?

5. How can your students create schoolwide or communitywide initiatives that can help with climate anxiety?

6. What connections do you see between climate anxiety and equity, and why is this important?

7. How can you use your school counselor or school social worker as a resource to help with climate anxiety?

8. Does your school or district have any general SEL activities or supports that can be translated/modified to address climate anxiety?

For Further Reading

FOR TEACHERS:

Biabani, Z. (2023). *Climate optimism: Celebrating systemic change around the world*. Mango Media.

Curtice, K. B. (2023). *Living resistance: An indigenous vision for seeking wholeness every day*. Brazos Press.

Huebner, D. (2021). *What to do when you worry too much: A kid's guide to overcoming anxiety*. American Psychological Association.

Johnson, A. E. (2022). *How to find joy in climate action* [Video]. YouTube. https://qrs.ly/ueg37f5

Olsen, A. (2020). *Body and earth: An experiential guide*. Wesleyan University Press.

Ray, S. J. (2020). *A field guide to climate anxiety: How to keep your cool on a warming planet*. University of California Press.

Wray, B. (2023). *Generation dread: Finding purpose in an age of climate anxiety*. Hachette UK.

FOR STUDENTS:

Ages 8–10

Celano, M., & Collins, M. (2023). *Something happened to our planet: Kids tackle the climate crisis*. American Psychological Association.

Long, M. (2021). *Kids on the march: 15 stories of speaking out, protesting, and fighting for justice*. Algonquin Young Readers.

Margolin, J. (2020). *Youth to power: Your voice and how to use it*. Hachette UK.

Wittenstein, B. (2023). *The day the river caught fire: How the Cuyahoga River exploded and ignited the earth day movement*. Simon and Schuster.

PART IV

HOW DO I INTEGRATE CLIMATE CHANGE EDUCATION INTO MY SCHOOL AND MY CURRICULUM?

Source: istock.com/Wavebreakmedia

CHAPTER SEVEN

CONNECTING CLIMATE CHANGE TO NATIONAL TEACHING AND LEARNING STANDARDS

I'm a real believer that creativity comes from limits, not freedom.

—Jon Stewart

THIS CHAPTER WILL DISCUSS

- The national learning standards across disciplines; the Next Generation Science Standards and Common Core State Standards in English Language Arts and Mathematics; and connections to the College, Career, and Civic Life Framework for Social Studies State Standards

- Strategies and grade-level specific ideas for integrating climate change in standards-aligned lessons; and

- Resources and tools for teaching standards-aligned climate change lessons

As with any new educational initiative, we as teachers must be mindful of the broader curricular landscape when adopting changes. Keeping context in mind is especially important when we integrate topics like climate change that can be seen as controversial by some people. Standards drive many curricular decisions and provide the limits to the frameworks within which teachers can plan and implement instruction. Such standards can also serve as a scaffold and justification—those who might oppose teachers integrating climate change into their classrooms have weaker arguments when the instruction is grounded in standards. Finally, and perhaps most importantly, standards provide the guidelines to allow teachers to showcase innovation and creativity.

In this chapter, we will look specifically at the Next Generation Science Standards along with Common Core State Standards in English Language Arts and Mathematics and the College, Career, and Civic Life (C3) Framework for Social Studies and identify easy-to-implement strategies for integrating climate change seamlessly using the standards.

STARTING FROM OUR ASSETS: THE NEXT GENERATION SCIENCE STANDARDS

The Next Generation Science Standards (NGSS) were launched in 2013, following the National Research Council's 2012 *Framework for K–12 Science Education* (National Research Council et al., 2012; NGSS Lead States, 2013). According to the National Science Teaching Association (NSTA, n.d.), these standards have been adopted by 20 states and all other states (except Florida) have created standards based on the *Framework for K–12 Science Education*. The NSTA endorses the use of the NGSS as they require students to use science content to solve problems and seek connections across ideas, rather than simply memorize facts. These standards were a long time coming: They were the first national science standards to be released in the United States since the 1996 National Science Education Standards, and they included major changes in the way in which science teaching and learning was presented. Some of these changes were simple and straightforward, such as including engineering content alongside science. Others changed the way in which standards were organized, such as specifying explicit grade levels for the standards K–5, rather than organizing them by grade band (K–2 and 3–5).

Assigning standards to particular grade levels K–5, rather than grade bands, provides children with more equitable access to science. This is especially important for topics like climate change that build and grow in complexity as students get older. Students from marginalized groups are often the most mobile and might attend several different schools over the course of their elementary years. When standards focus on grade bands, it's possible that some children might learn the same science content every year. When each year has specific ideas, we increase the likelihood that children learn a broader scope of ideas.

TIPS TO MAKE A DIFFERENCE: Turn the Tap!

Shirley Anthony, Branch Elementary, Muroc, CA

1. Don't let the water run when washing your hands.
2. Use reusable water bottles.

CLIMATE CHANGE AND THE NGSS

Among the other innovations offered by the NGSS, for the first time in national standards, Global Climate Change appeared as a disciplinary core idea. This disciplinary core idea is introduced in middle school and continues into high school. This content addition ensures that climate change must be taught to middle and high school students across the country, in those states that have adopted the standards. However, the inclusion of climate change in the NGSS did not happen without conflict. The Heartland Institute, a prominent climate change denial organization, sent 300,000+ copies of its publication *Why Scientists Disagree About Global Warming* to U.S. teachers in 2017. This effort was part of a broader campaign to promote skepticism about climate science in educational settings (Hirji, 2019). Regardless of pushback, middle and high school classrooms across the country have been including climate change in their lessons since 2014.

Yet, this addition at the middle and high school level begs the question: What can teachers who work with children *before* middle and high school do to ensure their students are prepared to learn about climate change?

Q: We all know climate change is real, but are there still some districts in the United States not validating the science and therefore not teaching it?

Wendy L. Welshans, Director of Forman Rainforest Project, Litchfield, CT

A: In states that have adopted the NGSS, teachers are required to teach about climate change in middle and high school science classes. Other states have different requirements, and there are some schools that do not teach climate change at all.

Interestingly, when we search for performance expectations related to Global Climate Change, we can see that there are no explicit and direct connections to standards at earlier grade levels. However, there are fundamental performance expectations contained in other disciplinary core ideas that lay the foundation for addressing climate change at a number of grade levels.

The most obvious of these are Human Impacts on Earth's Systems and Weather and Climate, but teachers should not feel limited to addressing climate change, or the prerequisite ideas for understanding climate change, in just these science topics.

Although teaching young children the difference between weather and climate is age appropriate and comprehensible, it is not always as simple as it seems. In many languages, such as Spanish, the words for weather and climate are the same. This means that supporting our English Language Learners in this context requires more than simply translating; we must provide the appropriate context to differentiate between the two ideas.

The Human Impacts on Earth's Systems disciplinary core idea is included in performance expectations as early as kindergarten. One example can be found below.

> *Students who demonstrate understanding can:*
>
> *K-ESS3-3. Communicate solutions that will reduce the impact of humans on the land, water, air, and/or other living things in the local environment.*

The idea that students can communicate ideas related to reducing human impacts is hopeful, solutions-oriented, and absolutely appropriate for kindergarteners. Five- and 6-year-olds may not be able to comprehend chemical reactions associated with burning fossil fuels, but they can clearly see smoke emissions from cars' exhaust and compare them to the lack of emissions generated by walking or riding a bike. Creating a "bike to school" campaign can be a fun way to invite children to think about reducing human impacts that lays the foundation for further investigations down the road.

Young children can also consider ways in which ecosystems change over time, how heat can change the speed at which air particles move, and what the differences are between weather and climate. As a result, with some simple changes in how teachers present science, NGSS-aligned K–5 lessons can clearly provide introductory climate change instruction.

Success Story: Climate Change and English Language Learners

Naomi Elliott, Auburn School District, Auburn, WA

For the past 4 years Auburn School District in Washington State has used GLAD (Guided Language Acquisition Design) strategies and science units throughout the school year. In our multilingual student summer school programs we work in conjunction with the King County Library System to teach the sciences. We also have used Orange County Department of Education Project GLAD strategies to teach entire climate change units, even during COVID. I am a beekeeper, and I conducted a Google Classroom meeting to demonstrate a beehive inspection with our multilingual students (Figure 7.1).

FIGURE 7.1 • Beekeeping demonstration

Source: istock.com/ Kateryna Kukota

THE COMMON CORE STATE STANDARDS

If ever there were a buzzword in education in the United States, we can say with certainty that for the past 15 years, "Common Core" was it. The Common Core State Standards (CCSS) were developed in 2007, using a thorough research process integrating information about how students learn and what skills will be needed to prepare children for the future (National Governors Association, 2010). Released in 2010, these national standards in both English Language Arts (ELA) and Mathematics reshaped the way in which these critical subjects have been taught. Specifically, skills within these standards are emphasized alongside disciplinary content, not unlike the way in which the NGSS emphasizes the act of doing science along with the content-based ideas. These standards include Anchor Standards, which link skills and topics within ELA and mathematics content areas to college and career readiness. At the time of this writing, the CCSS have been adopted or adapted widely—41 of the 50 states are using the CCSS or standards based on them, along with five of the six U.S. territories.

Much of the backlash about the CCSS wasn't about the standards themselves. Rather, it was about textbooks and other items marketed as being "aligned" to the standards and a misunderstanding that standards are not curriculum, just guidelines around which we build curriculum.

These standards have not been adopted without controversy, and much of the controversy comes from individuals who do not work in the field of education. It should be clear that the standards do not prescribe any specific methods of teaching or strategies. Yet, many textbooks published after their adoption indicated that they were "CCSS-aligned." As a result, many assumed that the strategies favored by these various textbooks were somehow part of the common core, but a simple look at the standards themselves, found at corestandards.org, will demonstrate that this isn't the case.

. . . .

Q&A   Q: What are ways we can weave these lessons of climate change into ELA, math, and religion classes, rather than just in science and social studies? Are there interdisciplinary units that can be easily implemented at various grade levels?

Elizabeth Duff-Russo, Old Saint Mary's School, Chicago, IL

A: Climate change can be integrated across disciplines individually, such as a topic for researching or a dataset for a math class, but also through interdisciplinary units of inquiry. In fact, researchers recommend using interdisciplinary approaches to enhance children's abilities to make connections across ideas. In ELA, climate change can be a starting point for reading and writing activities. Some more strategies related to ELA are highlighted throughout this chapter. In religion class, lessons about decision making and stewardship of our planet provide excellent opportunities for discussing our changing climate as well.

English Language Arts Common Core State Standards (CCSS-ELA)

The CCSS-ELA are organized into seven key categories:

- Reading Literature;

- Reading Informational Text;

- Reading Foundational Skills;

- Writing;

- Speaking and Listening;

- Language; and

- Range, Quality, and Complexity.

In each category, there are sub-ideas or anchor standards with a variety of ideas at each grade level. These ideas build upon one another and connect across grade levels.

TIPS TO MAKE A DIFFERENCE: Put Away the Plastic!
Janett Akerman, Cypress-Fairbanks Independent School District, Cypress, TX

1. Stop using plastic straws and cutlery.

INTEGRATING CLIMATE CHANGE IN READING

Three of the major CCSS-ELA categories focus specifically on reading. These categories each offer their own opportunities for integrating climate change. Silvhiany and colleagues (2023) offer many suggestions for integrating climate fiction into English classes, but this concept is not limited to the upper grades alone. For example, the following standard, in Reading Literature, is written at the Kindergarten level:

CCSS.ELA-LITERACY.RL.K.1

With prompting and support, ask and answer questions about key details in a text.

The "K" in this code indicates that the standard is at the kindergarten level, "L" tells us that this is a literature standard, and the "1" indicates it is the first one in this category. The same standard is expanded upon at each grade level to ensure students' learning experiences are sequential and connected over time. For example, the first literature standard in fourth grade is as follows:

CCSS.ELA-LITERACY.RL.4.1

Refer to details and examples in a text when explaining what the text says explicitly and when drawing inferences from the text.

Can climate change education be integrated with reading when using standards-aligned lessons? This example, which focuses on identifying and later using details in a text, certainly lends itself to climate change topics.

For example, a teacher could use a grade-level-appropriate children's book about weather around the world, such as Marilyn Singer's *On the Same Day in March*, to spark conversations about differences between weather and climate—a foundational idea for understanding climate change.

However, reading is not related to literature alone. When we examine the reading standards related to informational text, there are even further opportunities for climate change instruction. An example at the eighth-grade level follows:

CCSS.ELA-LITERACY.RI.8.7

Evaluate the advantages and disadvantages of using different mediums (e.g., print or digital text, video, multimedia) to present a particular topic or idea.

Note that the "I" after R indicates this is an informational text standard while the 8.7 tells us that this is the seventh standard in this category at the eighth-grade level. This particular standard offers students the opportunity to research a climate-related topic using a multitude of resources and identify strengths and weaknesses. Like the literature standards, this standard also becomes more complex as students advance. For example, at the second-grade level, this idea is expressed as follows:

CCSS.ELA-LITERACY.RI.2.7

Explain how specific images (e.g., a diagram showing how a machine works) contribute to and clarify a text.

Using informational text can also be a productive strategy for integrating climate change, especially as it provides opportunities for addressing various text features such as diagrams. For example, the website Newsela (https://newsela.com/) contains current events news articles organized by grade level, which can be especially helpful for students learning to read and interpret graphs or describe the effects of climate change (Figure 7.2).

FIGURE 7.2 • Map of Climate Zones in the United States

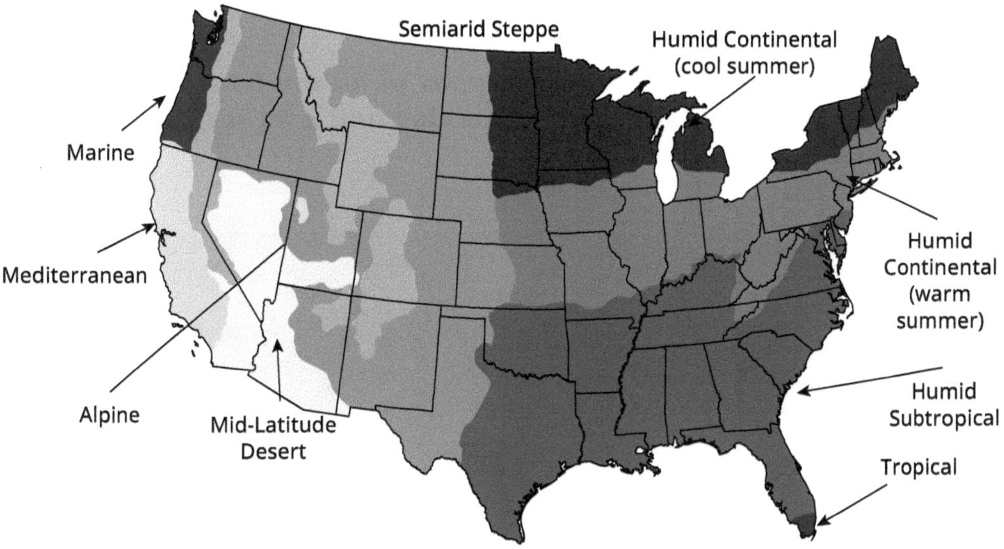

Source: PICRYL

INTEGRATING CLIMATE CHANGE IN WRITING

When we consider writing to the CCSS-ELA standards, there is even more opportunity to integrate climate change education. For example, the seventh-grade standard that follows offers a straightforward approach to writing about climate change.

> Text features such as the climate map featured in Figure 7.2 help students to make sense of text as they're reading.

CCSS.ELA-LITERACY.W.7.1

Write arguments to support claims with clear reasons and relevant evidence.

Using the same format as the reading standards, the "W" indicates this is a writing standard, while "7.1" indicates that this is the first standard in this category in seventh grade. This is a clear example of an opportunity for climate change instruction through writing. Like the others, the first-grade and 11th–12th-grade standards that follow show us how this category of standard becomes more sophisticated in each grade.

CCSS.ELA-LITERACY.W.1.2

Write informative/explanatory texts in which they name a topic, supply some facts about the topic, and provide some sense of closure.

CCSS.ELA-LITERACY.W.11-12.1

Write arguments to support claims in an analysis of substantive topics or texts, using valid reasoning and relevant and sufficient evidence.

 ## Success Story: Writing About Climate Change Isn't Just for Elementary School!

Benjamin Taylor, High School Principal, Clark County Schools, Kahoka, MO

I asked students to write an argumentative essay about climate change. They were allowed to present and defend either stance—"climate change is happening and we need to make changes" or "climate change isn't real and this is a cyclical part of nature." Students were required to find 3–4 pieces of evidence that supported their stance (evidence had to come from peer-reviewed studies and/or expert analysis—experts being PhDs in the areas they were presenting on). They also had to find 1–3 pieces of evidence from the opposing stance to present and attempt to refute. I found that while many students took the stance that climate change is fake, they quickly found that they weren't able to produce credible evidence to support that stance and that most of the rhetoric presenting climate change as fake was from "influencers" or politicians who weren't experts in the field.

- -

 Q: How do you incorporate climate change into a lesson when it is not a standard?

Renae Henry, Westfall Middle School, Williamsport, OH

A: There are several places in the science curriculum where climate change can be incorporated. For example,

- The Energy Unit: The law of conservation of energy states that energy cannot be made or destroyed; it can only be changed in form. Ask your students where the energy from fossil fuels comes from. By probing student understanding, you can take your students all the way back to the Sun, to plants that lived during the Carboniferous Period, to today's underground reserves of oil, natural gas, and coal. Using more energy transfers, students can now take those fossil fuels to the electrical energy used in their homes. Start at the power plant: The heat energy from burning fossil fuels boils water, producing steam. This steam is used to turn the turbines (mechanical energy) and run the generator (copper wire/magnet), which results in electrical energy. At this point, the class can learn about the role of fossil fuels in pollution and climate change. Students can also study the energy transfers involved with other energy sources, such as solar, nuclear, and wind power, as alternatives to fossil fuels.

- Ecology: Many teachers add lessons on climate change when covering the standard How Do Humans Interact With Their Environment? You can discuss how climate change affects ecosystems, biodiversity, and the distribution of species. Discuss the potential (and the current reality) for species extinction and changes in migration patterns.

- Meteorology: When exploring the Earth's climate system, including the atmosphere, hydrosphere, lithosphere, and biosphere, you can discuss how changes in one component can impact the entire system. Students can also investigate the role of greenhouse gases in trapping heat and affecting weather patterns, precipitation, and extreme weather events.

Climate change isn't just science! In history class, you can explore how past societies dealt with environmental challenges. Art and literature classes can inspire creative expression about the beauty of our planet and the need to protect it. Even social studies discussions about government and policy can involve exploring solutions for a sustainable future.

- -

Mathematics Common Core State Standards (CCSS-M)

Not unlike their NGSS counterparts, the CCSS-M are organized by grade level by both practice (the way in which mathematicians do their work) and domain (the branch of mathematics). The standards for mathematical practice are grouped in the following categories:

- Make sense of problems and persevere in solving them;

- Reason abstractly and quantitatively;

- Construct viable arguments and critique the reasoning of others;

- Model with mathematics;

- Use appropriate tools strategically;

- Attend to precision;

- Look for and make use of structure; and

- Look for and express regularity in repeated reasoning.

The domains are as follows:

- Counting & Cardinality;

- Operations & Algebraic Thinking;

- Number & Operations in Base 10;

- Number & Operations–Fractions;

- Measurement & Data;

- Geometry;

- Ratios & Proportional Relationships;

- The Number System;

- Expressions & Equations;

- Functions; and

- Statistics & Probability.

Like the CCSS-ELA standards, the CCSS-M are structured in a way that demonstrates how ideas become more complex over time.

Using a Critical Mathematics Education (CME) approach, Abtahi and colleagues (2017) argue that mathematics teachers have a moral responsibility to prepare their students with the mathematical skills to understand climate data. Not surprisingly, one key mathematics domain that lends itself quite easily to climate change is Measurement & Data. Understanding differences over time—whether trends in weather or frequency of events—is a foundational idea that underlies climate change. This concept is introduced in kindergarten, and by second grade students are representing and interpreting data in a number of different formats. For example, the standard below is at the third-grade level:

CCSS.MATH.CONTENT.3.MD.B.3

Draw a scaled picture graph and a scaled bar graph to represent a data set with several categories. Solve one- and two-step "how many more" and "how many less" problems using information presented in scaled bar graphs.

The "3" in this standard indicates that this is a third-grade standard, while the "MD" tells the reader that it is about measurement and data. A teacher could easily use this standard to help students understand changes in frequency in tropical storms or incidents of wildfires, some common effects of human-caused climate change. In later grades, more nuanced investigations grounded in statistics and probability are covered:

CCSS.MATH.CONTENT.HSS.MD.A.2

Calculate the expected value of a random variable; interpret it as the mean of the probability distribution.

This standard includes "HS," which indicates it is at the high school level, while again, the "MD" notes that it is also about measurement and data. As global temperatures continue to rise, there are more frequent wildfires and forest fires in general (Figure 7.3). You can use data related to trends in wildfire frequency to ask students to predict the likelihood or frequency of those events in the future.

FIGURE 7.3 • Forest Fire

Source: Istock.com/mack2happy

Yet, climate change instruction in a mathematics context should not be limited to measurement alone. There are many other opportunities to use mathematics skills to unpack ideas about climate change. Think about this fifth-grade geometry standard:

CCSS.MATH.CONTENT.5.G.A.1

Graph points on the coordinate plane to solve real-world and mathematical problems.

Some of the most engaging climate change lessons are grounded in climate solutions. Wind farms, both onshore and offshore, are excellent alternatives to burning fossil fuels. However, decisions about where to place wind turbines can be hard to make and require thinking about multiple factors: migrating bird patterns, wind patterns, and suitability of ground (or seafloor) cover are just a few. Using coordinate planes to model these factors can help students consider the complex factors that interact when making these kinds of decisions (Figure 7.4). This mathematical concept is introduced in fifth grade and develops further into middle school, as demonstrated in the seventh-grade standard below:

FIGURE 7.4 • Map of Planned Wind Turbine Placement at an Onshore Wind Farm in Scotland

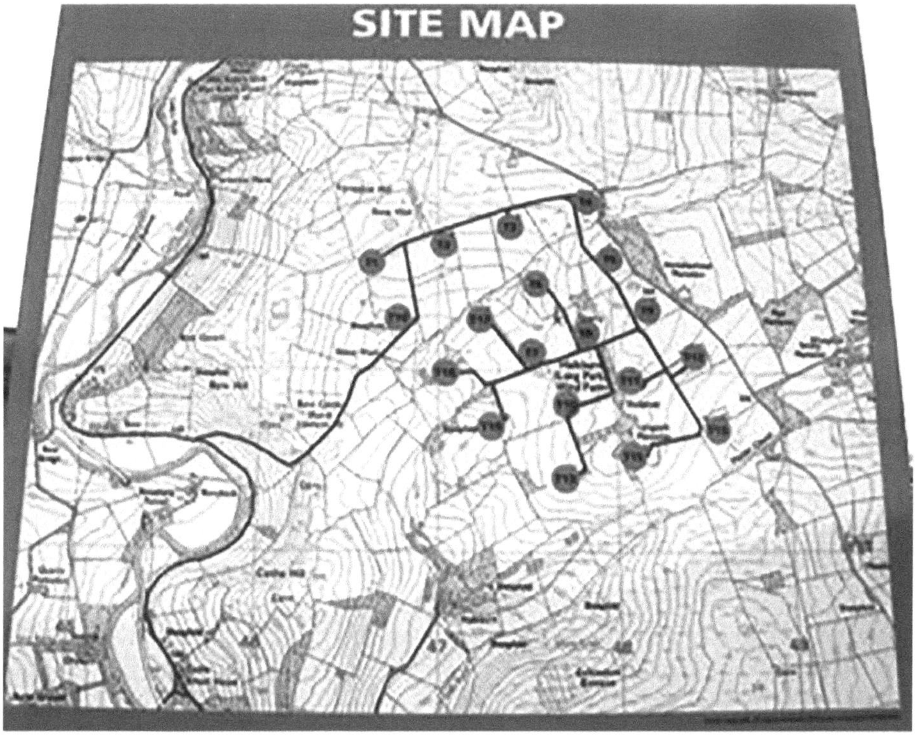

Source: Map of Long Park Wind Farm by M. J. Richardson geograph.org.uk/p/5402214, cc-by-sa/2.0

CCSS.MATH.CONTENT.7.G.B.6

Solve real-world and mathematical problems involving area, volume and surface area of two- and three-dimensional objects composed of triangles, quadrilaterals, polygons, cubes, and right prisms.

> **Project SEA's curricular materials are offered online for free and include a fifth-grade lesson using a *Battleship*-type game in which students can model where to plant wind farms. qrs.ly/ o2g3eoi**

SOCIAL STUDIES AND CLIMATE CHANGE

In 2013, the National Council for the Social Studies (NCSS) published a framework for social studies standards with a similar vision to the NGSS and CCSS: the College, Career, and Civic Life Framework for Social Studies State Standards, better known as the C3 Framework (NCSS, 2022). Rather than prescribing specific content to cover in social studies courses, the C3 Framework provides clear guidance in the form of inquiry arcs or pathways that teachers can use to construct coherent learning sequences. The C3 Framework consists of four key dimensions.

- Dimension 1: Developing Questions and Planning Inquiries
- Dimension 2: Applying Disciplinary Tools and Concepts
  - These concepts are further broken down into civics, economics, geography, and history.
- Dimension 3: Evaluating Sources and Using Evidence
- Dimension 4: Communicating Conclusions and Taking Informed Action

Here are some possible inquiry arcs on climate change that teachers can implement with the key dimensions:

Secondary Students

Dimension 1: Developing Questions and Planning Inquiries

- Students can brainstorm questions about climate change's impact on historical events, like the Dust Bowl and its effect on migration patterns in the United States.

- Another inquiry could focus on potential scenarios and how societies might adapt to rising sea levels.

Dimension 2: Applying Disciplinary Tools and Concepts

- Civics: Analyze policies like carbon pricing or international climate agreements and their effectiveness.

- Economics: Explore the economic costs of climate change (e.g., extreme weather events) and potential benefits of renewable energy investments.

- Geography: Examine the geographical distribution of climate change impacts and how they influence resource availability in different regions.

- History: Investigate past civilizations that collapsed due to environmental changes and analyze how societies can learn from these examples.

Dimension 3: Evaluating Sources and Using Evidence

- Students can compare and contrast scientific data on climate change from different sources, assessing their credibility.

- Analyze historical documents and images to understand past climate patterns and their influence on human societies.

Dimension 4: Communicating Conclusions and Taking Informed Action

- Students can present their research findings on climate change, advocating for solutions through presentations, debates, or mock policy proposals.

- Research local environmental initiatives and explore ways to get involved in community action.

The C3 Framework's core principles can also be adapted for younger learners to introduce them to climate change in an age-appropriate and engaging way. Here's how the four key dimensions can be used:

1. **Developing Questions and Planning Inquiries**
   - **Spark Curiosity:** Use age-appropriate stories, pictures, or videos that depict unusual weather events or environmental changes. Ask open-ended questions like "Why do you think the animals are having trouble finding water?" or "What would happen if it rained all the time?" Encourage student questions and brainstorm together.
   - **Simple Investigations:** Plan hands-on activities to introduce basic climate concepts. For example, students can observe how sunlight warms the Earth using a terrarium or experiment with melting ice cubes to understand rising temperatures.

2. **Applying Disciplinary Tools and Concepts**
   - **Geography for Little Learners:** Use maps and globes to show different locations and discuss how weather patterns can vary. Introduce basic vocabulary like "hot" and "cold" climates and how they affect the environment.
   - **Simplified Civics:** Introduce the concept of caring for our planet. Discuss simple ways people can help, like conserving water or throwing away trash properly.

3. **Evaluating Sources and Using Evidence**
   - **Focus on Observations:** Encourage students to use their senses to observe the world around them. They can record their observations in weather journals, drawing or writing about daily weather patterns.
   - **Age-Appropriate Resources:** Use reliable resources like children's books with clear illustrations and simple explanations about climate change and its effects.

4. **Communicating Conclusions and Taking Informed Action**
   - **Creative Expression:** Students can express their understanding of ways to protect the environment through drawings, songs, or short stories.
   - **Community Action:** Organize age-appropriate activities like planting a tree in the schoolyard, participating in a local clean-up event, or creating posters promoting water conservation.

Collaboration Between Subject Areas

The C3 Framework also encourages collaboration between social studies and other disciplines like science. Teachers can design units that explore the scientific aspects of climate change alongside its social and historical implications.

Here are some ideas for secondary students:

1. Climate Change and Historical Events
   - Social Studies: Analyze historical documents and data on past climate events like the Little Ice Age. Explore its impact on agricultural practices, societal structures, and population shifts in Europe.
   - Science: Research the scientific mechanisms behind the Little Ice Age, such as volcanic eruptions and changes in solar activity. Analyze historical temperature data and ice core records to understand past climate fluctuations.

2. The Future of Food and Climate Change
   - Social Studies: Investigate the economic and political implications of climate change for global food production and distribution. Analyze potential food shortages and explore policy solutions to ensure food security.
   - Science: Research the impact of climate change on agricultural yields, such as rising temperatures, changing precipitation patterns, and extreme weather events. Explore scientific advancements in drought-resistant crops and sustainable farming practices.

3. Climate Change and Public Policy

   - Social Studies: Analyze the historical development of environmental policies and international agreements on climate change mitigation. Debate the effectiveness of different policy approaches like carbon pricing or cap-and-trade systems.

   - Science: Research the scientific basis for different policy approaches and their potential environmental and economic impacts. Analyze climate modeling data to predict future climate scenarios under various policy interventions.

4. Climate Change and Indigenous Knowledge

   - Social Studies: Explore the traditional knowledge and practices of indigenous communities living in harmony with their environment for generations. Analyze how these communities have adapted to changing climate patterns.

   - Science: Investigate how indigenous knowledge systems can inform scientific research on climate change adaptation and resource management. Analyze the potential for integrating traditional ecological knowledge with modern scientific approaches.

5. The Ethics of Climate Change

   - Social Studies: Examine the ethical implications of climate change, such as the disproportionate impact on developing countries and future generations. Discuss the concept of climate justice and international cooperation for a sustainable future.

   - Science: Research the science behind the concept of tipping points in the climate system and potential irreversible environmental damage. Analyze the ethical considerations of geoengineering solutions to mitigate climate change.

Here are possible collaborations for younger students:

1. Storytelling and Inquiry

   - Social Studies: We can begin by reading a story about a fictional town facing unusual weather patterns. Maybe it's raining more than usual, causing floods, or there's a long drought making it difficult to grow crops.

   - Science: Students can then brainstorm reasons why the weather might be changing. This sparks curiosity and encourages them to think about the concept of climate change.

2. Exploring the World
   - Social Studies: We can virtually travel the world (through pictures or videos) and see how different places experience climate change. Students can compare their own local weather patterns to others and discuss how climate affects people's lives.
   - Science: Introduce the concept of "average weather" and how it's different from short-term changes. Students can learn about factors like temperature, precipitation, and wind patterns that contribute to climate.

3. Creative Problem Solving
   - Social Studies: Students can design solutions for the fictional town facing climate challenges. Maybe they brainstorm ways to conserve water during a drought or come up with ideas to prevent floods.
   - Science: Explore simple ways to reduce our impact on the environment, like using less energy at home or planting trees. Students can create posters or drawings to promote these solutions.

4. Collaboration and Action
   - Social Studies: Partner with the school garden or local environmental organization. Students can learn about sustainable gardening practices or participate in a community clean-up project.
   - Science: Explore renewable energy sources like wind or solar power. Students can create simple models of these technologies to understand how they work.

Though specific content and topics are not laid out in the C3 Framework, it can be used as a way to explore climate change through the lens of social studies. Climate change is listed as a key glossary topic in the framework:

> *Climate change: Long-term significant variations in average weather conditions on Earth, particularly in temperatures and precipitation, that are caused by either natural or human induced processes. Example: Alterations in the physical dynamics of Earth's atmosphere that affect the climate may result from natural phenomena, such as extensive volcanic eruptions, or human practices, such as burning fossil fuels. (NCSS, 2022, p. 103)*

The idea that human populations have moved over time due to climate variability can serve as a jumping-off point for an inquiry into climate change. Students will need to think about the physical geography of human settlements and how that has changed over the course of history. Furthermore, students can investigate reasons for emigrating to another country and how changing populations can affect resource use or economics. The C3 Framework offers additional suggestions for inquiries focused on climate change and can help teachers to ensure that social studies topics are also considered when crafting interdisciplinary units around climate. Here are some suggestions:

- Social Justice: Investigate the unequal distribution of climate change impacts and how marginalized communities are disproportionately affected.

- Human Rights: Analyze how climate change can lead to displacement and potential human rights violations.

- Technology and Innovation: Explore the role of technological advancements in mitigating climate change (e.g., renewable energy sources) and adapting to its effects.

INTEGRATING ACROSS SEVERAL CONTENT AREAS

The NGSS, CCSS, and C3 Framework offer obvious opportunities for exploring the phenomena around climate change, the difference between weather and climate, the ways we can advocate for climate action, and the way we can visualize (and numerically represent) data to use as evidence to support or refute claims. As a result, we can use them as frameworks for structuring learning that integrates across content areas. Studies suggest that using an interdisciplinary approach to climate change instruction leads to more meaningful learning for students (Dolan, 2021; Leve et al., 2023).

The standards themselves provide a framework to truly make interdisciplinary investigations come to life. Imagine your school green team decided to start a composting project for fruit and vegetable scraps in the school cafeteria. How could this tie into standards-based instruction? How could it help children to learn more about climate change?

In fifth grade, the NGSS include some very clear and specific guidance on this very topic with the following performance expectation:

Students who demonstrate understanding can:

5-LS2-1. Develop a model to describe the movement of matter among plants, animals, decomposers, and the environment.

Starting with simple weekly observations, children can say a lot about the way animals (humans, and perhaps worms or other bugs) interact with plant matter. Over time, as the scraps become compost, the role of decomposers will become clear. Using simple drawings alongside photographs, students can have real-time data to inform their models. As they wait for changes or weekly observations, they can spend time reading informational texts about compost and writing newsletters for the school community, their parents, and teachers. Finally, students can measure and compare temperature inside and outside the composter, and calculate mass before and after the composting process. A cafeteria composter isn't simply a nice way to reduce waste in a school—it's a wealth of learning opportunities for students (Figure 7.5).

FIGURE 7.5 • An Outdoor Food Composter

Source: Istock.com/Piotr_malczyk

Though waste reduction is an inherently sustainable act, students might need some help connecting the act of composting with climate change. Again, informational texts can play an important role in building this understanding. The science is clear: Excess food waste can lead to increases in greenhouse gas emissions—from the waste itself to the fuel needed to transport it. Keeping this waste in a composter, where the end product can be used to fertilize school or community vegetable gardens, provides an opportunity for circular systems that reduce waste and enhance efficiency. And using that compost to fertilize a school garden provides further opportunities for children to engage in interdisciplinary learning. It's also an excellent way to give students the chance to get involved and make a difference, which we know offers them hope for the future (see Chapter 5).

At the second-grade level, the NGSS offer this performance expectation:

> *Students who demonstrate understanding can:*
>
> *2-LS2-1. Plan and conduct an investigation to determine if plants need sunlight and water to grow.*

Young children, even in the early childhood grades, can plant, write about, care for, measure, draw, and finally eat the products of their school garden. The simple act of composting food waste can start as an activity for one grade level and lend itself to schoolwide collaboration and inquiry in a standards-based environment.

You can probably see by now: The standards that guide instruction should not be seen as limiting factors to teachers' creativity. Rather, they can serve as a set of criteria to guide exploration.

WHERE DO I FIND STANDARDS-ALIGNED CLIMATE CHANGE TEACHING RESOURCES?

At first blush, yes, learning standards can feel overwhelming. But when read carefully, with climate change in mind, they can be used as great jumping-off points for planning instruction. But don't feel like you have to write every lesson from scratch! There are some excellent tools freely available to support teachers' climate change instruction.

· ·

 Q: What curriculum resources are available that show how humans are contributing to climate change?

Joan Gillman, The Browning School, New York City, NY

A: There are many expert-reviewed resources from reputable organizations for teaching about human contributions to climate change. Read on to learn more.

· ·

SubjectToClimate (subjecttoclimate.org) provides free resources for teaching about climate change, from teacher professional development to lessons, units, and activities. The site allows visitors to search by type of resource—from short readings or videos that can be used to enhance instruction to complete standards-aligned lesson plans with linked editable Google Slides presentations and handouts for students. SubjectToClimate offers multiple entry points for teachers just beginning to integrate climate change into their teaching, to seasoned experts looking for some more variety and updates to their repertoires. Teachers can feel confident using these resources as they are reviewed by teachers for developmental appropriateness and scientists for content accuracy.

Another great place to look for climate change teaching resources is the teacher professional organizations.

- The National Science Teaching Association (NSTA, nsta.org) also provides a searchable database of resources. Teachers can enter key terms or specific NGSS performance expectations and receive a plethora of expert-reviewed instructional materials.

- The National Council for Teachers of English (NCTE) released a Resolution on Literacy Teaching on Climate Change in 2019 (https://qrs.ly/b9g37f6).

- NCTE sponsors presentations that offer teacher- and professor-created resources that can be adapted for classroom use in English Language Arts (https://qrs.ly/axg37f8).

- Though they do not have dedicated resources for teaching about climate change, the National Council for Teachers of Mathematics (NCTM) endorses the teaching of mathematics through phenomena and modeling. Both problems related to climate change and solutions to these problems provide many opportunities for discussing phenomena in our natural world.

Where are your go-to places for finding good lessons and resources?

However, teachers don't always need to search solely with standards in mind. A multitude of other reputable groups and organizations offer additional climate change teaching resources to integrate into existing curricula or build new units around, once a teacher has identified a standard and is looking for additional tools to share with students:

- NASA's Climate Kids (https://climatekids.nasa.gov/) is an interactive website with games, videos, readings, and slide shows focused on many different climate-related topics.

- Rethinking Schools (https://rethinkingschools.org/) is a magazine for teachers offering lesson ideas and personal vignettes focused on activism. This site is easily searchable and includes many climate change and climate justice resources.

- Green Teacher (https://greenteacher.com/) is a magazine dedicated to environmental education broadly, with many ideas and activities focused on climate change.

- PBS Learning Media (https://whyy.pbslearningmedia.org/) is an easily searchable tool with complete lesson plans, videos, and student handouts. This site integrates climate change among many other topics.

Climate change is perhaps the most critical and influential issue of our lifetimes, and as we've been discussing, it is sometimes seen as controversial. But as educators we owe it to our students to discuss this topic, its causes, and potential solutions, so they are empowered to solve the problems humanity is certain to face in the future. As we have argued in earlier chapters, using learning standards as the framework for exploring climate change content can help teachers to justify instructional decisions if they face pushback or confrontation.

Here are some suggestions for creating standards-aligned climate change lessons:

1. Before searching for new activities, review your existing curriculum and assess places where you can make small shifts to integrate climate change examples.

2. Build from students' ideas! When students come to class with questions about climate change, even if you can't respond in the moment, use those questions as starting points for the future.

3. Connect to your school community! Whenever possible, make sure your climate change instruction can connect to bigger issues within your school and greater community to build relevance and salience.

LEARNING FROM OUR COLLEAGUES
Using Persuasive Writing to Teach Climate Change

Ms. Chan and Mrs. Schafer teach inclusive third grade in northern New Jersey. Their classroom is full of books, flexible seating choices, artwork, plants, and sunshine. Early in the school day, after completing some daily housekeeping activities, the children leave their pods of desks to join their teachers on the rug at the front of the classroom.

(Continued)

(Continued)

Ms. Chan asked, "What do we remember about persuasive writing? Why would we use writing to persuade someone of something?"

Mrs. Schafer jumped in, "Do you remember when we used persuasive writing earlier this year in third grade?"

A boy shyly lifts his head and tentatively raises his hand.

"Yes Luke," Ms. Chan responds, "Do you want to share?"

Luke, feeling just a little surer of himself recalls, "Well, we wrote letters to the service dog people about having a dog visit our class!"

"That's right!" exclaimed Mrs. Schafer, "What kinds of things did we say to the service dog people?"

With this prompt, Rita chimes in, "We learned that service dogs help people with disabilities from watching a video, and we wanted to persuade them to bring one to visit our class so we could learn more."

"Super!" Ms. Chan exclaimed. "Well, today, we're going to learn about another kind of persuasive writing. We're going to learn about petitions and eventually write one. Has anyone heard the word petition *before? Do you think you could guess what it means?"*

There were no hands raised or head nods, so Ms. Chan moved on. "A petition is a letter that a people or group of people write to ask for something to change. It sends a strong message. Then, after that letter is written, the writer asks other people who agree to sign in agreement. When the person in charge receives the letter, they know this isn't the concern of just one person; it is something important to many people."

Mrs. Schafer asked, "Can you see how a petition is a different kind of persuasive writing? More than just a letter on its own?"

The children nodded in agreement.

"What have we noticed about the weather these past few months?" Ms. Chan followed. The students were quick to respond.

"It is SO rainy!"

"It has been raining since December almost every day!"

"Even when it isn't raining the grass is too soggy for us to play outside."

"Exactly!" exclaimed Ms. Chan, "And when we can't play outside on the grass, we sure do get antsy! We can't all fit on the basketball court, and even more, not everyone wants to play basketball."

Mrs. Schafer added, "Do you know some reasons for all this rain? Do you remember what we learned in science?"

Jack responded, "Well, the climate is changing. That means that weather is going to be less predictable, and around here, we're getting A LOT more storms."

"You're right," said Ms. Chan. "But there is something we can do to try to solve this problem. There are plants that can help keep the soil in place we might want to add to our schoolyard. We can also add better drainage, so that the grass doesn't get so soggy. But we can't do that by ourselves. We're going to need help."

Annie raised her hand, "Maybe we could write a petition and get the whole school to sign! Then we won't have to miss so much recess when it gets so rainy."

Mrs. Schafer smiled and shared, "I think you're right, but we need to do some research first!"

"So today, we're going to learn more about petitions, especially petitions that kids have written that have been successful. Next week, we're going to the library to learn about plants that can help keep our soil in place, and after that we'll talk with the groundskeepers about drainage in our playground. Then, after we've done our research, we can write a petition." Ms. Chan noted.

The children stayed seated on the carpet and watched several videos about successful petitions written by kids on change.org, including the one that sparked Crayola's marker recycling program (Crayola, 2024).

After class, Ms. Chan explained that she needed to teach about persuasive writing, and this was a way to connect writing to the effects of climate change her students feel daily. As a result, the children had a chance to see many examples of student activism and action, connect their own experiences to a bigger phenomenon, and use the opportunity to take action themselves.

Reflection Questions

1. When you think about integrating climate change in your lessons, what gets you most excited?

2. What do you see as the biggest challenges to teaching about climate change in your school? What about the biggest assets?

3. What are some topics and tried-and-true lessons you use that can be adapted to integrate climate change?

4. Who are the colleagues in your school or district that you can connect with to generate collaborative climate change lessons?

5. Which standards at your grade level or in your content area lend themselves best to climate change?

6. What climate questions come up frequently from your students? How can you use these to prompt lessons?

7. What are the local effects of climate change that your students experience? Can you use those as jumping-off points for future lessons?

For Further Reading

FOR TEACHERS

Edutopia. (2023, September). *Making climate change connections in every class*. qrs.ly/k2g3eoj

Kamenetz, A. (2024, February). The climate change lesson plans teachers need and don't have. *KQED Mindshift.* https://qrs.ly/6tg37fh

Worth, K. (2022). *Miseducation: How climate change is taught in America*. Columbia University Press.

FOR STUDENTS
Ages 4–9

Barr, C., & Williams, S. (2021). *The story of climate change: A first book about how we can help save our planet*. Frances Lincoln Children's Books.

Ages 5–8

Reynolds, P. H. (2019). *Say something!* Scholastic.

Ages 5–9

Meadows, M. (2024). *Green machines and other amazing eco-inventions.* Random House.

CHAPTER EIGHT

LEARNING FROM THE NEW JERSEY EXPERIENCE

....

Teaching our kids about climate change can make a difference in their ability to succeed in our changing economy. That's why I've led the charge to put in place a climate curriculum in schools, making NJ the first and only state in the nation to do so.

—*Tammy S. Murphy, First Lady of New Jersey*

THIS CHAPTER WILL DISCUSS

- A brief history of climate change education in New Jersey
- The process by which comprehensive climate change standards were developed and adopted across grade levels and subject areas K–12
- The pathways other states have taken to achieve similar goals; and
- Suggestions for implementing climate change education elsewhere

In June 2020, New Jersey's First Lady, Tammy Snyder Murphy, announced that the state would become the first in the nation to integrate climate change into learning standards across grade levels and subject areas (Office of the Governor, 2020). This announcement built upon prior commitments to climate change instruction. In 2014, New Jersey adopted the Next Generation Science Standards, which—as we discussed in the last chapter—include climate change ideas in science during middle and high school. Expanding the scope of this commitment to include all subjects and grades allows teachers and children to view this global issue as comprehensive and interdisciplinary, as it is.

 LAUREN: THIS IS MY STORY

Having spent my career focused on enhancing scientific literacy and the health of our planet through teaching and learning, I was thrilled to learn of Mrs. Murphy's priorities as First Lady of New Jersey. Though great curricular materials exist, finding time in a school day to implement anything "extra" is a tremendous challenge. With standards in place, New Jersey made this priority an actionable one. Though standards are not the only strategy for implementing comprehensive climate change education, they do represent a clear path other states might wish to follow. I had the good fortune of being asked to review the standards as part of the development process as well as to provide feedback on their implementation. This resulted in a recommendations report and series of preliminary research projects that helped them hit the ground running. Though we are early in the process, it is clear that children across New Jersey are building meaningful understanding around the way our climate is changing, like the ones pictured in Figure 8.1 below, planting native plants in their school garden.

FIGURE 8.1 • Students at Eldridge Park School in Lawrence, New Jersey, planting native species in a school garden.

Source: Kristin Burke

This chapter will detail the way in which these standards came to be, and the beginning steps of how they are being implemented, as a roadmap for other states. We will also explore current work on state standards in California, Connecticut, Maine, and New York.

> Standards are not curriculum. They are simply the guidelines used to select or create curriculum. Including climate change in learning standards requires the topic to be included in lessons but does not describe how or when to do so.

CLIMATE CHANGE IN NEW JERSEY

Although climate change affects all inhabitants of Earth, as we have discussed elsewhere in this book, it affects some more than others. In New Jersey, in recent years, we've started to pay more attention to the way in which the effects of climate change impact the state's citizens and ecosystems (Figure 8.2).

FIGURE 8.2 • Flooding on Rutgers University's Campus after Hurricane Ida, 2021

Source: istock.com/Sarah J Lee

Q: How do I go about making this topic applicable to second graders so that they will understand the science of climate change?

Mrs. Rogers, Caston Elementary School, Rochester, IN

A: One great way to get young learners involved in climate change education is connecting it to the plants and animals around us. Examining the effects of climate change, such as flooding, on the living things in our schoolyard can ensure that second graders have a personal connection to the topic. The mathematics and vocabulary don't have to be presented at the adult level. Rather, connect with second graders on a personal level to allow them to unpack their learning within their own context.

Effects of Climate Change in New Jersey

According to scientists, New Jersey experiences disproportionate effects of climate change relative to other places in the United States and around the world (New Jersey Department of Environmental Protection, 2020). In 2019, Governor Phil Murphy signed an executive order establishing a state chief resilience officer and mandating the development of a formal scientific report on climate change in the state (Exec. Order #89, 2019). In response to this order, in 2020, the state's Department of Environmental Protection released a report on climate change, detailing the specific effects experienced by New Jersey's nine million residents (New Jersey Department of Environmental Protection, 2020):

- Annual predicted precipitation increases from 4–11% by 2050

- Sea level rise at faster rates than the rest of the United States

- Longer and hotter summer heatwaves

- Drought conditions that could last from three to six months in a given year

- Lower crop and livestock stability, and therefore food supply challenges, due to climate-induced temperature and precipitation changes

- Increased air pollution, and resultant expected health challenges, particularly in the most vulnerable populations (see Figure 8.3)

FIGURE 8.3 • Elmwood Park, New Jersey, after a flooding event in late 2023.

Source: iStock.com/Johnrob

This report emphasizes that the most damaging effects of climate change will be faced by children, elderly individuals urban communities, and communities that lack infrastructure for mitigation of climate effects, such as those without many permeable surfaces, dedicated cooling stations, or green infrastructure. Along with this report, the Murphy administration also established key governmental structures to study the effects of climate change and identify strategies for mitigation and remediation.

. . . .

Q&A   **Q:** How do we encourage public schools to decrease their footprint in their cafeteria?

Kim Decker, Dyersburg City Schools, Dyersburg, TN

A: One useful tool for decreasing a school's carbon footprint is decreasing food waste. Bring a scale into your school's cafeteria and challenge students to weigh their food waste. Tally the total each day and see if they are able to decrease the amount of food waste entering the landfills over the course of a week. Perhaps you can inspire further changes in the kitchen with these actions!

. . . .

Systemic Approaches to Studying and Mitigating Climate Change in New Jersey and Elsewhere

The Murphy administration implemented several key plans to identify and combat the ways in which New Jersey's changing climate impacts its population. These plans include setting up formal structures such as the Statewide Heat Resilience Action Plan,[1] featuring step-by-step guidance for helping those affected by extreme heat, and the Flood Resource Toolkit,[2] which provides guidance for those experiencing floods.

What roles do teachers play in making sure that the most vulnerable among us have the tools they need to mitigate the effects of climate change?

These guides demonstrate a commitment to understanding and dealing with the challenges that climate change can bring, from a systemic state-wide perspective. They also provide teachers with opportunities for unpacking primary sources so that students can learn about real-time problems and solutions to climate change in their classrooms. It is perhaps not surprising that the state also turned its attention to education. Recent research, such as a predictive study conducted by Cordero, Centano, and Todd (2020), suggests that widespread climate education could account for a nearly 20-gigaton reduction in atmospheric carbon emissions—putting education at among the top 25% of potential solutions listed by Project Drawdown.

Project Drawdown is a nonprofit organization dedicated to using science-based approaches to build climate solutions. Their mission is to "help the world stop climate change—as quickly, safely, and equitably as possible." https://drawdown.org/

Globally, leaders are calling for education as a tool for action against the effects of climate change, too. "The UN Framework Convention on Climate Change, the Paris Agreement and the associated Action for Climate Empowerment (ACE) agenda call on governments to educate, empower and engage all stakeholders and major groups on policies and actions relating to climate change" (UNESCO, 2021).

---

[1] https://dep.nj.gov/climatechange/resilience/resilience-action-plans

[2] https://dep.nj.gov/climatechange/resilience/flood-resource-toolkit/

IMPLEMENTING CLIMATE CHANGE EDUCATION STANDARDS

As a state, New Jersey demonstrated that it took climate change seriously, with comprehensive programs to study and mitigate the effects across sectors. Yet, operationalizing these programs is different from planning them. Teachers in New Jersey had mixed levels of confidence and understanding regarding what climate change was and how to teach it. In a recent study surveying 166 New Jersey teachers, many teachers reported feeling mixed levels of comfort teaching about climate change, and several conflated climate change with other environmental issues such as marine plastic pollution (Madden, Ammentorp, et al., 2023). Yet, the findings also revealed that teachers were eager to learn more about teaching climate change to enhance their own professional practice.

TIPS TO MAKE A DIFFERENCE: Stop the Drip
Debbie Bond, PACE Academy, Columbia, SC

1. Lather with the water off when washing your hair.

Georgia Brewer, Marion School District, Marion, AR

2. Make sure you set your washing machine on high spin to reduce the amount of time clothes need in the dryer.

Soon after the announcement that New Jersey would adopt comprehensive climate change education standards, the nonprofit Sustainable Jersey for Schools, in partnership with the New Jersey School Boards Association, commissioned a report to identify the state's needs in advance of implementation. Their *Report on K–12 Climate Change Education Needs in New Jersey* was published in February 2022, approximately eight months before teachers would begin using them in their day-to-day work (Madden, 2022). The report considered the opinions of a multitude of experts: teacher-leaders, school administrators, higher education faculty, and environmental educators. These experts were asked to identify the biggest needs faced by collaborator groups through several rounds of surveys and discussions. Findings were categorized into four key areas:

- Access to high quality curricular resources

- Professional learning opportunities for teachers and other school staff

- Community-based climate change connections

- Support from administrators and school boards in implementing these new standards

Consider writing an op-ed or blog piece for a local newspaper to share your work in teaching climate change: It might have a ripple effect!

These key areas are reflected in our own research in preparation for this book (see the Editor's Note at the beginning of the book).

· ·

 Q: Is there an easy way to explain the role of oceans as a carbon sink?

Andrew McCullough, Brunswick High School, Brunswick, ME

A: Imagine Earth's oceans as giant sponges. The plants and algae photosynthesize and take in a large portion of the carbon dioxide we release, preventing it from accumulating solely in the atmosphere and causing further warming. However, just like a sponge eventually gets saturated, the oceans' capacity to absorb carbon dioxide is not limitless. This simplified explanation effectively conveys three key aspects of the ocean's role as a carbon sink:

- **Absorption:** Oceans absorb a significant amount of atmospheric CO_2.

- **Storage:** This CO_2 is stored within the oceans, mitigating its warming effect on the atmosphere.

- **Consequences:** Ocean acidification is a negative consequence of this absorption process. Ocean acidification threatens sea life and habitats.

· ·

The findings suggested that to fully enact the vision of comprehensive climate change education, teachers needed teaching tools; time to prepare; and support from colleagues, administrators, school boards, and community members. A survey of teachers across the state supported these findings (Madden, Heddy, et al., 2023). Teachers want help! (This is why we wrote this book!)

What the Standards Look Like

The New Jersey Climate Change Education Standards for seven key subject areas were shared with teachers in spring 2022:

- Visual and Performing Arts

- Comprehensive Health and Physical Education

- Science

- Social Studies

- World Languages

- Computer Science & Design Thinking

- Career Readiness, Life Literacies, and Key Skills

They were implemented first in September at the start of the academic year. On the State Department of Education's website,[3] the standards are organized by grade band: K–2, 3–5, 6–8, and 9–12. Dropdown menus allow site visitors to see all the standards at a given grade band, sorted by subject (see Figure 8.4 for a K–2 example).

TIPS TO MAKE A DIFFERENCE: Avoid Busy Drive Times
Shanna Dowd, Wingate Andrews High, High Point, NC

1. Plan travel to avoid traffic as a way to save gas.

---

[3]https://www.nj.gov/education/climate/learning/gradeband/

FIGURE 8.4 • K–2 Climate Change Standards for Visual and Performing Arts

Kindergarten Through Grade 2	⌃

Visual and Performing Arts

Enduring Understandings	Performance Expectations
As dance is experienced, all personal experience, knowledge and contexts are integrated and synthesized to interpret meaning.	1.12 Cn 10b: Using an inquiry-based set of questions to examine global issues, including climate change as a topic of dance.
Artist's appreciation of media artworks is influenced by their interests, experiences, understandings, and purposes. Identifying the qualities and characteristics of media artworks improves the individual's aesthetic and empathetic awareness.	1.2.2.Re7b: Identify, share and describe a variety of media artworks created from different experiences in response to global issues including climate change.
As theater is created and experienced, personal experiences and knowledge are synthesized to interpret meaning and analyze the way in which the world may be understood.	1.4.2.Cn11a: With prompting and support, identify similarities and differences in stories and various art forms from one's own community and from multiple cultures in a guided drama (e.g. process drama, story drama, creative drama) experience about global issues, including climate change.
People develop ideas and understandings of society, culture and history through their interactions with and analysis of art.	1.5.2.Cn11b. Describe why people from different places and times make art about different issues, including climate change.

Source: New Jersey Department of Education (2024a).

These standards do not replace important subject area content with ideas about climate change. Rather, they point out opportunities for teachers to integrate climate change at junctures where it would be an appropriate connection or real-life example. Let's look at the social studies standards for Grades 3–5:

> For this important core idea about geography, "Regions form and change as a result of unique physical characteristics conditions, economies, and cultures," children will engage in the following performance expectation:

> 6.1.5.GeoPP.2: Describe how landforms, climate and weather, and availability of resources have impacted where and how people live and work in different regions of New Jersey and the United States.

This standard provides clear and straightforward opportunities for discussing maps, aerial photographs, and weather data to discuss the impacts of climate change, such as the image in Figure 8.5.

FIGURE 8.5 • Destruction at a New Jersey Shore Amusement Park After Hurricane Sandy in 2012

Source: istock.com/skrum

 TIPS TO MAKE A DIFFERENCE: Get Cozy!

Kim Demarest, Sault Area Public Schools, Sault Ste. Marie, MI

1. To save food, make one meal a week from leftovers (like stone soup!).

2. Place lots of fun soft snug blankets on seating at home and keep the thermostat turned down.

3. Wear a hat outside to stay warmer in the cold weather.

How Do the Guidelines for English Language Arts and Mathematics Differ?

Browsing the New Jersey climate change standards' website, a viewer might wonder where English Language Arts (ELA) and Mathematics fit in. This is especially curious as these subjects tend to provide the bulk of the curriculum in the elementary years. Given the timeframe for standards adoption

What are some ways you can use climate change examples during more traditional ELA or mathematics instruction?

in New Jersey, the ELA and Mathematics standards were updated a few years later, with a scheduled implementation in the 2024–25 academic year. These standards came with companion guides that can support teachers weaving climate change into their instruction in these important content areas.

 Q: How do I get students involved in slowing climate change?

Marianne Zupanc, La Jolla Country Day School, La Jolla, CA

A: It's very important to get students involved, but as educators we want to make sure students don't feel the burden of fixing climate change on their own. We should teach students about individual and collective responses to climate change. Encouraging students to take individual actions can help them feel empowered, and asking them to evaluate the decisions they will make as adults in the voting booth and with their money can be even more impactful. Even before they reach adulthood, students can use their voices to advocate for political candidates and decisions that have positive outcomes for the planet.

THE LARGER PICTURE OF CLIMATE CHANGE EDUCATION IN THE UNITED STATES

Q&A **Q:** How does pollution of the oceans contribute to climate change?

Lanette Lanchester, Connecting Waters Charter School, Waterford, CA

A: Pollutants can affect the oceans in many different ways. For example, physical items like trash floating in the water can block algae from photosynthesizing and capturing carbon from the atmosphere. Other pollutants, such as runoff containing fertilizers, can cause algal blooms. When algae die, decomposers break them down, consuming oxygen and

Success Story: Recycling Electronics

Janet Villas, New Gardens Friends School, Greensboro, NC

In my experience, the best climate-related project is to run an electronics recycling drive. Your students will be shocked at the amount of junk we all have (Figure 8.6). I often recycle the wires for scrap and donate the cash to a worthy cause. Involve your students in recycling paper, plastic, etc. and ask your custodian where it all goes. Recently, our Upper School Environmental Science class was challenged to get 100 items donated to their E-waste Drive. They were pleased to announce they collected 130 items. The smaller items went to a county electronics drive, and the smartphones and tablets will go to #GorillasOnTheLine, an organization that supports gorilla habitats in Africa.

FIGURE 8.6 • Upper School Students at the Nee Gardens Friends School Electronics Drive

Source: Janet Villas

producing carbon dioxide, which can lead to the creation of anoxic dead zones. These algae can also block light from reaching organisms deeper beneath the ocean's surface, changing water temperature and therefore circulation patterns.

· ·

New Jersey provides a unique case in that it's learning standards *require* that climate change education be included in K–12 classroom instruction. This adoption is certainly different from the norm. The National Center for Education Statistics (NCES) conducted a nationwide study on how climate is being taught in schools across the United States (Plutzer et al., 2016). This study starts by emphasizing the critical importance of *classroom* teaching and learning. Of course, informal learning centers like parks and nature centers along with media-based learning contributes strongly to individuals' understanding of science, but the things children learn in K–12 school reach *all* sectors of society. The authors surveyed secondary science teachers from across all 50 states about a variety of climate change–related topics and the results were, not surprisingly, that climate change instruction varied quite a bit from teacher to teacher. See Chapter 1 for a broader discussion of how climate change is addressed in schools throughout the United States.

> Informal learning can be rewarding, but it is also inherently inequitable. Not all families have the assets needed—time, finances, and transportation to name a few—to provide children with opportunities to engage with learning environments outside of K–12 classrooms. These inequities can be mitigated with meaningful in-class instruction and family engagement through notes or electronic communication sent home with students.

It should also be made clear: New Jersey's progress on climate change education took place through executive, rather than legislative, action. As a result, these standards were developed and evaluated by the state's Department of Education and school board fairly quickly after the announcement. Their launch was also followed up with support: The state provided $4.5 million in grant funding for schools to prepare for climate change education during the 2022–23 academic year, the first full year of implementation (New Jersey Department of Education, 2023). The following academic year, New Jersey appointed a Senior Advisor on Climate Change Education to ensure the roll out of the standards was meeting the needs of teachers and schools (Office of the Governor, 2023). Soon after this announcement, the state provided funding opportunities, for schools as well as for institutions of higher education, emphasizing community-based partnerships to provide regional centers for climate change education support across the state (New Jersey Department of Education, 2024b, 2024c). With this sort of statewide organization, the recommendations from the earlier implementation report (Madden, 2022) stand a better chance of being realized. Other states, such as California, Connecticut, and Maine also built momentum for statewide efforts through the legislative process. Contacting your individual representatives may be a more effective process than reaching out to the governor's office.

> To date, Italy is the only country requiring climate change instruction starting in the early years. In 2019, Italy's education minister, Lorenzo Fioramonti, announced that all schools would be required to cover climate change and sustainable development for 33 hours each school year for all grade levels and subject areas (Jones, 2019).

TIPS TO MAKE A DIFFERENCE: Reduce Your Impact

Joan Gillman, The Browning School, New York City, NY

1. Use silverware as opposed to plastic disposable forks, spoons, and knives.
2. Donate your used clothes and toys if they are still in good shape rather than throwing them away.

Natalye James, Breck School, Golden Valley, MN

3. Use smaller lightbulbs (try holiday lights!) to illuminate the room.
4. Turn off the projector when not using.
5. Teach meaningful paper use.

Kristina Klammer, Beaver Country Day School, Chestnut Hill, MA

6. Reduce the number of days on which you consume meat (especially red meat).

California's Experience

By population, California is the largest state in the United States, with its 38 million residents comprising 12% of the United States population. As a result, educational initiatives in California influence a significant portion of the country overall. In 2019, in response to nationwide calls for climate change education in K–12 settings, the Environmental and Climate Change Literacy

Projects (ECCLPs) were formed. The ECCLPs are a collaborative partnership between preK–12 teachers, higher education professionals representing all 33 University of California and California State University campuses, environmental advocates, policy makers, and nonprofits. Together the ECCLPs use a justice, equity, diversity, and inclusion perspective to advance climate change literacy for youth and families across their state.

These projects include working with both preservice and practicing preK–12 teachers to create and implement climate change education using culturally relevant and solutions-oriented interdisciplinary learning. The ECCLPs' work is ongoing and comprehensive. It includes working with teacher credentialing programs and agencies to ensure those serving the classrooms of the future are well-prepared to enhance climate literacy in their future classrooms, identifying best practices for climate change education in group convenings of experts across sectors, and developing a bipartisan state task force prepared to advocate for widespread climate change literacy. At the time of this publication, the ECCLPs are working to identify existing strategies for integrating climate change in teacher credentialing programs, creating practical frameworks to guide future efforts, and conducting research to ensure evidence-based practices are used to enhance climate literacy.

Connecticut's Experience

In 2018, Connecticut State Representative Christine Palm proposed legislation to mandate climate change education beginning in fifth grade (Yang, 2022). Though studies revealed that climate change was already being covered in about 90% of the state's classroom, thanks in part to Connecticut being a state that adopted the Next Generation Science Standards, Palm presented CT House Bill 5285 with broad support from professionals throughout the education sector—superintendents, union representatives, teachers, and student-activists connected with the youth-led Sunrise Movement (Monk, 2022). This bill received bipartisan support and was followed by specific legislation around social studies education K–12. The state uses the National Council for the Social Studies' (NCSS) C3 Framework to guide its social studies standards and the ones focused directly on climate change (NCSS, 2013). The C3 Framework asks teachers to pose problems that require students to explore from multiple perspectives: civics, economics, geography, and history. Much like the NGSS, the C3 Framework provides a clear starting point for climate change instruction. Educators in Connecticut were able to continue to push for the inclusion of climate change in social studies as well. The Connecticut Department of Energy and Environmental Protection published guidelines for teachers and practical tools for integrating climate change into their classrooms on their website: https://qrs.ly/lrg37fm.

Source: istock.com/jacoblund

Maine's Experience

In the late 2010s, youth-led climate action came to the fore globally, and in Maine these youth leaders and activists came together to influence education. By late 2020, Maine's governor's office had a formal climate action plan in place outlining mitigation strategies for the effects of climate change, but this plan lacked guidance on education. A youth-led intergenerational group of students, educators, and community leaders affiliated with the Maine Environmental Education Association administered a survey to learn more about teachers' needs with respect to teaching about climate change. This group approached the governor's office and used statewide survey data to elevate the voices of teachers who indicated that they needed support and resources for teaching about climate change. These activists partnered with state representative Lydia Blume to craft a bill in 2022 that would provide grants for teacher professional development around climate change.

This bill was first denied by the state's legislative council, but Rep. Blume encouraged the group to request the decision be overturned. The group followed through with a teach-in for the legislative council and organized testimony from a multitude of collaborator groups including the Maine Youth Climate Justice Coalition. Eventually the bill, HP 1409 (Blume, 2022), passed both the house and senate and was signed by Governor Mills. This bill provided $2.1 million in funding to support climate education in schools across the state through teacher professional development and the organization of a Maine-specific climate change education hub, hosted by SubjectToClimate (https://subjecttoclimate.org/).

New York's Experience

Climate change education is not a new idea in New York, though the journey to passing legislation requiring teachers to implement the topic has been bumpy (Figure 8.7). In the 2019–2020 legislative session there were five climate education bills being considered in New York. By the 2021–2022 legislative session, a total of eight climate change education bills were assigned to committee, with goals ranging from codifying more specific climate change instruction within science and social studies classes to including grant funding for teachers to engage in professional learning around the topic (Branch, 2024a). As of the publication of this book, a bill by Manhattan representative Linda Rosenthal is in committee, waiting on a vote (Rosenthal, 2024).

FIGURE 8.7 • Activists marching in the Brooklyn Pride Parade.

Source: istock.com/Andrew Poulin

However, more progress has been made in New York City, while the state at large works to coalesce on a cohesive statewide plan. New York City's mayor's office hosts an Office of Climate and Environmental Justice, which, in collaboration with the state's Department of Environmental Protection, has created a New York City–specific climate change education module, ensuring that children living in the city have access to critical information regarding the place-based effects of climate change that impact their daily lives (City of New York, 2024). These lessons cover a broad range of topics, from greenhouse gases and urban heat islands to activism and green career pathways, and are accompanied by resources for teachers to use for their own professional learning. These modules are currently being implemented across New York City's five boroughs and are accompanied by districtwide "Climate Action Days" throughout the year to encourage students to apply what they've learned about climate change to relevant topics (New York City Department of Education, 2024).

Experiences Elsewhere

Across the United States, climate education action has begun to take off. Many plans have been formalized and codified in different ways, such as New Jersey's executive action that resulted in comprehensive climate change standards across subjects, and Connecticut and Maine's legislative approach to change policies supporting this work, and California's statewide network connecting collaborators across sectors. Though smaller in scope, other efforts have grown across the nation.

For example, in Indiana, the Department of Education worked in partnership with the Climate Change Research Center at Purdue University to craft a climate change education framework that identifies instructional resources for teachers and key science topics that connect directly to learning standards, to ensure teachers have access to scientifically accurate information and tools on the topic (Baker, 2021). Together these groups held a two-day virtual workshop for teachers to support implementation of these tools across Indiana. Similarly, Washington State has provided $4 million in grants to support teachers in professional development efforts related to climate science (Goerz, 2021). Other states, such as Virginia and New Hampshire, have made attempts to promote legislation supporting climate

> What are some ways organizations and individuals in your state collaborate on climate change education initiatives? How might you contribute to these efforts?

change education, but with mixed success. For example, the Virginia legislature recently passed a bill that would provide teachers with instructional materials about climate change, though it wouldn't require schools to use these materials in their teaching (Branch, 2024b). A similar resolution is under consideration in the New Hampshire legislature, which would also provide teachers with instructional materials (Branch, 2023). It follows that using examples from places like Maine and Connecticut to engage with the legislative process, it is certainly possible that further progress will be made across the nation.

HOW DO I ADVANCE THE CAUSE OF CLIMATE CHANGE EDUCATION IN MY STATE?

Whether trailblazing the path with policy-building initiatives like New Jersey, or providing tools and guidance for teachers to use like Indiana, states across the country are beginning to purposefully input climate change into K–12 spaces. There is certainly not one right way to start, but certain factors come up throughout each of these examples.

1. Collaborate! In each state profiled, it took the collaboration of many individuals, organizations, and perspectives for the group to find some success. Start by asking your colleagues and school administrators to work together to identify places that it makes sense for *you* to integrate climate change education in your setting. Next, look to professional groups like teachers' unions. These groups can help you to shape a clear and shared vision that includes the voices of many students and families. Connect with community organizations like boys and girls clubs, faith-based centers, and civic groups to let them know you're interested in offering this kind of work. Make sure to include youth voices in your collaboration and keep good records of your meetings. Having a shared vision and clear plan helps advocacy efforts down the road.

2. Find a hero! With a prominent voice, messages can be heard by larger audiences. When New Jersey's First Lady Tammy Murphy announced her intention to implement widespread climate change education across the state, many listened. In Connecticut and Maine, elected officials helped to shape the vision and planning. Partnering with leaders and people of influence can help you to mobilize quickly.

3. Consider multiple entry points! Think about the many ways in which climate change education can take root in a school, district, or state. It might make sense to start by adding climate-related children's literature in elementary classrooms and advocating for specific standards to be implemented statewide to support this kind of integration. It could help to work directly with teacher credentialing programs to make sure future teachers entering the profession are well prepared, as is the case in California. Studying examples of place-based effects of climate change on your schoolyard could also provide teachers and students alike with starting points for conversations that build into curricular units. Providing teachers with time to examine their existing curricula for places to integrate climate change–specific examples can also help ensure the topic is included in a meaningful way, connected to other efforts at your school.

LEARNING FROM OUR COLLEAGUES
Teaching the New Silk Road

Mrs. North teaches eighth-grade Social Studies in central New Jersey. With 5 years of teaching experience under her belt, she has found her stride in the classroom and welcomes students in with a smile each class period. Her classroom walls are covered in photos of past students and Lizzo posters, making the room a warm and welcoming spot for her teenage students to land. Climate change, policies around it, and the shifting geographical features that result from its effects have always been part of her curriculum. However, with the launch of the state's new climate change standards, she's made some purposeful efforts to integrate it into her world history instruction.

On a rainy October morning, Mrs. North's students enter the classroom and open their Chromebooks right away to dive back into some earlier work on the Silk Road[4] and trade with China, marking up maps and reviewing past reading assignments. Mrs. North then led a short discussion reviewing some key events and ideas related to the Silk Road. Next, Mrs. North said, "I'd like to show you videos on the New Silk Road created for a Western audience made by Chinese government officials recently." The class watched intently, then moved on to discuss similarities and differences between these two historical periods and debate the pros and cons of a New Silk Road (Figure 8.8).

FIGURE 8.8 • Container Ships Traveling the New Silk Road

Source: istock.com/sefa ozel

(Continued)

---

[4]The term *Silk Road* refers to the ancient trade routes between China and the West during the Roman Empire. The *New Silk Road* is the term journalists use to refer to China's Belt and Road Initiative connecting Pakistan and China and supporting more trade between China and other countries across the globe.

(Continued)

Next, Mrs. North posed the question, "So, how does this kind of trade over long distances impact our climate?" Stumped for a minute, the eighth graders were quiet. Luka shyly raised his hand and shared that there would surely be increases in CO_2 emissions from heavy ship traffic. With several students nodding in agreement, Mrs. North asked some more questions, checking for students' understanding about the relationship between these emissions and temperature. Later, Jasmine mentioned the recent whale strandings that had taken place along the coast of New York and New Jersey and said that her mom told her these were due, in part, to the higher traffic of container ships. Yet Xiaxuo chimed in, "What about the plastic? Most of the stuff on those ships is plastic, right? And doesn't that mean we're using more oil to make it?" Rather than answering, Mrs. North tossed the question back to the class, who generally agreed.

Jamie asked to come to the front of the room, and Mrs. North agreed. On the whiteboard, he drew a flow chart connecting plastic goods to factories, factories to oil, and oil to oil refineries. He took a step back, scrunched his nose and shifted his posture a bit to take it in. The student turned to his classmates and said, "Yeah. It's a lot. Like a whole lot. It's everywhere. We're doing a lot to add carbon to the atmosphere and we don't really think about it. When I look at my water bottle, it's definitely not the first thing to come to mind. But yeah. It's here. And we need to do something different to get past it."

Mrs. North wrapped up the class with some housekeeping items and thanked her students for contributing so meaningfully to the group's conversation. She promised them that the next day, they'd consider what some other futures could look like.

Reflection Questions

1. Do you anticipate any roadblocks to introducing climate change in your school? If so, what are they? What are some ways to overcome or circumvent them?

2. What are your successes with regard to climate change education? Have you shared these with your colleagues and community?

3. Who are the climate heroes in your state? Can you identify people of influence who might be able to help you get started integrating climate change?

4. What are some of the ways your state's policies have made you proud? Can you build from those successes?

5. Which groups of collaborators are most likely to get on board with climate change education? Community groups? Students? Teachers? How can you connect with them?

6. What are your community assets? Can you draw on them to support climate education implementation?

7. What do you think the best first step is for you?

For Further Reading

RESOURCES FOR TEACHERS

Filion, L. (2023). But what about the polar bears? Centering student interests in place-based learning. *Edutopia*. https://qrs.ly/k2g3eoj

Leslie, C. W., Tallmadge, J., Wessels, T., & Zwinger, A. (2005). *Into the field: A guide to locally focused teaching*. Nature Literacy Series No. 3. Orion Society Press.

Madden, L. (2022). *Report on K–12 climate change education needs in New Jersey*. New Jersey School Boards Association. https://qrs.ly/8tg37fo

Sobel, D. (1998). *Mapmaking with children: Sense of place education in the elementary years*. Heinemann.

For up-to-date reporting on the climate crisis in New Jersey, NJ, Advance Media environmental reporter Steven Rodas' work can be found at https://qrs.ly/j5g37fv

RESOURCES FOR STUDENTS

Ages 5–8

Yezerski, T. (2011). *Meadowlands: A wetland survival story*. Farrar, Straus and Giroux.

Ages 8–12

Greenfield, R. (2021). *Be the change: Rob Greenfield's call to kids making a difference in a messed-up world*. Greystone.

Zissu, A. (2021). *Earth squad: 50 people who are saving the planet*. Running Press.

APPENDIX
Online Teacher Resources

. . . .

CHAPTER 1

Calculate Your Carbon Footprint: https://qrs.ly/bbg3gk4

The Climate Initiative: https://www.theclimateinitiative.org/

Climate Superhero!: https://qrs.ly/m3g3gka

Generation180: https://generation180.org/

Global Youth Statement on Climate Change and COP26 Outcomes: https://qrs.ly/dcg36w9

Kids Fight Climate Change: https://www.kidsfightclimatechange.org/

Mission 1.5: https://qrs.ly/dgg3gk9

UNICEF Online Climate Course: https://qrs.ly/vkg36w0

United Nations #ActNow Campaign: https://qrs.ly/jeg3gk1

United Nations Youth in Action—Climate Action: https://qrs.ly/n1g3gk7

YOUNGO: https://qrs.ly/2fg3gkg

Zinn Education Project: https://qrs.ly/c5g36sv

Climate Simulations

The Earth Overshoot Day Calculator: https://qrs.ly/ghg3gki

En-ROADS: https://qrs.ly/k1g378q

NASA's Climate Time Machine: https://qrs.ly/hqg3gno

The Yale Climate Change Opinion Maps: https://qrs.ly/exg378v

CHAPTER 2

The Cranky Uncle Teacher's Guide: https://crankyuncle.com/wpcontent/uploads/2021/01/Cranky_Teachers_Guide_v1.pdf

Generation Skeptics: https://www.generationskeptics.org

Skeptical Science: https://qrs.ly/jlg3gkk

A Scientific Guide to the Skeptic's Handbook: https://qrs.ly/t2g37a7

SubjectToClimate: https://qrs.ly/utg3gkt

Generation Skeptics Lessons

Grade 6–12 Climate Sleuths—Identifying Climate Misconceptions: https://qrs.ly/83g37a2

Grade 6–12 Follow the Money Trail!: https://qrs.ly/ohg37a0

CHAPTER 3

Climate Central: https://www.climatecentral.org/

Climate Feedback: https://climatefeedback.org/

Climate Literacy and Energy Awareness Network (CLEAN): https://cleanet.org/about/

The Climate Reality Project: https://www.climaterealityproject.org/climate-101

Coursera: The Science and Modeling of Climate Change: https://qrs.ly/8zg3gky

The CRAAP Test: https://qrs.ly/z4g37b9

EPA Climate Change: https://qrs.ly/n3g37b7

EPA Climate Change for Kids: https://qrs.ly/mqg37bg

Fact Checker: https://www.washingtonpost.com/politics/fact-checker/

Climate.gov Climate Models: https://www.climate.gov/maps-data/climate-data-primer/predicting-climate/climate-models

IPCC Facts for Kids: https://qrs.ly/5kg37ba

Lead Stories: https://leadstories.com/

NASA Climate Change: https://climate.nasa.gov/

NASA Climate Kids: https://qrs.ly/wgg3ep3

NASA Kids' Club: https://qrs.ly/qmg3eo3

The National Center for Atmospheric Research (NCAR) Community Earth System Model (CESM): https://www.cesm.ucar.edu

The National Center for Science Education's Teaching Climate Change: https://ncse.ngo/teaching-climate-change

National Geographic Climate Change Education: https://education.nationalgeographic.org/ (type "climate change" into search bar for hundreds of good resources)

National Geographic Education: https://qrs.ly/vbg37bi

National Oceanic and Atmospheric Administration (NOAA) Climate Data Center: https://qrs.ly/4qg37b5

The New York Times What's Going on in This Graph?: https://qrs.ly/u5g37aa

Project Drawdown: https://drawdown.org/

Project Drawdown's list of researched and ranked solutions: https://qrs.ly/8bg3gkx

Snopes.com: https://www.snopes.com/

Teach About Climate Change With 30 Graphs From *The New York Times:* https://qrs.ly/elg37ab

The Vostok Core & Milankovitch Cycles Climate Applet: https://qrs.ly/y9g3gkw

What's Your AI IQ? Lesson: https://qrs.ly/rag37bm

World Wildlife Fund (WWF) Climate Change: https://qrs.ly/hug3eo1

CHAPTER 4

Carbon Footprint Assessment: https://qrs.ly/8cg37bx

Citizen Science Projects: https://qrs.ly/hsg37c4

Communicate With Your Kids About Climate Change: https://qrs.ly/w1g3gl5

Community Garden or Urban Farming: https://qrs.ly/qkg37by

Energy Efficiency Audit: https://qrs.ly/sqg37c0

Model Greenhouse: https://qrs.ly/3kg3dgw

National Center for Science Education (NCSE): https://ncse.ngo/

National Science Teaching Association (NSTA): https://www.nsta.org/

Parenting in an Age of Climate Change: https://qrs.ly/6mg3gl1

Street Epistemology: https://qrs.ly/dcg37bv

Yale Climate Connections: https://climatecommunication.yale.edu/

CHAPTER 5

California Communities Environmental Health Screening Tool: CalEnviroScreen 4.0: qrs.ly/ukgh6z1

Climate Central's Coastal Risk Screening Tool: Affordable Housing at Risk of Flooding: https://qrs.ly/wzg3dhc

Climate Crisis NCTS: https://qrs.ly/axg37f8

EPA's Environmental Justice Screening and Mapping Tool: https://www.epa.gov/ejscreen

Grist's Imagine 2200 Project: https://qrs.ly/ulg3eot

NASA's Climate Kids: https://climatekids.nasa.gov/

PBS Learning Media: https://whyy.pbslearningmedia.org/

SubjectToClimate: https://www.subjecttoclimate.org

CHAPTER 6

ACLU: Students' Rights: Speech, Walkouts, and Other Protests: https://qrs.ly/2zg37ey

The Audre Lorde Project: https://qrs.ly/xxg37f0

Climate-Aware Therapist Directory: https://qrs.ly/tsg3gm3

Climate Psychiatry Alliance: https://www.climatepsychiatry.org/

Climate Psychology Alliance North America: https://www.climatepsychology.us/

Climate Psychology Alliance North America: An Educator's Guide to Climate Emotions: https://qrs.ly/ljg37ek

Climate Psychology Alliance United Kingdom: https://qrs.ly/ohg3gm4

Design for Change: https://qrs.ly/wog37ci

EcoAnxious Stories: https://qrs.ly/fhg3gmh

EcoRise: Introduce Your Students to Climate Resilience: https://qrs.ly/hdg37dw

Gen Dread: A Newsletter About Staying Sane in the Climate Crisis (Substack): https://qrs.ly/6jg3gmi

Global Goals 13: Climate Action: https://qrs.ly/rwg37cc

Good Grief Network: 10 Steps to Resilience & Empowerment in a Chaotic Climate: https://www.goodgriefnetwork.org/

NASA Climate Kids: Green Careers: https://qrs.ly/9ig37et

SubjectToClimate: https://qrs.ly/clg37c5

SubjectToClimate Lab Activities: https://qrs.ly/23g37c8

Sunrise Movement: Electoral Organizing Campaign: https://qrs.ly/uxg37ez

Sunrise Movement: Green New Deal for Communities: https://qrs.ly/adg3gmk

SustainUs: U.S. Youth for Justice and Sustainability: https://sustainus.org/

Time for Kids: Climate Jobs: https://qrs.ly/pmg3dhn

World's Largest Lesson: Climate Action: https://qrs.ly/e3g37gh

Youth vs Apocalypse: https://www.youthvsapocalypse.org

CHAPTER 7

Climate Generation Resource Library: https://qrs.ly/1vg3eo9

Green Teacher: https://greenteacher.com/

IMF Climate Change Indicators Dashboard: https://qrs.ly/ztg37en

NASA's Climate Kids: https://climatekids.nasa.gov/

NASA's Global Temperature Data: https://qrs.ly/k7g37ep

The National Council for Teachers of English (NCTE)'s Resolution on Literacy Teaching on Climate Change in 2019: https://qrs.ly/b9g37f6

NOAA's Climate Data Online: https://qrs.ly/hvg37eo

NOAA's Maps & Data: https://www.climate.gov/maps-data

Our Children's Trust: State Legal Actions: https://qrs.ly/xng37ee

PBS Learning Media: https://qrs.ly/sig37e6

Project Drawdown Climate Solutions Library: https://drawdown.org/solutions

Project SEA Curriculum: https://qrs.ly/o2g3eoi

Rethinking Schools: https://rethinkingschools.org/

Stanford University Middle School Curriculum: Introduction to Climate Change: https://qrs.ly/a9g3gnc

SubjectToClimate: https://qrs.ly/1pg3eos

World Bank's Climate Change Database: https://qrs.ly/a7g3eoc

CHAPTER 8

Climate Emergency: Feedback Loops (video): https://qrs.ly/46g3gml

Connecticut Department of Energy and Environmental Protection Environmental Curriculum Topics: https://qrs.ly/lrg37fm

New Jersey Climate Change Education Standards: https://www.nj.gov/education/climate/learning/gradeband

Project Drawdown: https://drawdown.org/

Steven Rodas, environmental reporter, NJ Advance Media: https://qrs.ly/j5g37fv

REFERENCES

Abbott, A. (2005) Gut feeling secures medical Nobel for Australian doctors. *Nature, 437*, 801. https://doi.org/10.1038/437801a

Abtahi, Y., Gøtze, P., Steffensen, L., Barwell, R., & Hauge, K. H. (2017). Teaching climate change in mathematics classrooms: An ethical responsibility. Philosophy of Mathematics Education Journal, 32, 1–18. https://hvlopen.brage.unit.no/hvlopen-xmlui/bitstream/handle/11250/2993623/Abtahi.pdf

Agrawal, S. (2023, October 10). *Climate change took them to "dark places." Now these Californians are doing something about it.* CalMatters. https://calmatters.org/health/mental-health/2023/10/climate-change-california-youth-mental-health/

Allan, R. P., Arias, P. A., Berger, S., Canadell, J. G., Cassou, C., Chen, D., Cherchi, A., Connors, S. L., Coppola, E., Cruz, F. A., Diongue-Niang, A., Doblas-Reyes, F. J., Douville, H., Driouech, F., Edwards, T. L., Engelbrecht, F., Eyring, V., Fischer, E., Flato, G. M., . . . Zickfeld, K. (2021). *Summary for policymakers.* IPCC. www.ipcc.ch/report/ar6/wg1/downloads/report/IPCC_AR6_WGI_SPM.pdf

Alter, J. (2020, September 29). Climate change was on the ballot with Jimmy Carter in 1980—though no one knew it at the time. *Time.*

Anders, C. (2024, June 23). World breaks 1,400 temperature records in a week as heat waves sweep globe. Semafor. www.semafor.com/article/06/23/2024/world-breaks-1400-temperature-records-heat- waves-sweep-globe

Baker, A. (2021). *IDOE announces new climate change education framework in partnership with Purdue.* https://education.purdue.edu/2021/01/idoe-announces-new-climate-change-education-framework-in-partnership-with-purdue/

Ballew, M. T., Pearson, A. R., Schuldt, J. P., Kotcher, J. E., Maibach, E. W., Rosenthal, S. A., & Leiserowitz, A. (2021). Is the political divide on climate change narrower for people of color? Evidence from a decade of U.S. polling. *Journal of Environmental Psychology, 77*, Article 101680. https://www.sciencedirect.com/science/article/abs/pii/S027249442100133X

Ballew, M., Maibach, E., Kotcher, J., Bergquist, P., Rosenthal, S., Marlon, J., & Leiserowitz, A. (2020, April 16). *Which racial/ethnic groups care most about climate change.* Yale Program on Climate Change Communication: Climate Note. https://climatecommunication.yale.edu/publications/race-and-climate-change/

Bartlett, S. (2008). Climate change and urban children: Impacts and implications for adaptation in low- and middle-income countries. *Environment and Urbanization, 20*, 501–519.

BBC. (2020, September 18). Environment: Do you want a 'green job' in the future? *BBC.* https://www.bbc.co.uk/newsround/54191148

Berberian, A. G., Gonzalez, D. J. X., & Cushing, L. J. (2022). Racial disparities in climate change–related health effects in the United States. *Current Environmental Health Reports, 9*(3), 451–464. https://doi.org/10.1007/s40572-022-00360-w

Bigelow, B., & Swinehart, T. (Eds.). (2014). *A people's curriculum for the earth: Teaching climate change and the environmental crisis.* Rethinking Schools.

Blue California News Center. (2022, April 21). *New poll finds climate change is taking a toll on Gen Z mental health while also inspiring youth to act.* https://news.blueshieldca.com/2022/04/21/new-poll-finds-climate-change-is-taking-a-toll-on-gen-z-mental-health-while-also-inspiring-youth-to-take-action

Blue Shield of California. (2022). *Youth climate survey 2022.* https://s3.ama zonaws.com/cms.ipressroom.com/347/files/20223/Blue+Shield+of+California+ N e x t G e t n + Y o u t h + C l i m a t e + Survey+2022+Report_FINAL.pdf

Blume. (2022). *Bill HP 1409.* https:// legislature.maine.gov/bills/getPDF .asp?paper=HP1409&item=1&snum=130

Branch, G. (2023). *A climate change education resolution in New Hampshire.* https://ncse.ngo/climate-change-educa tion-resolution-new-hampshire

Branch, G. (2024a). *Climate change education legislation dies in New York.* https://ncse .ngo/climate-change-education-legisla tion-dies-new-york

Branch, G. (2024b). *NCSE featured in coverage of Virginia climate change education legislation.* https://ncse.ngo/ ncse-featured-coverage-virginia-cli mate-change-education-legislation

Browne, G. (2022, July 11). The climate anxiety discussion has a whiteness problem. *Wired.* https://www.wired.com/story/climate-anxiety-whiteness-problem/

Bruce, C. S., & Edwards, S. L. (2018). Information literacy: Evaluating web resources. Libraries Unlimited.

Bryant, B. (Ed.). (1995). *Environmental justice: Issues, policies, and solutions.* Island Press.

Bullard, R. D. (1993). The legacy of American apartheid and environmental racism. *John's J. Legal Comment, 9,* 445.

Burke, S., Sanson, S., & van Hoorn, J. (2018). The psychological effects of climate change on children. *Current Psychiatry Reports, 20,* 35.

Cama, T. (2023, October 24). *Quiz show: GOP deploys new climate messaging tactic.* E&E News by POLITICO. www.eenews.net/ articles/quiz-show-gop-deploys-new-cli mate-messaging-tactic/

Campbell, E., Kotchner, J., Maibach, E., Rosenthal, S., & Leiserowitz, A. (2022). *Who is willing to participate in non-violent civil disobedience for the climate?* Yale Program on Climate Change Communication. https://climatecom munication.yale.edu/publications/ who-is-willing-to-participate-in-non-violent-civil-disobedience-for-the-climate/

Carbon Capture and Storage Association. (2021). *Carbon capture and storage: A vital solution for climate action.* https:// www.ccsassociation.org/

Carman, J., Ballew, M., Lu, D., Leiserowitz, A., Maibach, E., Rosenthal, S., Kotcher, J., Goddard, E., Low, J., Marlon, J., Verner, M., Lee, S., Myers, T., Goldberg, M., Badullovich, N., Mason, T., Aguilar, A., Ongelungel, S. M., Sahlin, K., . . . Torres, G. (2023). *Climate change in the American mind: Climate justice, Spring 2023.* Yale University and George Mason University. Yale Program on Climate Change Communication.

Carrington, D. (2024a, May 8). 'Hopeless and broken': Why the world's top climate scientists are in despair. *The Guardian,* Guardian News and Media. www.theguardian.com/environment/ ng-interactive/2024/may/08/hopeless-and-broken-why-the-worlds-top-cli mate-scientists-are-in-despair

Carrington, D. (2024b, May 8). World's top climate scientists expect global heating to blast past 1.5C target. *The Guardian,* Guardian News and Media. www.the guardian.com/environment/article/ 2024/may/08/world-scientists-cli mate-failure-survey-global-temperature

Caulfield, M. (2019). Critical thinking in the age of fake news: Why it matters and how to get better at it. Ingram International.

Caulfield, M. (2019). *SIFT (The four moves).* Hapgood. https://hapgood.us/ 2019/06/19/sift-the-four-moves/

CCI. (2024). *California Climate Investments.* www.caclimateinvestments.ca.gov/

Centers for Disease Control. (2023, April 27). *Youth Risk Behavior Surveillance System (YRBSS).* https://www.cdc.gov/ healthyyouth/data/yrbs/index.htm

Chase, M. (2024, January 4). A look at America's first direct air capture facility.

Earth.Org.earth.org/americas-first-direct-air-capture-facility-opens-in-california

Cherry, L. (director). (2013, July 20). *Dreaming in green*. YouTube. https://www.youtube.com/watch?v=ylOVx2NMQWw

Citizens' Climate Lobby. (2024, February 20). *The basics of carbon fee and dividend*. https://citizensclimatelobby.org/basics-carbon-fee-dividend

City of Austin. (2021, September). *Austin climate equity plan*. AustinTexas.gov. https://www.austintexas.gov/page/austin-climate-equity-plan

City of Miami. (2021, September 15). *Miami forever carbon neutral: Growing the new green economy*. https://www.miamigov.com/files/bd7c8b23-60be-471f-8410-6743af168401/City-of-Miami-New-Green-Economy-Overview.pdf

City of New York. (2024). *Climate change education module*. https://www.nyc.gov/site/dep/environment/climate-change-education-module.page

Clark, J. (2023, August 15). Is what we're recycling actually getting recycled? HowStuffWorks, Science. science.howstuffworks.com/environmental/conservation/issues/recycling-reality.htm

Climate Central. (2024). *Hurricane Helene and climate shift index: Ocean, September 23, 2024*. https://csi.climatecentral.org/ocean?card=cyclone-state&chosenCyclone=al092024&cyclones=al092024&firstDate=2024-09-23&lat=12.02266&lng=-66.26953&tcState=7&zoom=4

Climate Reality Project. (2021). *How the climate crisis is impacting Bangladesh*. https://www.climaterealityproject.org/blog/how-climate-crisis-impacting-bangladesh

CO2.Earth. (2024, December 9). *Daily CO2*. https://www.co2.earth/daily-co2

Coffey, Y., Bhullar, N., Durkin, J., Islam, M. S., & Usher, K. (2021). Understanding eco-anxiety: A systematic scoping review of current literature and identified knowledge gaps. *The Journal of Climate Change and Health*, 3, Article 100047.

Columbia Climate School. (2021). Attribution science: Linking climate change to extreme weather. *State of the Planet*, Columbia University. news.climate.columbia.edu/2021/10/04/attribution-science-linking-climate-change-to-extreme-weather/

Cook, J. (2020). *Cranky uncle vs. climate change: How to Understand and respond to climate science deniers*. Citadel Press.

Cook, J. (2024). *Cranky uncle*. https://crankyuncle.com/author/crankyuncle/

Cook, J., Nuccitelli, D., Green, S. A., Jacobs, P., & Anderegg, W. R. (2013). Quantifying the consensus on anthropogenic global warming in the scientific literature. *Environmental Research Letters*, 8(2), Article 024024.

Cook, J., Oreskes, N., Doran, P. T., Anderegg, W. R., Verheggen, B., Maibach, E. W., Carlton, J. S., Lewandowsky, S., Skuce, A. G., Green, S. A., Nuccitelli, D., Jacobs, P., Richardson, M., Winkler, B., Painting, R., & Rice, K. (2016). Consensus on consensus: A synthesis of consensus estimates on human-caused global warming. *Environmental Research Letters*, 11, 1–7. https://doi.org/10.1088/1748-9326/11/4/048002

Cordero, E. C., Centeno, D., & Todd, A. M. (2020). The role of climate change education on individual lifetime carbon emissions. *PLOS ONE*, 15(2), Article e0206266. https://doi.org/10.1371/journal.pone.0206266

Cordero, E. C., Centeno, D., & Todd, A. M. (2020). The role of climate change education on individual lifetime carbon emissions. *PloS One*, 15(2), e0206266.

Crayola. (2024). Crayola colorcycle. https://www.crayola.com/colorcycle.aspx

Dayton, L., Balaban, A., Scherkoske, M., & Latkin, C. (2023). Family communication about climate change in the United States. *Journal of Prevention*, 44(4), 373–387. https://doi.org/10.1007/s10935-022-00712-0

Dolan, A. M. (Ed.). (2021). *Teaching climate change in primary schools: An interdisciplinary approach*. Routledge.

Dream in Green. (2008, December). *The green schools challenge*. https://dreamingreen.org/the-dream-in-green-academy/

Duarte, F. (2024, June 13). Amount of data created daily (2024). *Exploding Topics*. explodingtopics.com/blog/data-generated-per-day.

Earth.Org. (2024, November 19). The quiet rise of carbon capture in Europe. *Earth.org*. https://earth.org/the-quiet-rise-of-carbon-capture-in-europe/

Edge Delta. (2024, March 11). *How much data is created per day? Unveiling the daily data deluge*. edgedelta.com/company/blog/how-much-data-is-created-per-day

Environmental Protection Agency (EPA). (2020, September 8). Overview of greenhouse gases. 19january2021snapshot.epa.gov/ghgemissions/overview-greenhouse-gases_.html

Environmental Protection Agency. (2023, June 1). *Summary of Inflation Reduction Act*. EPA. https://www.epa.gov/system/files/documents/2022-12/12%2009%202022_OAR%20IRA%20Overview_vPublic.pdf

EPA. (2020, September 8). *Overview of greenhouse gases*. Environmental Protection Agency. 19january2021snapshot.epa.gov/ghgemissions/overview-greenhouse-gases_.html

EPA. (2022). *Regulatory impact analysis for proposed federal implementation plan addressing regional ozone transport for the 2015 ozone national ambient air quality standard*. www.epa.gov/system/files/documents/2022-03/transport_ria_proposal_fip_2015_ozone_naaqs_2022-02.pdf

Exec. Order 89. (2019). *nj.gov*. https://nj.gov/infobank/eo/056murphy/pdf/EO-89.pdf

Facing History and Ourselves. (2023, September 26). *Straight A's for facilitating crucial conversations*. https://www.facinghistory.org/resource-library/straight-facilitating-crucial-conversations

Fernbach, P. (2013, November 15). The illusion of understanding: Phil Fernbach at TEDxGoldenGatePark. *YouTube*. https://www.youtube.com/watch?v=2SlbsnaSNNM&ab_channel=TEDxTalks

Fielding, J. A. (2019). Rethinking CRAAP: Getting students thinking like fact-checkers in evaluating web sources. College & Research Libraries News, 80(11), 620–622. https://doi.org/10.5860/crln.80.11.620

Flynn, C., & Jordan, S. (2024, June). The peoples' climate vote 2024. *UNDP*. www.undp.org/publications/peoples-climate-vote-2024

Forschungsverbund Berlin. (2019, July 23). Climate changes faster than animals adapt. *ScienceDaily*. www.sciencedaily.com/releases/2019/07/190723121912.htm

Forster, P., Storelvmo, T., Armour, K., Collins, W., Dufresne, J.-L., Frame, D., Lunt, D. J., Mauritsen, T., Palmer, M. D., Watanabe, M., Wild, M., & Zhang, H. (2021). The earth's energy budget, climate feedbacks, and climate sensitivity. In V. Masson-Delmotte (Ed.), *Climate change 2021: The physical science basis. Contribution of Working Group I to the Sixth Assessment Report of the Intergovernmental Panel on Climate Change* (pp. 923–1054). Cambridge University Press. https://www.ipcc.ch/report/ar6/wg1/chapter/chapter-7/

Freeman, S., Eddy, S. L., McDonough, M., Polk, M., & Tinker, M. (2014). Active learning increases student performance in science, engineering, and mathematics. *Proceedings of the National Academy of Sciences, 111*(23), 8410–8415. https://www.pnas.org/doi/abs/10.1073/pnas.1319030111

Friedlingstein, P., Le Quéré, C., Peters, G. P., Andrew, R. M., Canadell, J. G., Jackson, R. B., . . . & Zhou, L. (2024). *Global Carbon Budget 2024*. Earth System Science Data. https://www.sciencedaily.com/releases/2024/11/241112191227.htm

Funk, C. (2021). *Key findings: How Americans' attitudes about climate change differ by generation, party and other factors*. Pew Research Center. https://www.pewresearch.org/short-reads/2021/05/26/key-findings-how-americans-attitudes-about-climate-change-differ-by-generation-party-and-other-factors/

Furnham, A., & Robinson, C. (2022). Correlates of belief in climate change: Demographics, ideology and belief systems. *Acta Psychologica, 230,* Article 103775.https://doi.org/10.1016/j.actpsy.2022.103775

Gallup. (2023, May 17). *Environment.* Gallup. Com; news.gallup.com/poll/1615/environment.aspx

Generation180. (2023). *Students and parents spark progress toward 100% clean energy.* Generation180. https://generation180.org/blog/students-and-parents-spark-progress-toward-100-clean-energy/

Global Cement and Concrete Association. (2020). *2050 climate ambition.* https://gccassociation.org/climate-ambition/

Godden, N. J., Farrant, B. M., Yallup Farrant, J., Heyink, E., Carot Collins, E., Burgemeister, B., Tabeshfar, M., Barrow, J., West, M., Kieft, J., Rothwell, M., Leviston, Z., Bailey, S., Blaise, M., & Cooper, T. (2021). Climate change, activism, and supporting the mental health of children and young people: Perspectives from Western Australia. *Journal of Paediatrics and Child Health, 57*(11), 1759–1764.

Goerz, T. (2021). *In Washington state, classrooms are putting climate change at the forefront of K-12 education.* https://www.dailyuw.com/science/article_15d1c-d4c-8101-11e9-a344-6f9c8af8f5bc.html

Gramling, C. (2024). Climate change fueled the fury of hurricanes Helene and Milton. *Science News.* https://www.sciencenews.org/article/climate-change-hurricanes-helene-milton

Grass, R., & Agyeman, J. (2002). *Second national people of color environmental leadership Summit-Summit II.* Summit II National Office.

Gray, J. A., & McNaughton, N. (2000). *The neuropsychology of anxiety: An enquiry into the function of the septo-hippocampal system.* Oxford University Press.

Greshko, M., & National Geographic Staff. (2019, September 26). *Mass extinction facts and information.* National Geographic. www.nationalgeographic.com/science/article/mass-extinction

Guggenheim, D. (2006). *An inconvenient truth.* Paramount Vantage.

Haidt, J. (2006). *The happiness hypothesis: Finding modern truth in ancient wisdom.* Basic Books/Hachette Book Group.

Hansen, J. E., Sato, M., Simons, L., Nazarenko, L. S., Sangha, I., Kharecha, P., Zachos, J. C., von Schuckmann, K., Loeb, N. G., Osman, M. B., Jin, Q., Tselioudis, G., Jeong, E., Lacis, A., Ruedy, R., Russell, G., Cao, J., & Li, J. (2023). Global warming in the pipeline. *Oxford Open Climate Change, 3*(1), Article kgad008. https://doi.org/10.1093/oxfclm/kgad008

Heglar, M. A. (2019, February 18). *Climate change isn't the first existential threat.* Medium. https://zora.medium.com/sorry-yall-but-climate-change-ain-t-the-first-existential-threat-b3c999267aa0

Hickman, C., Marks, E., Pihkala, P., Clayton, S., Lewandowski, R. E., Mayall, E. E., Wray, B., Mellor, C., & Van Susteren, L. (2021). Climate anxiety in children and young people and their beliefs about government responses to climate change: A global survey. *The Lancet Planetary Health, 5*(12), e863–e873.

Hirji, Z. (2019, December 16). *Climate change mailers sent to thousands of teachers cast doubt on global warming.* BuzzFeed News. https://www.buzzfeednews.com/article/zahrahirji/climate-mailers-for-teachers#.osLBGJnLV

Hough, L. (2023, May 22). When we teach climate change: Tina Grotzer explains the challenge teachers face talking about the environment. *Harvard Graduation School of Education Magazine.* https://www.gse.harvard.edu/ideas/ed-magazine/23/05/when-we-teach-climate-change

HP. (2022). HP study finds climate crisis is changing parental decisions on purchasing, careers and even family size . *Press Center.* press.hp.com/us/

en/press-kits/2023/hp-sustainable-impact-report-2022.html

IEA. (2024). Renewables – Energy system. www.iea.org/energy-system/renewables

Intergovernmental Panel on Climate Change (IPCC). (2021). *Climate change 2021: The physical science basis.* Contribution of Working Group I to the Sixth Assessment Report of the Intergovernmental Panel on Climate Change. Cambridge University Press.

Intergovernmental Panel on Climate Change (IPCC). (2022). *Climate change 2022: Impacts, adaptation and vulnerability.* www.ipcc.ch/report/ar6/wg2/

International Energy Agency. (2020, September 14). *Going carbon negative: What are the technology options?* https://www.iea.org/commentaries/going-carbon-negative-what-are-the-technology-options

International Energy Agency. (2023, October 6). *Massive expansion of renewable power opens door to achieving global tripling goal set at COP28.* https://www.iea.org/news/massive-expansion-of-renewable-power-opens-door-to-achieving-global-tripling-goal-set-at-cop28

International Rescue Committee. (2023). *10 countries at risk of climate disaster.* https://www.rescue.org/article/10-countries-risk-climate-disaster

International Union for the Conservation of Nature. (2020). *Environmental degradation driving gender-based violence—ICUN study.* https://www.iucn.org/news/gender/202001/environmental-degradation-driving-gender-based-violence-iucn-study

Iowa State University. (2019, August 1). Species aren't adapting fast enough to cope with climate change. *ScienceDaily.* www.sciencedaily.com/releases/2019/08/190801111044.htm

IPCC. (2021). *Climate change 2021: The physical science basis.* Contribution of Working Group I to the Sixth Assessment Report of the Intergovernmental Panel on Climate Change [Masson-Delmotte, V., P. Zhai, A. Pirani, S. L. Connors, C. Péan, S. Berger, N. Caud, Y. Chen, L. Goldfarb, M. I. Gomis, M. Huang, K. Leitzell, E. Lonnoy, J. B. R. Matthews, T. K. Maycock, T. Waterfield, O. Yelekçi, R. Yu, and B. Zhou (Eds.)]. Cambridge University Press. https://doi.org/10.1017/9781009157896

IPCC. (2022). Summary for policymakers. In H.-O. Pörtner et al. (Eds.), *Climate change 2022: Impacts, adaptation, and vulnerability. Contribution of Working Group II to the Sixth Assessment Report of the Intergovernmental Panel on Climate Change* Cambridge University Press. https://www.ipcc.ch/report/ar6/wg2/downloads/report/IPCC_AR6_WGII_SummaryForPolicymakers.pdf

IPCC. (2023). *Climate change 2023: Synthesis report* (pp. 35–115). Contribution of Working Groups I, II and III to the Sixth Assessment Report of the Intergovernmental Panel on Climate Change [Core Writing Team, H. Lee and J. Romero (eds.)]. https://doi.org/10.59327/IPCC/AR6-9789291691647

IREC. (2023, July). *National solar jobs census 2022.* Interstate Renewable Energy Council. https://irecusa.org/census-executive-summary/

Jaquette Ray, S. (2021, March 21). Climate anxiety is an overwhelmingly white phenomenon. *Scientific American.* https://www.scientificamerican.com/article/the-unbearable-whiteness-of-climate-anxiety/

Jones, G. (2019). *Italy to make climate change study compulsory in schools.* https://www.reuters.com/article/idUSKBN1XF1E4/

Justice40 Initiative. (2022). *The White House.* https://www.whitehouse.gov/environmentaljustice/justice40/

Kamenetz, A. (2019, April 22). *Most teachers don't teach climate change; 4 In 5 parents wish they did.* National Public Radio. https://www.npr.org/2019/04/22/714262267/most-teachers-dont-teach-climate-change-4-in-5-parents-wish-they-did

Kamenetz, A. (2019, April 22). *Most teachers don't teach climate change; 4 in*

5 parents wish they did. National Public Radio. https://www.npr.org/2019/04/22/714262267/most-teachers-dont-teach-climate-change-4-in-5-parents-wish-they-did

Khan, A. E., Scheelbeek, P. F., Shilpi, A. B., Chan, Q., Mojumder, S. K., Rahman, A., Haines, A., & Vineis, P. (2014). Salinity in drinking water and the risk of (pre) eclampsia and gestational hypertension in coastal Bangladesh: a case-control study. *PloS one*, *9*(9), e108715. https://doi.org/10.1371/journal.pone.0108715

Khan, M. R. (2016). Natural fish resources see drastic decline. *The Daily Star*. https://www.thedailystar.net/frontpage/natural-fish-resources-see-drastic-decline-1256335

Kiest, K. (2023, July 6). Kids are educating parents on climate change... and parents are listening. *NOAA Sea Grant*. seagrant.noaa.gov/kids-are-educat ing-parents-on-climate-changeand-par ents-are-listening/

Konnikova, M. (2013, April 30). Why we need answers. *The New Yorker*. www.newyorker.com/tech/annals-of-technology/why-we-need-answers

Kwauk, C., & Winthrop, R. (2020, September 17). *Unleashing the creativity of teachers and students to combat climate change: An opportunity for global leadership*. Brookings. https://www.brookings.edu/articles/unleashing-the-creativity-of-teachers-and-students-to-combat-climate-change-an-opportunity-for-global-leadership/

Lawson, D. F., Stevenson, K. T., Peterson, M. N., Carrier, S. J., Strnad, R. L., & Seekamp, E. (2019). Children can foster climate change concern among their parents. *Nature Climate Change*, *9*, 458–462. www.nature.com/articles/s41558-019-0463-3

Learning for Justice. (2022). *Social justice standards: The learning for justice anti-bias framework*. https://www.learningforjustice.org/sites/default/files/2022-09/LFJ-Social-Justice-Standards-September-2022-09292022.pdf

Lei Win, T. (2019). These entrepreneurs are fighting for gender equality in farming. *Thomas Reuters Foundation*. https://www.globalcitizen.org/en/content/tech-innovation-women-farmers/

Leiserowitz, A., Maibach, E., Rosenthal, S., Kotcher, J., Carman, J., Neyens, L., Marlon, J., Lacroix, K., & Goldberg, M. (2021). Dramatic increase in public beliefs and worries about climate change. *Yale Program on Climate Change Communication*. https://climatecommunication.yale.edu/publications/dramatic-increase-in-public-beliefs-and-worries-about-climate-change/

Leiserowitz, A., Maibach, E., Rosenthal, S., Kotcher, J., Goddard, E., Carman, J., Verner, M., Ballew, M., Marlon, J., Lee, S., Myers, T., Goldberg, M., Badullovich, N., & Their, K. (2024, March 1). Global warming's six Americas, Fall 2023. *Yale Program on Climate Change Communication*. climatecommunication.yale.edu/publications/global-warmings-six-americas-fall-2023/

Leitch, A. (2012). Evaluating digital information in a multimedia world. Emerald Group Publishing.

Leve, A. K., Michel, H., & Harms, U. (2023). Implementing climate literacy in schools — what to teach our teachers? Climatic Change, 176, 134. https://doi.org/10.1007/s10584-023-03607-z

Leve, A. K., Michel, H., & Harms, U. (2023). Implementing climate literacy in schools — what to teach our teachers? Climatic Change, 176, 134. https://doi.org/10.1007/s10584-023-03607-z

Lopez, M. H., Krogstad, J. M., & Passel, J. S. (2023, September 5). Who is Hispanic? *Pew Research Center*. www.pewre search.org/short-reads/2023/09/05/who-is-hispanic

Madden, L. (2022). *Report on K-12 climate change education needs in New Jersey*. New Jersey School Boards Association. https://qrs.ly/8tg37fo

Madden, L., Ammentorp, L., Magee, N., & Taylor, G. (2023). Marine science, climate change, and the Next Generation

Science Standards: Understanding the knowledge and perspectives of K-8 New Jersey teachers. *Current: The Journal of Marine Education, 38*(1), 3–15. https://doi.org/10.5334/cjme.74

Madden, L., Heddy, E., Wang, M., Turner, J., Lindsay, S., & Perdew, I. (2023). *New Jersey teachers' perspectives on the implementation of K-12 climate change standards: Initial findings from surveys in June and December 2022.* SubjectToClimate.SubjecttoClimate.org; https://subjecttoclimate.nyc3.cdn.digitaloceanspaces.com/files/nj-climate-change-standards-implementation-paper.pdf

Majeed, H., & Lee, J. (2017). The impact of climate change on youth depression and mental health. *The Lancet Planetary Health, 1*(3), e94–e95.

Markolf, S., Azevedo, I. M. L., Muro, M., & Victor, D. G. (2022, March 9). *Pledges and progress: Steps toward greenhouse gas emissions reductions in the 100 largest cities across the United States.* Brookings Institute. https://www.brookings.edu/articles/pledges-and-progress-steps-toward-greenhouse-gas-emissions-reductions-in-the-100-largest-cities-across-the-united-states/

Marohn, K. (2023, April 10). *Minnesota House passes bill requiring carbon-free electricity by 2040.* MPR News. https://www.mprnews.org/story/2023/01/27/minnesota-house-passes-bill-requiring-carbonfree-electricity-by-2040

Mayer, R. E. (2012). Multimedia learning. Cambridge University Press.

McCarthy, J. (2020). Understanding why climate change impacts women more than men. *Global Citizen.* https://www.globalcitizen.org/en/content/how-climate-change-affects-women/

Mead, E., Roser-Renouf, C., Rimal, R. N., Flora, J. A., Maibach, E. W., & Leiserowitz, A. (2012). Information seeking about global climate change among adolescents: The role of risk perceptions, efficacy beliefs, and parental influences. *Atlantic Journal of Communication, 20*(1), 31–52.

Miami-Dade County Public Schools. (2024, June 17). *M-DCPS Awarded $8.8 Million EPA Grant for Electric Buses* https://www3.dadeschools.net/news/34077/details

Moench, M. (2023). New data shows a global surge in searches related to 'climate anxiety'. *Time.* https://time.com/6338759/climate-change-anxiety-google-search-trend/

Monk, G. (2022). *CT schools will soon be required to teach climate change.* https://ctmirror.org/2022/05/19/ct-schools-will-soon-be-required-to-teach-climate-change/

NASA. (2022). *Steamy relationships: How atmospheric water vapor amplifies earth's greenhouse effect.* climate.nasa.gov/explore/ask-nasa-climate/3143/steamy-relationships-how-atmospheric-water-vapor-amplifies-earths-greenhouse-effect/

NASA. (2023). Land-ocean temperature index classroom data sheet. https://www.nasa.gov/wp-content/uploads/2023/06/land-oceantempindexclassroomdatasheet.pdf

NASA. (2024). *Climate change.* NASA Science. science.nasa.gov/climate-change/

NASA. (2024). Solar system temperatures. NASA Science. science.nasa.gov/resource/solar-system-temperatures/

National Caucus of Environmental Legislators. (2023, May 9). *These states are working in 2023 to limit climate pollution from buildings.* www.ncelenviro.org/articles/these-states-are-working-in-2023-to-limit-climate-pollution-from-buildings/

National Centers for Environmental Information. (2022, January). *Monthly global climate report for annual 2021.* https://www.ncei.noaa.gov/access/monitoring/monthly-report/global/202113

National Centers for Environmental Information. (n.d.). *Billion-dollar weather and climate disasters.* National Oceanic and Atmospheric Administration. https://www.ncei.noaa.gov/access/billions/

National Council for the Social Studies (NCSS). (2013). *The College, Career, and Civic life (C3) framework for social studies state standards: Guidance for enhancing the rigor of K-12 Civics, Economics, Geography, and History.* https://www.socialstudies.org/system/files/2022/c3-framework-for-social-studies-rev0617.2.pdf

National Council for the Social Studies. (2022). The college, career, and civic life (C3) framework for social studies state standards: Guidance for enhancing the rigor of K–12 civics, economics, geography, and history (Rev. ed.). https://www.socialstudies.org/sites/default/files/c3/C3-Framework-for-Social-Studies.pdf

National Governors Association. (2010). Common core state standards.

National Oceanic and Atmospheric Administration. (2023). The sea breeze. www.noaa.gov/jetstream/ocean/sea-breeze

National Research Council, Division of Behavioral, Board on Science Education, & Committee on a Conceptual Framework for New K-12 Science Education Standards. (2012). A framework for K-12 science education: Practices, crosscutting concepts, and core ideas. National Academies Press.

National Science Teaching Association (NSTA). (n.d.). Science standards. https://www.nsta.org/science-standards

New Jersey Department of Education. (2023, February 13). *Notice of Grant Opportunity (NGO): Climate awareness education: Implementing the New Jersey Student Learning Standards (NJSLS) for climate change.* https://www.nj.gov/education/broadcasts/2023/feb/15/NGO-ClimateAwarenessEducationImplementingtheNJSLSforClimateChange.pdf

New Jersey Department of Education. (2024a). *Climate change education by grade band.* https://www.nj.gov/education/climate/learning/gradeband/

New Jersey Department of Education. (2024b). *Expanding access to climate change and NJ student learning through climate change learning collaborative-competitive.* https://www.nj.gov/education/grants/opportunities/2024/24-WB06-G02.shtml

New Jersey Department of Education. (2024c). *Expanding access to climate change education and NJ student learning standards through interdisciplinary learning and community resilience projects-competitive.* https://www.nj.gov/education/grants/opportunities/2024/24-WB05-G02.shtml

New Jersey Department of Environmental Protection. (2020). *Scientific report on climate change.* Author. https://dep.nj.gov/wp-content/uploads/climatechange/nj-scientific-report-2020.pdf

New York City Department of Education. (2024). *Climate action days.* https://www.schools.nyc.gov/school-life/space-and-facilities/sustainability/climate-action-days

NGSS Lead States. (2013). *Next Generation Science Standards: For states, by states.* National Academies Press.

NGSS Lead States. (2013). Next generation science standards: For states, by states. National Academies Press.

Niels Bohr Library & Archives. (2023). The discovery of global warming. history. aip.org/climate/20ctrend.htm#:~:text=The%20warming%20up%20to%201940,or%20by%20random%20volcanic%20eruptions

NOAA National Centers for Environmental information. (2024, January). Climate at a glance: Global time series. https://www.ncei.noaa.gov/access/monitoring/climate-at-a-glance/global/time-series

NOAA. (2023, January 10). *2022 U.S. billion-dollar weather and climate disasters in historical context.* https://www.climate.gov/news-features/blogs/beyond-data/2022-us-billion-dollar-weather-and-climate-disasters-historical

Ocean Cleanup. (2021). *How it works.* https://theoceancleanup.com/

Office of the Governor. (2020, June 3). *First lady Tammy Murphy announces New Jersey will be first state in the nation to incorporate climate change across education guidelines* for K-12 schools [Press Release]. https://nj.gov/governor/news/news/562020/approved/20200603b.shtml

Office of the Governor. (2023, September 26). *Governor, first lady Tammy Murphy and New Jersey Department of Education establish first-in-the-nation office of climate change education.* https://www.nj.gov/governor/news/news/562023/20230926a.shtml

OpenSecrets. (2023). *Sen. James M Inhofe campaign finance summary.* www.opensecrets.org/members-of-congress/james-m-inhofe/summary?cid=N00005582

Our Testing: Dangerous Dirt. (2014). *G. W. Carver Samsung solve for tomorrow.* carversamsung.weebly.com/our-testing-dangerous-dirt.html

Oxfam. (2018). *Hurricane Maria puts a disproportionate burden on women.* https://www.oxfamamerica.org/explore/stories/hurricane-maria-put-a-disproportionate-burden-on-women/

Patnaik, A., Son, J., Feng, A., & Ade, C. (2020). *Racial disparities and climate change.* PSCI. psci.princeton.edu/tips/2020/8/15/racial-disparities-and-climate-change

Plutzer, E., & Hannah, A. L. (2016, March). *Mixed messages-how climate change is taught in America's schools.* NCSE. https://ncse.ngo/files/MixedMessagesReport.pdf

Plutzer, E., Hannah, A. L., Rosenau, J., McCaffrey, M. S., Berbeco, M., & Reid, A. H. (2016). *Mixed messages: How climate is taught in America's Schools.* National Center for Science Education. http://ncse.com/files/MixedMessages.pdf

Porras-Salazar, J. A., Wyon, D. P., Piderit-Moreno, B., Contreras-Espinoza, S., & Wargocki, P. (2018). Reducing classroom temperature in a tropical climate improved the thermal comfort and the performance of elementary school pupils. *Indoor Air, 28*(6), 892–904. https://doi.org/10.1111/ina.12501

Prager, A., & Samson, S. (2019). The fight against Nigeria's northeast terrorism is also a battle against climate change. *Quartz.* https://qz.com/africa/1730868/fighting-boko-haram-and-climate-change-in-nigeria

Project Drawdown. (2023, September). Drawdown solutions. https://drawdown.org/solutions

Rapin, K. (2023, July 28). Climate conversation groups are an outlet for Americans anxious about climate change. *Teen Vogue.* https://www.teenvogue.com/story/climate-conversation-groups

Raymond, N. (2024). *Hawaii agrees to 'groundbreaking' settlement of youth climate change case.* Reuters. www.reuters.com/legal/hawaii-agrees-settle-youth-climate-change-lawsuit-2024-06-21/

Reincke, C., Bredenoord, A., & Mil, M. (2020). From deficit to dialogue in science communication: The dialogue communication model requires additional roles from scientists. *EMBO Reports, 21,* Article e51278. https://doi.org/10.15252/embr.202051278

Revelle, R. (1982). Carbon dioxide and world climate. *Scientific American, 247*(2), 35–43. http://www.jstor.org/stable/24966657

Revelle, R., & Suess, H. E. (1957). Carbon dioxide exchange between atmosphere and ocean and the question of an increase of atmospheric CO_2 during the past decades. *Tellus, 9*(1), 18–27. https://doi.org/10.3402/tellusa.v9i1.9075

Revill, J., & MacSwan, A. (2022). Worst melt year on record for Swiss glaciers, data shows. *Reuters.* www.reuters.com/business/environment/worst-melt-year-record-swiss-glaciers-data-shows-2022-09-27/

Ritchie, H. (2021). How have the world's energy sources changed over the last two centuries? Our World in Data. https://ourworldindata.org/global-energy-200-years

Rojo, M. (2019). Women weather climate change in Senegal. *Dw.* https://www.dw.com/en/the-women-left-to-face-climate-change-and-over-fishing-alone/a-47709246

Rosenthal, L. (2024). *New York State Assembly Bill 1516511*. https://www.billtrack50.com/billdetail/1516511

Schlosberg, D., & Collins, L. B. (2014). From environmental to climate justice: Climate change and the discourse of environmental justice. *WIREs Climate Change, 5*, 359–374. https://doi.org/10.1002/wcc.275

Schmidt, M. W., & Hertzberg, J. E. (2011). Abrupt climate change during the last ice age. *Nature Education Knowledge, 3*(10), 11.

Schulte, E. (2023, March 17). Experts debunk viral post claiming 1,100 scientists say there's no climate emergency. *Inside Climate News*. insideclimatenews.org/news/23082022/experts-debunk-viral-post-claiming-1100-scientists-say-theres-no-climate-emergency/

Schwartz, S. E., Benoit, L., Clayton, S., Parnes, M. F., Swenson, L., & Lowe, S. R. (2023). Climate change anxiety and mental health: Environmental activism as buffer. *Current Psychology, 42*(20), 16708–16721.

Silvhiany, S., Kurniawan, D., & Safrina, S. (2023). Climate change awareness in ELT: Ethnography in connected learning and ecojustice pedagogy. Journal of English Language Teaching Innovations and Materials (Jeltim), 5(2), 91–109.

Stevenson, K., & Peterson, N. (2015). Motivating action through fostering climate change hope and concern and avoiding despair among adolescents. *Sustainability, 8*(1), 6. http://doi.org/10.3390/su8010006

Sylvie, A. (2021). Applied critical thinking in strategy: Tools and a simulation using a live case. *Journal of Education for Business, 96*(4), 252–259, https://doi.org/10.1080/08832323.2020.1792395

The Climate Reality Project. (2021, July 1). *6 interactive tools to better understand the climate crisis*. www.climaterealityproject.org/blog/6-interactive-tools-better-understand-climate-crisis

Thunberg, G. (2019, January 25). *Address at World Economic Forum: Our house is on fire*. https://awpc.cattcenter.iastate.edu/2019/12/02/address-at-davos-our-house-is-on-fire-jan-25-2019/

Tigue, K. (2023, August 15). Montana youth sued their government over climate change and won. Here's why that's a big deal. *Inside Climate News*. insideclimatenews.org/news/15082023/montana-youth-climate-lawsuit-ruling-big-deal

Trecek-King, M. (2022, February 28). A life preserver for staying afloat in a sea of misinformation. *Center for Inquiry*, Skeptical Inquirer. skepticalinquirer.org/2022/02/a-life-preserver-for-staying-afloat-in-a-sea-of-misinformation/

Trecek-King, M. (2024, January 22). Guide to the most common logical fallacies. *Thinking Is Power*. thinkingispower.com/logical-fallacies/

Turner, B. (2023, October 23). Gulf stream weakening now 99% certain, and ramifications will be global. *Space.Com*, Space. www.space.com/gulf-stream-weakening-certain-global-ramifications

U.S. Department of Energy. (2023). *U.S. energy and employment report 2023* (Version 2). https://www.energy.gov/sites/default/files/2023-06/2023%20USEER%20REPORT-v2.pdf

U.S. Department of the Treasury. (2024, March 13). *The Inflation Reduction Act: A place-based analysis*. home.treasury.gov/news/featured-stories/the-inflation-reduction-act-a-place-based-analysis

U.S. Environmental Protection Agency. (2021). *Climate change and social vulnerability in the United States: A focus on six impacts* (EPA 430-R-21-003). https://www.epa.gov/cira/social-vulnerability-report

U.S. Environmental Protection Agency. (2024). Causes of climate change. https://www.epa.gov/climatechange-science/causes-climate-change

U.S. Environmental Protection Agency. (2024). *White House Environmental Justice Advisory Council*. https://www.epa.gov/environmentaljustice/

white-house-environmental-justice-advisory-council

U.S. Senate Committee on Energy and Natural Resources. (1988). *Transcript of pivotal climate-change hearing 1988.* U.S. Government Printing Office.

UNESCO. (2021). *Climate change education.* https://www.unesco.org/en/node/66349

UNICEF. (2021). *The climate crisis is a child rights crisis: Introducing the children's climate risk index.* https://www.unicef.org/reports/climate-crisis-child-rights-crisis

Union of Concerned Scientists. (2021). *The benefits of electrification: Moving toward a carbon-free future.* https://www.ucsusa.org/resources/benefits-renewable-energy-use

United Nations Environment Programme. (2021). *Making peace with nature: A scientific blueprint to tackle the climate, biodiversity and pollution emergencies.* https://www.unep.org/resources/making-peace-nature

United Nations Environment Programme. (2023). *Scientific assessment of the ozone layer depletion: 2022.* www.unep.org/resources/publication/scientific-assessment-ozone-layer-depletion-2022

United Nations Food and Agriculture Organization. (2024). *Why is gender equality and rural women's empowerment central to the work of FAO?* https://www.fao.org/gender/background/en

United Nations Framework Convention on Climate Change (UNFCCC). (2020). *Just transition of the workforce, and the creation of decent work and quality jobs.* Technical Paper. https://unfccc.int/sites/default/files/resource/Just%20transition.pdf

United Nations. (n.d.). *The 17 goals.* https://sdgs.un.org/goals

USDA. (2024). *Growing seasons in a changing climate.* Climate Hubs. Retrieved May 3, 2024, from www.climatehubs.usda.gov/growing-seasons-changing-climate

Vazquez, B. (2021, December 20). Science saves lives (6–12). *ScienceSaves*, The Center for Inquiry. sciencesaves.org/2021/12/20/science-saves-lives-6-12/.

Vosoughi, S., Roy, D., & Aral, S. (2018). The spread of true and false news online. *Science, 359*(6380), 1146–1151. https://doi.org/10.1126/science.aap9559

Waite, K. (2024). Teaching for environmental justice: Learning from the film "Manzanar, Diverted: When Water Becomes Dust." *Social Education, 88*(3), 148–152. https://www.socialstudies.org/social-education/88/3

Warfield, Z. J., & Kolhatkar, S. (2021, November 21). *Introduction: A new social justice.* Yes Magazine. https://www.yesmagazine.org/issue/a-new-social-justice/2021/11/15/new-social-justice

Whitaker, R. C., Phillips, S. M., & Orzol, S. M. (2006). Food insecurity and the risks of depression and anxiety in mothers and behavior problems in their preschool-aged children. *Pediatrics, 118*(3), e859–e868.

White, R. (2024). Study warns of largest U.S. cities to face "significant flooding." *Newsweek.* https://www.newsweek.com/us-cities-rising-sea-levels-risk-1876399

Wihbey, J. (2023, February 22). The forgotten story of Jimmy Carter's White House solar panels. *Yale Climate Connections.* yaleclimateconnections.org/2023/02/the-forgotten-story-of-jimmy-carters-white-house-solar-panels/

Will, M., & Prothero, A. (2022, November 29). Teens know climate change is real. They want schools to teach more about it. *Education Week.* www.edweek.org/teaching-learning/teens-know-climate-change-is-real-they-want-schools-to-teach-more-about-it/2022/11

Wineburg, S., Breakstone, J., Ziv, N., & Smith, M. (2020). Educating for misunderstanding: How approaches to teaching digital literacy make students susceptible to scammers, rogues, bad actors, and hate mongers (Working Paper A-21322). Stanford History Working Group.

World Meteorological Organization. (1986). *Report of the international conference on the assessment of the role of carbon dioxide and of other greenhouse gases in climate variations and associated impacts,* Villach, Austria, October 9–15, 1985.

World Meteorological Organization. (2024, June 4). *Global temperature is likely to exceed 1.5°C above pre-industrial level temporarily in next 5 years.* wmo.int/news/media-centre/global-temperature-likely-exceed-15degc-above-pre-industrial-level-temporarily-next-5-years

World Resources Institute. (2020). *Creating a sustainable food future.* https://research.wri.org/wrr-food

Worth, K. (2021). *Miseducation: How climate change is taught in America.* Columbia Global Reports.

Xiang, P., Zhang, H., Geng, L., Zhou, K., & Wu, Y. (2019). Individualist-collectivist differences in climate change inaction: The role of perceived intractability. *Frontiers in Psychology, 10,* Article 187. https://doi.org/10.3389/fpsyg.2019.00187

Yale Climate Connections. (2021). *The link between climate change and terrorism.* https://yaleclimateconnections.org/2021/11/the-link-between-climate-change-and-terrorism/

Yang, M. (2022). *'Face it head on': Connecticut makes climate change studies compulsory.* https://www.theguardian.com/education/2022/dec/17/climate-change-studies-connecticut

Zivin, J., & Shrader, J. (2016). Temperature extremes, health, and human capital. *The Future of Children, 26,* 31–50.

INDEX

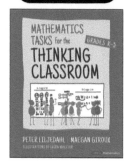
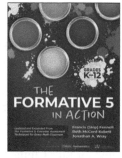

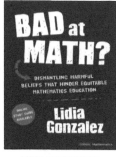

**JENNIFER M. BAY-WILLIAMS,
JOHN J. SANGIOVANNI, ROSALBA SERRANO,
SHERRI MARTINIE, JENNIFER SUH,
C. DAVID WALTERS, SUSIE KATT**

Because fluency is so much more than
basic facts and algorithms.
Grades K–8

**MARIA DEL ROSARIO
ZAVALA,
JULIA MARIA AGUIRRE**

Discover innovative equity-
based culturally responsive
mathematics instruction that
unlocks the mathematical
heart of each student.
Grades K–8

**IVANNIA SOTO,
THEODORE RUIZ SAGUN,
MICHAEL BEIERSDORF**

Focus on the literacy
opportunities that multilingual
students can achieve when
language scaffolds are
taught alongside rigorous
math and science content.
Grades K–8

**JOHN J. SANGIOVANNI, SUSIE KATT,
LATRENDA D. KNIGHTEN, GEORGINA RIVERA,
FREDERICK L. DILLON, AYANNA D. PERRY,
ANDREA CHENG, JENNIFER OUTZS, KAREN MESMER,
ENYA GRANDOS, KEVIN GANT, LAURA SHAFER**

Actionable answers to your most pressing
questions about teaching elementary math,
secondary math, and secondary science.

Elementary, Secondary

**CHRISTA JACKSON, KRISTIN L. COOK,
SARAH B. BUSH,
MARGARET MOHR-SCHROEDER,
CATHRINE MAIORCA, THOMAS ROBERTS**

Help educators create integrated STEM
learning experiences that are inclusive for all
students and allow them to experience STEM
as scientists, innovators, mathematicians,
creators, engineers, and technology experts!

Grades PreK–5 and Grades 6–12

A Sage Company

Helping educators make the greatest impact

CORWIN HAS ONE MISSION: to enhance education through intentional professional learning.

We build long-term relationships with our authors, educators, clients, and associations who partner with us to develop and continuously improve the best evidence-based practices that establish and support lifelong learning.